USING THE STRENGTHS PERSPECTIVE IN SOCIAL WORK PRACTICE

USING THE STRENGTHS PERSPECTIVE IN SOCIAL WORK PRACTICE

A Positive Approach for the Helping Professions

MORLEY D. GLICKEN

Professor Emeritus of Social Work
California State University, San Bernardino
and Executive Director
The Institute for Positive Growth: A Strengths-Based Research,
Treatment, and Training Cooperative

Boston ■ New York ■ San Francisco
Mexico City ■ Montreal ■ Toronto ■ London ■ Madrid ■ Munich ■ Paris
Hong Kong ■ Singapore ■ Tokyo ■ Cape Town ■ Sydney

Series Editor: *Patricia Quinlin*
Editorial Assistant: *Annemarie Kennedy*
Editorial-Production Administrator: *Joe Sweeney*
Editorial-Production Service: *Denise Botelho, Colophon*
Composition Buyer: *Linda Cox*
Manufacturing Buyer: *JoAnne Sweeney*
Cover Administrator: *Joel Gendron*
Text Composition: *Modern Graphics*

For related titles and support materials, visit our online catalog at www.ablongman.com.

Between the time Website information is gathered and then published, it is not unusual for some sites to have closed. Also, the transcription of URLs can result in typographical errors. The publisher would appreciate notification where these errors occur so that they may be corrected in subsequent editions.

Library of Congress Cataloging-in-Publication Data

Glicken, Morley D.
    Using the strengths perspective in social work practice: A positive approach for the helping professions / by Morley D. Glicken.
      p. cm.
    Includes bibliographical references and index.
    ISBN 0-205-33512-8 (alk. paper)
    1. Social service—Psychological aspects. 2. Resilience (Personality trait) I. Title.

HV41.G64 2003
361'.06—dc21

2003050447

Printed in the United States of America

10 9 8 7 6 5 4 3 2 1   RRD-VA   09 08 07 06 05 04 03

This book is dedicated to the abused and maltreated children who show us that harm to the body and the spirit can be overcome with amazing demonstrations of resilience. For those children who haven't been so fortunate to overcome the terrible impact of their maltreatment, this book will hopefully serve as a promise that people often change, grow, and overcome adversity through the helping impulse of others, and through the cultural, religious, and spiritual guidance that often serves us in our darkest moments. My sister Gladys Smith, my daughter Amy Glicken, and my parents Rose and Sam Glicken are the resilient people I admire so much. I wanted to write a book in whose presence their approach to life would be captured. I hope I've accomplished this in my book, and send out a special thank you for their love, encouragement, and support.

CONTENTS

■ ■ ■ ■ ■

CHAPTER THREE
The Strengths Perspective:
Psychosocial Assessments   36

CHAPTER FOUR
The Strengths Perspective and the Client–Worker
Relationship   48

PART III   THE IMPORTANCE OF CULTURE:
TWO EXAMPLES   103

CHAPTER EIGHT

Utilizing the Strengths Perspective
with the Culturally Traditional Latino Client in Crisis
(with Mina A. Garza)   105

CHAPTER NINE

The Ethnically Asian Client in Crisis
and the Strengths Perspective: A Collectivist Approach
(with Steven M. Ino)   117

PART IV   THE STRENGTHS PERSPECTIVE WITH SPECIAL POPULATIONS   137

CHAPTER TEN
The Strengths Perspective with Abusive Clients and Their Victims   139

The idea that people can resolve serious social and emotional problems by focusing on the strengths in their lives is an elegant concept, but one at odds with many current notions of psychotherapy that focus on what's wrong with people. The strengths perspective is interested in showing how the day-to-day work that most of us do to keep ourselves going, even in the midst of crisis, is the basis for a more effective way of helping people. Furthermore, the strengths perspective suggests that even without the help of trained professionals, many people in deep despair show resilience and actually resolve their problems by using the positive influences of family, community, support networks, religious and spiritual beliefs, and a philosophy of life that not only guides them through moments of sorrow, but actually enhances and improves their social and emotional lives.

While the purpose of this book is to show clinicians how to use the strengths perspective, it is also to suggest that much is to be learned from the amazingly resilient people who navigate the troubled waters of life's traumas. Many social and emotional problems that currently require treatment by trained mental health professionals can be resolved when people use the natural resources in their lives. All too little is known about resilience, but from a strengths point of view, it is the key to understanding how people cope with life difficulties and how they often come out of a crisis stronger and more certain of their goals, desires, and directions in life.

Reviewing the research on the effectiveness of counseling and psychotherapy in preparation of this book was an unsettling experience. Much of the effectiveness research is based on the opinion of therapists about client improvement, client satisfaction reports, and improvement on instruments intended to measure social and emotional functioning. The real test of effectiveness, however, is social functioning. Does the client function better socially as a result of treatment? Does he or she work better, show more success at school, commit fewer acts of violence, and show the signs of good citizenship that include community concern and involvement? Using social functioning as a guide to measuring treatment effectiveness, the research on the effectiveness of psychotherapy is not reassuring. There is all too little evidence that professional helpers make an overall difference in the social functioning of the clients they treat. To be sure, we hope we make a difference, but the hard evidence is often lacking. In fact, Chapter 7 of this book, on natural helpers, suggests that a body of literature exists on self-help groups led by nonprofessionals that shows great promise in terms of improved social functioning of group members. These self-help groups generally focus on affirmation, unconditional acceptance, and positive reinforcement, conditions of therapy sometimes not found in the work done by professional helpers.

People do not get better when the locus of help is on what is wrong with them. They get better when the worker and the client actively identify the client's strengths—those behavioral processes, values, beliefs, cultural imperatives, religious involvements, spiritual convictions, support networks, friendships, and a host of more subtle life issues that move the client in a positive direction and whose focus permits a loving, tender, and caring relationship between helper and client.

In the strengths perspective, the client involves the helper in a journey of understanding. That journey is often defined by a sense of astonishment that the client would allow him or her to view the client's often-painful inner world. It is a world of hurt and sorrow, coupled, to be sure, with a world of heroism, bravery, loving devotion, sensitivity to others, a helping impulse, and the amazing moments in time when even the most hardened and destructive reach out to others and act in ways that can only fill us with immense joy at the unpredictability of the human spirit. It is an approach to helping that uses what works for people to dominate the discussion of how those in difficulty can change for the better. For the depressed client who struggles with the urge to give up, every day must be an act of bravery to bathe, dress, take care of family, work, pay bills, and nurture children, spouses, and other loved ones. Most of that behavior suggests an extraordinary effort to cope that is moving and heroic. The pathology model views that behavior in no specific way, choosing instead to focus on feelings of depression and the difficulty in making emotional progress. The strengths perspective wonders what prompts people to do as well as they do. It asks what internal and external mechanisms propel people to get on with life, even if the struggle is often more than they can take.

The strengths perspective believes that as clients begin to appreciate what is good, functional, and positive about themselves, the mechanisms used to achieve success in one area of life will transfer over to those areas of life that are more problematic. The essence of the strengths perspective is the belief that focusing on what is good about the client will provide more real gain than focusing on what is bad. And although this is more easily said than done, this book is about helping people who are in serious social and emotional difficulty, get well. Getting well means living with an absence of internal emotional pain and providing society with the benefits of people's talents and abilities. A practice approach that fails to encourage socially responsible behavior fails to truly help people.

This is a book for helping professionals. It is a "how to do it" book, in a sense, because it shows clinicians how to understand and apply the strengths perspective. It comes from almost 40 years of practice experience by the author, 35 of which have also been spent as a social work educator. Most of my career has been spent teaching students to apply empirically based theories to their practices. Similarly, this book comes from a belief that much of what is wrong with practice today is the inability of practitioners to be guided by research findings. I would not have written a book on the strengths perspective without the belief that its underpinnings are or will be available in the research literature.

This orientation to the empirical leads to an unusual feature in the book. At the end of every chapter, there is critical feedback on what has been covered throughout the chapter, the purpose of which is to provide a balanced and sometimes antagonistic response to what I have written. It is essential to all learning that other points of view be included in any discourse. This critical feedback, however grating it might be, hopefully serves that purpose.

This book is written for the brave and resolute among us who fight the daily battle of survival against all odds, and who often win. But it is particularly written for my daughter Amy and for my sister Gladys, who are the best examples I know of people who use the strengths perspective in their lives everyday and are wise, caring, and loving people as a result.

ACKNOWLEDGMENTS

When you write a book about something as new and unique as the strengths perspective, you recognize the debt you owe to the people who did so much of the early work. I want to particularly thank Drs. Dennis Saleebey, Charles Rapp, Ann Weick, and other former colleagues at the University of Kansas School of Social Welfare for their pioneering work. I also want to thank the scholars who recognized that some children have amazing recuperative powers and cope with traumas in ways that teach us about the wonders of the human spirit. Many resilient children have endured terrible assaults to their bodies and their spirits, and I would never want the reader to think that I discount the harm done by abusive adults to children in the United States. Child abuse is a problem that won't go away without a great national effort, one that must be led by the helping professions.

Megan Dwyer, my research assistant for this, my fourth book for Allyn and Bacon, has once again helped in ways that have been immeasurable. Dr. Neal Maser, founder of the Institute for Strengths-Based Communities in Santa Barbara has been very helpful in sharing information about community life. My co-authors on much of the work in Chapters 5, 8, and 9, respectivly—Liza Fraser, Mina Garza, and Steven Ino—were wonderful mentors into ideas about spirituality and cultures. I thank them for their patient understanding and guidance. Those who reviewed the manuscript offered helpful suggestions: Robert Blundo, University of North Carolina at Wilmington; Jean Nuernberger, Central Missouri State University; Ruth Pellow, University of Arkansas, Monticello; Martha K. Wilson, Boise State University; and David Worster, University of New Hampshire.

I grew up in a home in which the strengths perspective was practiced every day. My parents, Rose and Sam Glicken, were the tough, resilient Jewish immigrants of eastern Europe who believed that you got on with life and you never let life's sorrows affect you. Their support, encouragement, and resilient approach to life gave me a foundation that made writing this book a joy.

Two special people are examples of the strengths perspective. I am grateful to have them in my life. My sister Gladys Smith and my daughter Amy Glicken are wonderful examples of strong people who deal with life's adversities every day in ways that enhance and promote the human spirit. I love them both and I know that I could not have written this book without their presence in my life.

ABOUT THE AUTHOR

Dr. Morley Glicken, MSW, MPA, DSW is the former Dean of the Worden School of Social Service in San Antonio, California, the founding director of the Master of Social Work Department at California State University, San Bernardino, the past Director of the Master of Social Work Program at the University of Alabama, and the former Executive Director of Jewish Family Service of Greater Tucson.

Dr. Glicken received his bachelor's degree in Social Work with a minor in Psychology from the University of North Dakota. He holds a master of Social Work from the University of Washington, Seattle, and the master of Public Administration and doctor of Social Work degrees from the University of Utah in Salt Lake City, Utah. He is a member of Phi Kappa Phi Honorary Fraternity.

In addition to the two books published with Allyn and Bacon in 2002, *The Role of the Helping Professions in the Treatment of Victims and Perpetrators of Violence* (with Dale Sechrest) and *A Simple Guide to Social Research*, is his forthcoming title, *Violent Young Children* (Allyn and Bacon, 2004). Dr. Glicken has written over 50 articles for professional journals. He has held clinical social work licenses in Alabama and Kansas and is a member of the Academy of Certified Social Workers. He is currently Professor Emeritus in Social Work at California State University, San Bernardino and Director of the Institute for Positive Growth: A Research, Treatment and Training Cooperative in La Jolla, California. He can be reached online at mglicken.@msn.com.

THE CORE BELIEFS OF THE STRENGTHS PERSPECTIVE

In Part I, which includes Chapters 1 through 4, the core elements of the strengths perspective and the diagnostic approach used are discussed. After each chapter presents material on the strengths perspective, the reader will find dissenting opinions given by practitioners and academics. The purpose of the critical response section of this book is to provide the reader with alternative opinions regarding the material presented. It is hoped that this enables readers to be critical evaluators of those aspects of the strengths perspective they can or cannot use in their practices.

Chapter 1 is an overview of the core ideas of the strengths perspective. Chapter 2 includes the positive behaviors clinicians might consider in their overall evaluation of their clients' functioning. Chapter 3 shows the way that the strengths perspective might approach a psychosocial evaluation of a client, while Chapter 4 discusses the importance of the client–worker relationship. Although much of the material in Chapter 4 comes from the existing literature on the strengths perspective, many of the ideas presented here may differ from the writings of others who are working with the same material but who may view it differently. For additional ideas regarding the strengths perspective, the reader is encouraged to read the sources provided in the references section of each chapter. The strengths perspective is a fairly new approach, and as with all new approaches, opinions on the same material sometimes differ.

A feature of Part I that the reader will find throughout the book is the inclusion of case studies, the purpose of which is to show the reader how the strengths perspective might be applied in practice. Once again, the conclusions drawn by the reader might differ from those of the author. To help clarify those differences, integrative questions are posed at the end of each chapter. The reader should feel free to use these questions as a clarifying process. There are no right or wrong answers, and questions might still remain in the reader's mind, as they should.

CHAPTER ONE

INTRODUCTION TO THE STRENGTHS PERSPECTIVE

This chapter discusses the central themes of the strengths perspective and provides a response to some of the criticism of the approach found in the literature. Each chapter in the book will include at least one or more case studies to help the reader learn about the strengths perspective and its application to work with clients. A critical response to the material in each chapter is also included to give the reader a more balanced view. All discourse should permit dissent and this book does that in an active way. Whenever possible, the research literature has been used to help explain the strengths model.

While this book uses many references from the existing strengths perspective literature, the material presented may differ in some fundamental ways from other books on the strengths perspective. Further, the Positive Psychology movement of Martin Seligman has influenced the writing of this book in many significant ways. This is also true of the work of Eileen Gambrill and others on evidence-based practice, an approach to practice that is strongly congruent with the frame of reference used in this book. Because this is a book for practitioners, there are chapters included on such issues as mental illness, substance abuse, and abusive behavior. If a model of practice is to stand the test of realistic use in the field, then difficult problems that face the clinician in everyday practice should be included.

A DEFINITION OF THE STRENGTHS PERSPECTIVE

A review of the literature suggests the following definition of the strengths perspective: The strengths perspective is a way of viewing the positive behaviors of all clients by helping them see that problem areas are secondary to areas of strength and that out of what they do well can come helping solutions based upon the successful strategies they use daily in their lives to cope with a variety of important life issues, problems, and concerns.

ELEMENTS OF THE STRENGTHS PERSPECTIVE

The central elements of the strengths perspective provide the following common themes (Saleebey, 1985, 1992, 1994; Weick et al., 1989; Goldstein, 1990):

1. The strengths perspective focuses on the coping mechanisms, problem-solving skills, and decision-making processes that work well for clients and generally result in an abundance of positive and successful behaviors. There is usually more about clients that is positive and functional than is negative or dysfunctional. Helpers must reassess the way they diagnose client functioning to recognize these largely positive behaviors (Turner, 2002).

2. Clients have the innate ability to resolve problems when helpers show them that the majority of their life has been successful. This focus on positive behavior can be critical because it helps motivate and energize clients to effectively resolve problems areas in their lives and not to "give up" hope that they will improve.

3. Clients have the right to live their lives as they desire. Our task is to help them attend to problem areas as they see them interfering with their lives and, importantly, as clients request help. Obviously, the ethics of our professions prohibit us from helping clients do harmful or antisocial activities to themselves or to others.

4. Workers must do an "asset review" of the many positive behaviors that result in life success for the client.

5. Workers must have a basic understanding of their client's inner world because it may dramatically help in the healing process. That inner world includes recognition of spirituality, religious involvement, social and political philosophies, and the cultural beliefs that often shape a client's worldview. These deeply felt beliefs are crucial to the helping process because they are the core beliefs that help motivate clients to change.

6. Along with the client's inner life, workers can help by knowing their client's aspirations, dreams, hopes, and desires since they are the hidden motivators that help clients cope with serious social and emotional problems and continue in life even when the path seems hopeless.

7. Clients set the agenda for change and must be clear about what needs to be worked on and why. It is the worker's job to help clients clarify the agenda without manipulating it. An agenda developed by the worker will never feel comfortable to the client who may resist it completely.

8. Workers and clients often experience a sense of newness and even astonishment when clients tell their stories. This sense of astonishment suggests that the worker is openly and completely experiencing the client's story. There are no assumptions made about the client's behavior or a desire to diagnose the client at a very early stage in the relationship. At the initial point in treatment, workers should feel a sense of newness and clients a sense of relief as they struggle to understand the client's descriptions of experiences in life that have shaped them and have led to the problem for which they seek help.

9. Labeling in mental health often suggests client problems that may be difficult, if not impossible, to resolve. Axis 2 diagnoses of personality disorders or a diagnosis of any number of serious and chronic emotional conditions influence the way

clients view themselves. They may also negatively affect job and career opportunities, insurance coverage, and a host of realistic life issues. The strengths perspective does not use labels that imply pathology since they are often misleading, pejorative, unhelpful in treatment, or provide an excuse for not helping clients.

10. The strengths perspective always views clients in a hopeful and optimistic way, regardless of the complexity of the problem, the length of time the client has experienced the problem, or the difficulty the client has experienced in resolving the problem.

11. Workers do not begin the treatment process believing that they have the solution to the client's problem. Such a belief negates the client's essential role in change. Clients creates change, not helpers. Helpers offer suggestions or make interpretations, but clients ultimately implement change. In this sense, workers are facilitators, but clients always bring about change.

12. There must be a willingness to suspend orthodox notions of the worker-client relationship and to recognize that a professionally aloof therapeutic approach discourages change. Workers using the strengths perspective should be fully engaged, optimistic, and positive. They should react to their clients in an honest and open way by responding when clients needs support and encouragement, even if this occurs when workers are inconvenienced or away from the office. To be sure, rules can be established regarding the worker's time, but a few minutes of assurance away from the office when clients are grappling with problems may make all the difference in treatment.

13. There should be a willingness by workers to suspend value judgments about clients and their behavior. The strengths perspective is oriented toward what clients do well, and not what they do badly. This is a key component of the strengths perspective. It doesn't negate the problem or eliminate the fact that clients may be involved in behavior that is destructive to self or others. It does suggest that, to be very trite, you catch more flies with honey than you do with vinegar. Negative and judgmental worker responses about the client's behavior will almost always result in resentment and opposition to treatment by clients.

14. The strengths perspective is not an approach that ignores research. It is, in fact, very much aligned with knowledge-guided and evidence-based practice approaches to treatment. All practice must derive its underlying assumptions and beliefs from the research literature. This requires strengths perspective workers to gather data on the effectiveness of their own practice and to make modifications when it doesn't seem to work. It also requires workers to encourage clients to seek as much independent information about their treatment as possible. Workers using the strengths perspective might suggest lines of inquiry that help clients become better informed consumers who can work cooperatively with workers to determine the best available treatment approaches as defined by the most current research literature.

15. The struggle to overcome life problems usually contains elements that are healthy and positive. In listening to clients discuss their attempts to change, many examples of positive, purposeful and adaptive behavior can be found. As Saleebey (2000) writes, "Every maladaptive response or pattern of behavior may also contain the seeds of a struggle for health" (p. 129).

16. Workers must recognize that the social and cultural environments of their clients are rich in opportunities for support, encouragement, and assistance from others. Within the client's social environment are the families, friends, co-workers, religious leaders, neighbors, and acquaintances that form the client's external world. They offer potential for helping clients in many important ways and may be more significant, in the long term, than helpers. The worker's task is to help the client identify those people in their social and cultural environment who possess positive and reinforcing skills that can be used in times of need and to maintain gains made in treatment.

17. The enlistment of a support network to help clients is the beginning of the development of a community of helpers whose desire to help one person can be enlarged to help many others. The strengths perspective believes that all work done with individuals will ultimately have a positive impact on the lives of many people and that our work will have a synergistic impact on our communities and, ultimately, on society. This notion of help that touches many lives is a core ingredient of the strengths perspective.

18. There exist within any given geographic locale the natural or indigenous helpers who provide supportive, reinforcing, helpful advice, and positive modeling to people in difficulty. We should accept natural helpers as a positive force in the lives of our clients and enlist their assistance.

19. For the client, the end result of treatment using the strengths perspective is recognition of what they do well, a more socially responsible approach to life, and a more complete understanding of the many internal and external resources available to them to resolve future problems and to live happy and fulfilling lives.

20. For workers, the end result of using the strengths perspective is a very accepting view of human behavior. That acceptance includes positive recognition of the importance of their client's inner world, support networks, family, and culture. It also includes a sense that what we do with clients affects the larger world we live in. Helping people live socially responsible, ethical, and fulfilling lives is a much greater challenge and responsibility than symptom removal. Workers using the strengths perspective have a goal of preparing clients for responsible and virtuous living so that we all benefit from the worker's efforts.

In summary, the binding elements of the strengths perspective include the recognition that the client, not the worker, is the primary change agent. The worker's role is to listen, help the client process, and facilitate by focusing on positive behaviors that might be useful in coping with the client's current life situation. The strengths perspective is an optimistic approach to helping, but one that functions from a research-guided frame of reference. The strengths perspective recognizes the positive influences of support networks, family, culture, and religious and spiritual convictions and uses these positive influences in the helping process. The result of treatment using the strengths perspective is not only better client functioning, but also socially responsible client and worker behavior that have a positive and synergistic impact on the community in which clients and workers live, work, and interact with others.

AN UNEMPLOYED EXECUTIVE: A CASE STUDY

James Gibbons recently lost his high-paying position as head of a large community mental health clinic. The reasons for his removal were largely political. When James found out that he was to be fired, he went into a deep depression. Fearing that the depression would make future searches for work difficult, James sought therapy from a highly regarded clinical psychologist in his community. He admired her listening abilities and felt that she was kind, warm, and thoughtful. However, after each session, he would experience severe feelings of sadness and would return home and drink alcohol until he fell asleep. James had never abused alcohol before and began to worry that he was becoming addicted. He told the author,

> The therapist focused on the negative behavior that lead to the loss of work. She showed me how those behaviors had their origins in my relationship with my parents and how they had formed patterns in my life. Not once did she focus on my many positive accomplishments, or the fact that I've held a number of jobs successfully in the past. While I don't doubt the connection between my relationship with my parents and my job loss, that was a long time ago and I've done pretty well in my life since. It seems to me that therapy should provide optimism and focus on your successes. After five visits, I finally had enough. I found a more positive therapist, stopped feeling so depressed, and, thankfully, stopped drinking. When I explained to my prior therapist that her approach wasn't helping and that it just seemed to be creating other problems, she was nice enough about it but said that without exploring the past, you can't understand the present. Maybe that's true, but I'm a therapist and I've never found her approach to be especially helpful with my deeply troubled social work clients. It drudges up past failures and focuses the client on misery and defeat rather than optimism and hope.
>
> My new therapist is wonderful. He's reframed my current situation in a way that allows me to understand what went wrong on my job and to provide me with the confidence to put that behind me and look for new work. He's also helped me see the dysfunctional nature of the agency I worked for and to become better at spotting problems in an agency that might cause me trouble on a new job. We laugh a lot together. Rather than feeling depressed when I go home and needing a drink, I feel thoughtful, hopeful, and very optimistic. I'm grieving the loss of an important job and the fear of not being able to ever get anything quite as good, while at the same time I'm feeling quietly optimistic that I'll work through this experience and that something good will come of it. Maybe I'm deluding myself, and maybe my former therapist was right about the relationship between the past and the present. All I can say is that I'm energized enough to look for new work, while, with my former therapist, I could barely get up in the morning.

DISCUSSION

No one who is thoughtful about the relationship between wellness and treatment can discount any number of reasons for James's improvement. It could be that the *relationship* with the new therapist, not the approach, was the deciding reason for his improvement. And to be fair, it's possible that James would have improved had he remained with his prior therapist. No one can say for certain why people change, but the logic of his reaction to the initial treatment seems hard to deny. The treatment was increasing his distress at a time when he needed to feel better about himself, not worse. This distance between what a client needs to function well and the notion that pain

(continued)

CONTINUED

is a necessary part of the healing process is difficult to justify in light of the high drop-out rates in treatment. The client who stops treatment prematurely may go on to even more troubled behavior. Apparently, James's new therapist was able to get at much of the same material as his initial therapist by showing him that, in spite of the problems he'd experienced in the agency, he'd done very well in his life and that he will very likely do well in the future.

James's new therapist was asked how he dealt with James's painful feelings about the loss of work. He responded,

> I listened to Jim tell his story. It's important for me to fully understand what is happening from the client's point of view. Maybe that point of view is a little distorted, and perhaps it contains elements of denial and manipulation of the facts, but it's important to hear the client's side of an issue. The client is, after all, the one dealing with the pain. I seldom interrupt, and I encourage the client to take as much time as is necessary to tell me everything they want me to know. Jim took almost an hour to tell his story. He was in a deep state of grief over being fired for reasons that had nothing to do with his abilities. He had not been given needed support on the job and felt unwanted by the staff, who were unwilling to work with him and wanted nothing to do with the changes they had asked him to make, but refused to implement.
>
> With five minutes left in the first session, I said something like this: "Jim, you're grieving the loss of work and the pain associated with feeling betrayed. These are natural feelings, and you're right in feeling sad and depressed at times. But the very abilities that have taken you so far in life are the same abilities you can use to resolve this temporary setback. For almost all of your life, you've been a highly successful professional. It takes a concentrated body of knowledge and skill to attain your level of achievement. We're going to use the skills that made you successful professionally to help you resolve the issues at hand. As I see it, the issues you'd like help with include getting over feeling sad, increasing your level of energy so that you can apply for new work, and making certain that new jobs don't have hidden pools of quicksand that might lead to future problems at work. If that's a correct summary of what you'd like to work on, then let's focus on those past work experiences that were very positive and let's see if we can isolate the elements of past success to use in understanding what happened at the agency and to begin a new job search. In the process, you'll allow your grieving to end, and you'll begin to focus more and more on getting a great new job."
>
> And guess what? In three months, he went from being clinically depressed and perhaps suicidal to having a very good new position. In the context of talking about prior successes, he could readily see the mistakes he'd made in his current job and the cumulative issues that led up to the dismissal. He also saw some patterns of long-held beliefs and behaviors that sometimes worked badly for him. It didn't make him depressed to discover any of this, since he had gone from feeling hopeless and lost to feeling optimistic and energized. In my experience, clients change when they feel good about themselves, not when they feel bad. The idea of focusing on pathology rather than strength just seems wrong in light of what we know about motivating client change.
>
> Will Jim relapse into a depression? Will old feelings of failure return to haunt him on his new job? Will he make similar mistakes, and will they lead to failure? I doubt it, but no system of treatment can say with certainty what the long-term outcomes will be. To make more certain that he does well, however, we have a weekly long-distance telephone chat. I've identified several strengths perspective therapists in his area that he can use if problems occur, and I've given him all the videos we made of treatment so that he can replay them whenever he feels stuck. This is an approach that works very well, I think, and is often a source of pride to clients. Seeing the hard work they've done and the changes they've made can be very reinforcing and energizing. Therapy of any sort is educational, and it never hurts to reinforce learning through repetition.

CONCERNS REGARDING THE STRENGTHS PERSPECTIVE

Concerns about the strengths perspective that are sometimes expressed in the professional literature (Saleebey, 1996) are the following:

1. The strengths perspective is just positive thinking in disguise.
2. The strengths perspective is just a way of reframing misery.
3. The strengths perspective is Pollyannaish.
4. The strengths perspective is too superficial. Problems are really much more complex, and change is much more difficult than the approach suggests.
5. Skills in one area of life often cannot be transferred to other areas of life. If it were that simple, therapy would work more effectively than it does.
6. The pathology model is more scientific because it finds its base in the medical model.
7. Telling people that they have competencies does not lead to change.
8. The strengths perspective makes other clinicians the reason that clients don't improve.
9. The strengths perspective is unable (or unwilling) to differentiate healthy cultures, religions, and beliefs from those that are harmful. It is a part of the philosophy of the strengths perspective that there is innate good in most things. As a politically correct statement, that's lovely, but as science, it's invalid.
10. The strengths perspective uses new ideas related to self-healing and resilience that have potential to harm clients with serious physical and emotional conditions that require prompt, effective, and traditional treatment.

CONCERNS ABOUT THE VALUE BASE OF PRACTITIONERS

Another criticism of the strengths perspective is that it fails to define the responsibilities of the helping professions to create, through the work they do with their clients, a society that functions with dignity and virtue. Much of what is written in the strengths perspective literature focuses on the community as a helping vehicle, but when that help is provided, isn't there an expectation that clients will reciprocate by living socially responsible and virtuous lives? Ryff and Singer (1998) suggest that modern psychology has failed to develop a view of the client beyond the absence of dysfunctional behavior. Seligman (1999) has called for a taxonomy of strengths that promote resilience and responsibility in families and individuals. Sandage and Hill (2001) suggest that modern psychology has no model of the "good life" or the virtues that promote healthy individual and community behavior. In fact, they suggest that much of psychology, and perhaps much of the helping professions, have no model of the positive values that we should stress with our clients. Positive Psychology is a movement concerned with constructive social behaviors. The strengths perspective, in a sense, is an approach that focuses on the client as victim and the helper as the undoer of victimization rather than the teacher of healthy, socially desirable, and virtuous behaviors.

RESPONSE

There is merit to all of the arguments presented. It is, in fact, often very difficult to use skills in one area of life and transfer them to another, but it's not impossible. A growing body of literature would suggest that it is possible, even in the most traumatized and severely dysfunctional of people. Research on resilience in traumatized children and adults suggests that the commonly held beliefs about human development are untrue: (1) There are stages of observable and consistent human development; (2) childhood trauma almost always leads to adult psychopathology (Benard, 1994; Garmezy, 1994); and (3) there are social and economic conditions that are so troubling that they usually lead to social and emotional problems (Rutter, 1994).

One well-known study of resilience in children as they grow into adulthood is the longitudinal research begun in 1955 by Werner and Smith (1992). In their initial report, Werner and Smith (1982) found that one of every three children who were evaluated by several measures of early-life functioning to be at significant risk for adolescent problems, actually developed into well-functioning young adults by age 18. In their follow-up study, Werner and Smith (1992) report that two of three of the remaining two-thirds of children at risk had become caring and healthy adults by age 32. One of their primary theories was that people have "self-righting" capabilities. From their studies the authors concluded that some of the factors that lead to self-correction in life can be identified. They also concluded that a significant factor leading to better emotional health for many children is a consistent and caring relationship with at least one adult. This adult (in a few cases, it was a peer) does not have to be a family member or physically present all of the time. These relationships provide the child with a sense of protection and serve to initiate and develop the child's self-righting capacities. Werner and Smith believe that it is never too late to move from a lack of achievement and a feeling of hopelessness to a sense of achievement and fulfillment.

This finding is supported by similar findings of serious antisocial behavior in children. In summarizing the research on youth violence the Surgeon General noted that "most highly aggressive children or children with behavioral disorders do not become violent offenders" (Satcher, 2001, p. 9). Similarly, the Surgeon General reported that most youth violence begins in adolescence and ends with the transition to adulthood. If people didn't change, then these early-life behaviors would suggest that all violence in youth would certainly continue into adulthood. The report further suggested that the reasons for change in violent children relate to treatment programs, maturation, and biosocial factors (self-righting tendencies, or what has more recently been termed *resilience*) that influence the lives of even the most violent youthful offenders. This and other research suggests that people *do* change, often on their own, and that learning from prior experience appears to be an important reason for change. Consequently, the notion that skill in one area of life is transferable to another appears reasonable, and this idea, supported by a growing body of research, does not appear to be "Pollyannaish."

A person's positive view of life can have a significant impact on one's physical and emotional health, as is indicated by a longitudinal study of a Catholic order of women in the Midwest (Danner, Snowdon, & Friesen, 2001). Longitudinal studies of the many aspects of life span and illness among this population suggest that the personal statements written by very young women to enter the religious order correlate positively with life span. The more positive and affirming the personal statement written when applicants were in their late teens and early 20s, the longer their life spans, sometimes as long as 10 years beyond the mean length of life for the religious order, as a whole, and up to 20 years or more longer than that of the general population. Many of the women in the sample lived well into their 90s and beyond. In a sample of 650 nuns, six were over 100 years of age. Although some of the sample suffers serious physical problems, including dementia and Alzheimer's disease, the numbers are much smaller than in the general population, and the age of onset is usually much later in life. The reasons for increased life span in this population seem to be related to good health practices (for example, the order doesn't permit liquor or tobacco products, and foods are often fresh and with a focus on vegetables) and an environment that focuses on spiritual issues and helping others. The order also has a strong emphasis on maintaining a close, supportive relationship among its members so that when illness does arise, there is a network of positive and supportive help.

People who have had long-term problems often think of themselves in very negative ways. They define themselves as having serious problems, and the notion that they have positive abilities and talents is a belief that many clients initially dismiss. These negative feelings about self have often been reinforced by family, friends, and helping professionals. It is difficult to move clients away from long-held beliefs about the negative nature of their behaviors. Rather than being Pollyannaish, the strengths perspective requires hard work on the part of both the clients and workers. In the long run, that work results in much more optimistic and fulfilled clients. As Kaplan and Girard (1994) indicate, "People are more motivated to change when their strengths are supported [because] . . . the worker creates a language of strength, hope, and movement" (p. 53).

A key idea of the strengths perspective is that skills in one area of life can be transferred to other less functional areas of life. The criticism of this capacity of people to learn from their successes is difficult to understand. Contrary to the adage that people learn from their mistakes, people generally repeat their mistakes. Success is far more instructive and motivating than failure. On the face of it, the criticism that skill in one area of life is nontransferable to other areas of life contradicts the fact that people change in life, often for the better, and that in the midst of crisis they can do amazingly wonderful things. Anderson (1997) suggests the benefits of focusing on the positive qualities of children who have been sexually abused. She believes that the focus of work should not be on the damage done to the child but on the survival abilities of the child to cope with the abuse. This means that practitioners must look for themes of resilience in the "survival stories" of abused children and help children recognize the active role they played in surviving the abuse. Perhaps, as Anderson (1997) suggests, "The psychological scars will never disappear completely; however, focusing on the child's strengths and resiliency can help limit the power of sexual abuse over the child" (p. 597).

The criticism of the strengths perspective—that it reframes misery and somehow makes it a positive or politically correct condition—is also difficult to understand. There is nothing politically correct or romantic about misery. It is the desire to rid the client of misery that motivates the use of the strengths perspective and produces a knowledge-guided practitioner who understands the research literature, urges the client to become familiar with that literature, and engages the client in a cooperative approach to treatment. As Gambrill (1999) notes in her discussion of a knowledge-guided practice approach similar to the one proposed for the strengths perspective,

> Evidence-based practice requires an atmosphere in which critical appraisal of practice-related claims flourishes, and clients are involved as informed participants. A notable feature of EBP is attention to clients' values and expectations. Clients are involved as active participants in the decision-making processes. (p. 348)

Another criticism of the strengths perspective is that it claims support networks and culture, among others, are as effective, if not more effective, than treatment. Seligman (1995), in his review of a survey of *Consumer Reports* readers responding to a questionnaire about satisfaction with psychotherapy and other forms of treatment for emotional and social problems treatment, wrote, "[We need to test out the] Bayesian inference that psychotherapy works better than talking to friends, seeing an astrologer, or going to church [before claims of treatment effectiveness] can be made more confidently" (p. 11).

An argument can be made that psychotherapy is in its infancy. We have not as yet determined what works, why it works, and, if it does work, how long the positive impact of treatment will last. There is evidence, however, that self-help groups and natural healing are approaches that may be as effective and perhaps more effective than traditional psychotherapy. Seligman (1995), for example, in his report for *Consumer Reports* on the effectiveness of psychotherapy, noted, "Alcoholics Anonymous (AA) did especially well, . . . significantly bettering mental health professionals [in the treatment of alcohol and drug related problems]" (p. 10). Similarly, Seligman (1995) found only a marginal difference between the satisfaction with life and the happiness with treatment in clients having experienced long-term in-depth treatment (more than two years) as opposed to shorter-term more superficial treatment (six months or less).

Finally, regarding Seligman's concern about virtue and the good life, this chapter and Chapter 2 contain this author's belief that socially responsible behavior is a key indicator of the effectiveness of treatment. The questions Seligman raised, however, are important and represent a challenge to the helping professions to be more certain that treatment results in socially responsible behaviors.

CONCERNS ABOUT THE STRENGTHS PERSPECTIVE FROM PRACTITIONERS

Even with the arguments given in the prior section, there is continuing criticism of the strengths perspective from the practice community. A respected psychotherapist told the author,

It's a wonderful assumption that the defenses clients use to deal successfully with life can be transferred to problems they deal with less well and sometimes deal with very badly. Let's take intimacy as an example. Many people who have serious problems with intimacy do very well in careers and in other areas of life. Often the reason they do so well is that achievement is a form of compensation for poor skills in intimacy. The idea that you can transfer skills in achieving success in careers to issues of intimacy seems improbable to me. How can you transfer a skill that someone essentially lacks? And the answer is that it's extremely difficult.

Even the most superficial forms of therapy suggest that complex issues involving very complicated people skills are difficult for many of us to achieve. Love, long-term relationships, bonding, and lifelong friendships are all areas of life Americans find difficult to achieve. But when the issue of people skills is complicated by serious early-life traumas such as child abuse, domestic violence, or parental abandonment, I don't think anyone would say that treatment is easy. The reason treatment isn't easy is that many people who have been emotionally harmed along the way have few relevant transferable skills to use in overcoming problems with intimacy. Their lives are marked by mistake after mistake in relationships that often result in distressing emotional pain. If it were so simple to just continually act as a cheerleader for the client by focusing on their successes in life, people would have been cured a long time ago and we could all go home, after work, knowing that our job was that simple to do.

I know we live at a moment in time when all of us are looking for effective solutions to the problems clients bring to us, solutions that are quick, positive, and effective. Many of us want to think that if only we could mobilize our inner resources, or if we had people around us who were supportive and optimistic, that our dreams and aspirations would come true and we would all be happy. This is the mantra for a society that is unable to come to grips with the fact that there is a great deal of physical and emotional harm done to people in our society at early points in their development. That harm has long-term consequences. It doesn't permit many troubled people to use healthier coping skills or to deal with certain life issues in logical ways. The skills that others have aren't skills readily available to very troubled people. That's why troubled people are so attracted to every new fad that comes along. It's an attempt to use something new in place of the hard work that needs to be done to overcome long-term problems. Some troubled people become more spiritual, or they go back to their religious and cultural roots, or they surround themselves with people whom they believe care about them. But the intimate relationships and the sense of fulfillment and well-being they crave completely elude them. If spirituality, or religious observation, or dear friends were the answer to unhappiness, then all my clients who use those strategies would cure themselves.

But they don't get better. They remain miserable. They smile and tell you how wonderful their lives have become since they discovered their inner world, but the reality is that they suffer, and it's painful to watch. Anyone who cares about suffering and pain wants a solution, and they want it now. And while I applaud the new therapy movements with their positive and reaffirming messages, and surely there is much to be learned from them for any therapist who cares, it isn't the answer for all too many of my troubled clients who haven't an idea, not an inkling, of how to transfer what they do so well in their lives to issues of intimacy and love.

The truth is that helping people to become more intimate is a slow and often tedious process. It involves the development of trust. It means that clients have to be more forgiving of others and accept people with all of their faults. These are skills that are difficult to teach healthy people. For troubled people, they are difficult in the extreme. The simplicity of the strengths model is almost childlike to me. It assumes that people can get better because . . . well . . . because they can. If that were the case, a legion of people with serious mental health problems would be cured by now.

An academic and therapist the author spoke to put it another way:

I think I did something like the strengths perspective for a few years after graduate school. I was very pro-client and into positive reinforcement and being uncritical and positively and unconditionally accepting and empathic. Carl Rogers had a real impact on me. So I'd do my work, and the clients loved me. They were happy and smiling when they'd leave treatment. They'd send me cards on all the holidays and would bring me their creative writing, their artwork, and other forms of creative expression to show me how well they were doing in their lives. And when they'd leave treatment, it was all hugs, and laughter, and happiness. Like any good therapist, I'd call them often and check to see if the change was lasting. Within two months, they were back in therapy, usually with someone who offered no quick fix and who dealt with long-term treatment. And occasionally, I'd bump into them, my old clients, and they were doing better with the tough therapy, the therapy that made them delve into their sorrow than they had ever done with my happy therapy, my good time, cheerleading therapy.

People are complex, and the strengths model simplifies the complexities of why people become miserable. Issues that are long standing don't go away so easily. Many people don't have support systems, or a loving and helpful culture, or kind and concerned friends. They aren't really spiritual, and religion doesn't work for them. They are, in a sense, typically American. They are rootless and move from job to job until they hardly know *where* they are, let alone *who* they are. The focus of the strengths perspective is on creating emotional stability, I think, but many people in our society, to maintain jobs and careers, are required to live very chaotic and rootless lives. This instability permits very little introspection, and it wrecks havoc with relationships. The work many of us do in therapy is just keeping these wandering, rootless people together and, with enough time and help, assisting them to settle down emotionally. That's a very complex and exacting process, more than being endlessly positive with clients, I'm afraid.

RESPONSE TO PRACTITIONER CONCERNS

As the reader can see, the criticisms of the strengths perspective generally center on a conviction that the approach is overly simplistic and superficial. This concern is coupled with a strongly held belief within the helping professions that the length and depth of treatment have a positive impact on treatment effectiveness. As noted here, and as is noted elsewhere in this book, this is not a particularly persuasive argument. While the concern that a superficial approach will not be effective is a good concern to have, focusing on what is right about a person is a very in-depth process. Discovering positive attributes about clients is as complex and in-depth a process as finding out about negatives, and much more effective. As noted throughout this book, the strengths perspective has very broad application to a variety of complex client problems. However, this book provides those with concerns about the approach an opportunity to voice their concerns. Throughout the book, there are arguments heard from other professionals and concerns about the strengths perspective found in the professional literature. This book attempts to model the strengths perspective by including dissenting points of view. Helping others is a complicated and challenging venture. How better to make up one's mind about the approach than to include the dissenting opinions about the strengths perspective? That is what learning is about: making the best argument one can make, providing opposing points of view presented in an equally well argued way, and then letting you, the reader, decide which argument is most meaningful.

SUMMARY

In this chapter, the binding elements of the strengths perspective and the criticism of the approach are discussed. A case presentation describes how the approach works in practice, and several clinicians provide positive and negative responses to the approach from their own clinical experience. To involve readers in making their own decisions about the strengths perspective, a critical response section will be found at the end of most chapters. This is done to provide a provocative discourse and to help the reader decide what best to take from the material presented. It is not the book's intent to uncritically promote the strengths perspective. Instead, the book encourages readers to make up their own minds in a rational and thoughtful way. Perhaps this approach may offend or confuse the reader. Hopefully it will have the opposite effect.

INTEGRATIVE QUESTIONS

1. When a client experiences racism, poverty, poorly functioning institutions, childhood traumas, and a host of serious problems experienced by many of our clients, isn't it very difficult for the client to view life in a positive and optimistic way?

2. Many behaviors for which clients seek help are destructive. How can one work to change destructive behaviors when clients set the agenda for help?

3. Eileen Gambrill proposes a knowledge-guided approach to practice. Does this suggest that new approaches to treatment, such as the strengths perspective, would not be utilized until there were empirical data to suggest that they work? Is this a good idea in your view?

4. The criticisms of the strengths perspective seem to suggest that it is overly simplistic. Does this suggest that therapy is complex, time consuming, and difficult? What's your opinion about whether the strengths perspective seems simplistic?

5. Seligman suggests that treatment should be more than symptom removal and that virtuous, happy, and fulfilling behavior should be the objective of all therapy. Do you think this sets impossible standards for therapists who work with clients whose basic concern is, after all, the removal of troubling symptoms?

REFERENCES

American Psychiatric Association. (1994). *Diagnostic and statistical manual of mental disorders* (4th Ed.). Washington, DC: American Psychiatric Press.

Anderson, K. M. (November 1997). Uncovering survival abilities in children who have been sexually abused. *Families in Society: The Journal of Contemporary Human Services,* 78, 592–599.

Benard, B. (December 1994). Applications of resilience. Paper presented at a conference on the Role of Resilience in Drug Abuse, Alcohol Abuse, and Mental Illness, Washington, DC.

Danner, D.D., Snowdon, D.A., and Friesen, W.V. (2001). Positive emotions in early life and longevity: Findings from the nun study. *Journal of Personality and Social Psychology,* 80, 804–813.

Gambrill, E. (July 1999). Evidence-based practice: An alternative to authority-based practice. *Families in Society: The Journal of Contemporary Human Services,* 80, 341–350.

Garmezy, N. (1994). Reflections and commentary on risk, resilience, and development. In R.J. Haggerty, L.R. Sherrod, N. Garmezy, and M. Rutter (Eds.), *Stress, risk, and resilience in children and adolescents: Processes, mechanisms, and interventions* (pp. 1–18). Cambridge, England: Cambridge University Press.

Goldstein, H. (1990). Strength or pathology: Ethical and rhetorical contrasts in approaches to practice. *Families in Society,* 71, 267–275.

Kaplan, L., and Girard, J. (1994). *Strengthening high-risk families: A handbook for practitioners.* New York: Lexington Books.

Rutter, M. (1994). Stress research: Accomplishments and tasks ahead. In R.J. Haggerty, L.R. Sherrod, N. Garmezy, and M. Rutter (Eds.), *Stress, risk, and resilience in children and adolescents: Processes, mechanisms, and interventions* (pp. 354–385). Cambridge, England: Cambridge University Press.

Ryff, C.D., and Singer, B. (1998). The contours of positive human health. *Psychological Inquiry,* 9, 1–28.

Saleebey, D. (1985). In clinical social work practice, is the body politic? *Social Service Review,* 59, 578–592.

Saleebey, D. (1992). *The strengths perspective in social work practice.* White Plains, NY: Longman.

Saleebey, D. (1994). Culture, theory, and narrative: The intersection of meanings in practice. *Social Work,* 39, 352–359.

Saleebey, D. (1996). The strengths perspective in social work practice: Extensions and cautions. *Social Work,* 41, 296–305.

Saleebey, D. (2000). Power in the people: Strength and hope. *Advances in Social Work,* 1, 127–136.

Sandage, S.T., and Hill, P.C. (2001). The virtue of positive psychology: The rapprochement and challenge of an affirmative postmodern perspective. *Journal of the Theory of Social Behavior,* 31, 241–260.

Satcher, D. (2001). *Youth violence: A report of the surgeon general.* Washington, DC: U.S. Department of Health and Human Services, Office of the U.S. Surgeon General. Available online at: http://surgeongeneral.gov/library/youthviolence/report.html.

Seligman, M.E.P. (1995). The effectiveness of psychotherapy: The *Consumers Report* study. *American Psychologist,* 50, 965–974.

Seligman, M.E.P. (1999). The president's address. *American Psychologist,* 54, 559–562.

Turner, F. (2002). *Diagnosis in social work.* Toronto: Allyn & Bacon.

Walzer, M. (1983). *Spheres of justice*. New York: Basic Books.

Weick, A., Rapp, C., Sullivan, W.P., and Kisthardt, W. (1989). A strengths perspective for social work practice. *Social Work*, 34, 350–354.

Werner, E., and Smith, R.S. (1982). *Vulnerable but invincible*. New York: McGraw-Hill.

Werner, E., and Smith, R.S. (1992). *Overcoming the odds: High-risk children from birth to adulthood*. Ithaca, NY: Cornell University Press.

CHAPTER TWO

A STRENGTHS MODEL
OF DIAGNOSIS

THE STRENGTHS PERSPECTIVE AND
DIAGNOSTIC LABELING

A continual criticism of the DSM-IV (APA, 1994) is that it is overly focused on pathology (Saleebey, 1996). A client's uniqueness is seldom represented by a DSM-IV diagnosis, nor are the positive behaviors clients bring with them that often determine whether they will improve. As most clinicians know, it's not what's wrong with clients that helps in the change process, it's what's right. As Saleebey notes (1996), "The DSM-IV (American Psychiatric Association, 1994), although only seven years removed from its predecessor, has twice the volume of text on disorders. Victimhood has become big business (Saleebey, 1996, p. 296).

The strengths perspective individualizes a client by looking in a hopeful and optimistic way at the client's culture, family life, support network, coping abilities, past and current successes, and a number of otherwise ignored issues that often contribute to good mental health and can frequently be used in the helping process. Building on the strengths of a client seems much more likely to lead to change than focusing on the negatives.

In defense of the DSM-IV, the addition of a GAF (Global Assessment of Functioning) score on the five axes of the DSM-IV does permit a certain recognition of positive behavior. However, discussion with clinicians seeking third-party reimbursements suggests that GAF scores over 50 or 60 (with 100 representing perfectly healthy behavior) often result in a claim being denied because the client's functioning is too healthy. Clinicians, therefore, often artificially lower GAF scores to suggest poorer functioning than is the case, and tend to use diagnostic categories that are vague and nondescriptive. The DSM-IV, although not meant to be used that way, is often more political and financial than it is descriptive of the clients with whom we work. Clients may also find themselves locked into lifelong diagnostic categories by their medical providers and insurers that often have harmful effects on their lives because of adverse diagnostic labeling.

As an example of the negative impact of labeling, Markowitz (1998) believes that the stigma attached to a diagnosis of mental illness negatively affects clients who "may expect and experience rejection, in part, because they think less of themselves" (p. 343). The impact of perceived stigma by others who negatively view mental illness as a lifelong and problematic illness affects work opportunities and compounds feelings of low self-worth and depression (Markowitz, 1998). One could say the same thing about clients with an initial diagnosis of personality disorders or substance abuse. The inclination among employers is to view an initial diagnosis as lifelong, unchanging, and untreatable.

Although labeling for diagnostic purposes may be relevant for the medical field, diagnostic labels for mental health purposes are often poorly defined and pejorative. Far too many diagnoses are subjective and may ignore important indicators of health, including culture, gender, age, level of cognitive functioning, and other complex issues that affect a person's ability to cope with social or emotional problems. In the 1970s, many feminist writers correctly pointed out that diagnostic categories used by male therapists with female clients were more a function of prevailing stereotypes of women than accurate statements of their social or emotional functioning. Gay and lesbian clients have suffered the same degree of inaccuracy in labeling. For a long time, in fact, being gay or lesbian was considered an indication of dysfunctional behavior in earlier versions of the DSM. The same can often be said of people from other cultures and religions whose affiliations often result in diagnoses that are inaccurate and may affect their ability to work at jobs that consider certain diagnostic categories to be bad risks in the workplace. Labels harm people, and the most vulnerable among us—the poor, minority groups, women, immigrants, and the physically, emotionally, and socially disadvantaged—are those most harmed by labels.

The literature related to the treatment of minority clients is interesting to note in that authors often suggest both the need for positive views of people and frequently note the harm done by labeling. Franklin (1992), for example, suggests the following guidelines for effective practice with African American men who react negatively to the use of labeling:

1. *Confronting Negative and Acknowledging Positive Behaviors:* This guideline suggests that African American men should be recognized for their many strengths and that while troublesome behavior may need to be discussed, the worker must remember that the client is doing well in many aspects of his life and that positive behavior must be considered when confronting negative behavior.

2. *The Influence of Labels:* Franklin notes that African American men want to see themselves as "partners in treatment" and resent labels that suggest pathology. Labels send signals to African American men, who believe that these labels subtly or overtly suggest racism.

3. *Addressing Sexism and Racism:* Franklin indicates that African American men are particularly sensitive to sexist notions that berate or bash men. Helpers, according to Franklin, must be particularly careful not to generalize about male behavior. They

also must be aware that African American men are sensitive to racist notions that may include negative stereotypes of African American men.

4. *Cultural Congruence:* Franklin suggests that workers need to understand and value the black experience to be effective with African American men clients. Workers need to approach African American men with respect, concern, and awareness of the many factors that create tensions in their lives.

MEASURING STRENGTHS

The strengths perspective does not use negative labeling. It does, however, look for those positive attributes that may help clients resolve current problems. Although the strengths perspective doesn't deny that clients with repeated emotional difficulties might fall broadly into one of the diagnostic categories used by the DSM-IV, it finds no particular relevance to those categories, believing that they only create bias in those who treat and that they tend, for a large category of clients, to suggest that change is unlikely to take place. Consider the literature on borderline personalities or schizophrenia. In fact, many of the diagnostic categories in the DSM-IV under Personality Disorders (APA, 1994, p. 629) suggest limited potential for client change, causing reluctance by insurers and clinicians to even provide needed treatment. As Moxley and Washington (2001) note in writing about the strengths perspective in work with chemical dependence,

> It is not necessary to categorically view symptoms as deficits since many people coping with chemical dependency have acquired and groomed as strengths the routines, skills, abilities, and competencies that have proven useful in their careers of drug use. Strengths emerge and express themselves under many different conditions. A person's accommodation can contain many strengths. (p. 260)

Although elaborate reasons are often given by clinicians and insurers for not treating certain categories of clients, it still amounts to a system based on exclusion of help to clients who may have been inaccurately diagnosed. Furthermore, it is a system that misses an essential point: Almost all people, even those with long-term psychosocial difficulties, have many positive attributes. Those positive attributes form the strengths approach to treatment.

If we were to categorize the positive attributes of clients to provide overall functioning from a strengths perspective, what might those attributes be, and how might we provide a score that would have relevance to others?

Here are some criteria for measuring a client's level of positive functioning. A suggestion is to use a 10-point Likert Scale to give the client a rating. Perhaps a score of 1 would be the lowest possible level of strength and 10 might be the highest. Five (5) might be an average level of strength, and anything above 5 could be seen as a positive indication of a client's strength in a certain area. The higher the number on the Likert Scale, the more significant the strength. The following continuum, using a Likert Scale, might be helpful:

Likert Scale Measuring Level of Strength
1 —— 2 —— 3 —— 4 —— 5 —— 6 —— 7 —— 8 —— 9 ——10
Very Low   Low   Average   Medium High   Very High

FORTY-FIVE CLIENT STRENGTHS
TO CONSIDER IN DIAGNOSIS

The following positive behaviors should be considered when evaluating positive client behaviors:

1. *Coping Skills:* The ability to handle stressful and debilitating life issues and situations while still being productive and socially active. Good coping skills suggest that clients are resilient in times of stress and open to new ideas, new directions, and new pathways to resolve life crises. Coping skills might also be thought of as the "habits" clients have of successfully dealing with life difficulties. Credit should be given to clients for their ability to deal effectively with a wide range of issues. The ability to cope well in most areas of life should be considered a strength even if the client's coping abilities are not working well at present in certain areas of the client's life.

2. *Support Network:* Some questions we might ask to determine client support networks include the following: Do clients have a vital and significant support network composed of people who will actively help them whenever they are in need of assistance? Do clients respond in a positive and helpful way when others need help? Are the support networks composed of people with good judgment? Have people in the support network helped out in the past? In times of a crisis, could clients call on members of the support networks for assistance? Do support networks include old friends, some of them from a very early age in the client's life (showing an early ability to make and maintain long-term relationships)? Are clients in frequent contact with members of their support network? Are they able to distinguish the difference between friends and acquaintances, and to recognize the need for friendships? Do clients work at maintaining friendships, or do they leave it up to others to do the work? Do clients remember and participate in important life events with members of the support network including birthdays, anniversaries, or the death of significant people in a friend's life? Would they attend a special function for a friend even if it might be necessary to travel or to use scarce funds to attend the function?

3. *Prior Life Successes:* Have clients successfully achieved in the past in such areas as work, education, family life, and community contributions? When clients thinks about their lives prior to a current crisis, do they highly rate their level of achievement? It is important to recognize that clients define achievement. The worker should not have "caveats" on achievement by suggesting that it was accomplished for selfish or unworthy reasons. If the definition of achievement used by clients is unethical or involves harm to others, the best therapeutic stance is to remain neutral by neither praising nor criticizing clients for their level of achievement. There is ample opportunity to provide feedback in the course of treatment as clients explore related life issues and begin to understand the harmful effect their behavior may have had on others.

4. *Current Life Successes:* Even though clients might be currently experiencing a life crisis, would they rate their level of past success in a positive way? Are they able to separate their overall level of achievement from current life problems or do these problems define the way they view their overall levels of success in life?

5. *Cultural Strengths:* Are the client's cultural backgrounds positive about clients and their problems, or do they tend to isolate and condemn clients because of their problems? Do cultures tend to strongly oppose the abuse of alcoholism and drugs, and the abuse of spouses and children? Do they urge people to seek help for social and emotional problems, or do they have very pejorative views of the need to seek help? Do cultures value their traditions and history or do they view it in self-deprecating or negative ways?

6. *Problem-solving Skills:* Are clients usually able to solve life problems and is their judgment normally good? When trying to solve problems, do clients look for advice or help from friends, indigenous helpers, and people with expertise? Are they able to project the consequences of decisions made during periods of crisis into the future and are they able to accept their decisions as the best possible ones made at the time without criticizing themselves for decisions with unwanted or unexpected consequences?

7. *Level of Moral Development:* Are clients able to differentiate between their needs and the needs of others, and to make socially appropriate decisions? Do they place the needs of others above their own needs at critical moments? Would clients help family members or friends if they were experiencing difficulty? Do clients understand and obey the laws of the community? Are they honest and truthful and do they possess personal integrity? Anderson (1997) defines morality as the "expression of an informed conscience and is demonstrated through empathy, compassion, and caring toward others" (p. 596).

8. *Degree of Social Responsibility:* Do clients have a strong sense of a need to make the world, community, and neighborhood better places? Do they support social change and responsible involvement in social justice? Are they actively a part of their community and are they active politically? Do they make a point of voting and of being informed about social and political issues? Are they tolerant of other political beliefs and do they have friends who hold different political beliefs? Do they believe that it is their obligation to leave a positive legacy for future generations?

9. *Level of Motivation to Resolve the Presenting Problem:* Do clients see that they have significant responsibilities for changing the problem they're experiencing, or do they think that it's someone else's responsibility? Are they completing homework assignments given by the worker? Do they actively use the advice of the worker? Do they come on time for interviews, and do they pay fees on time? Does their inability to resolve the problem on their own cause them some degree of anxiety and do they see the negative ramifications of not resolving their problems?

10. *Educational Success:* This might be based on grades, special skills obtained through education, advanced degrees, special accomplishments, joy in learning, interest in new ideas, or the amount of reading done, particularly if it is relevant to the problems they're experiencing. Other issues might include their belief that education is a useful way of achieving social and financial security. Do they value learning? Will they use a learning model (reading, watching appropriate videotapes, going to workshops or lectures) as a part of their own treatment?

11. *Success in the Workplace:* This might be based on the length of time clients have held jobs, their history of promotions and salary increases indicating good work, special skills that make them highly employable, extra training received to do new work, retraining if an old job is obsolete, and a good work record. Other questions to determine strength might be: Do they value work? Would it make them upset to be out of work? Do they have a strong work ethic? Are they loyal to their employer? If they were downsized or otherwise unemployed, would they be able to form plans to obtain new work? Would they be able to put aside anger at the organization that laid them off and get on with the task of finding a new job or career, or consider retraining for new work opportunities?

12. *Interpersonal Skills:* This strength notes the ability of clients to relate to others in a positive and effective way and might include good eye contact, effective use of language, and appropriate communication skills. One way to gauge communication skills is to consider the ability of clients to communicate well with their workers and to develop an effective helping relationship.

13. *Personal Appearance:* Are clients neatly groomed when meeting with workers? Even though they may lack financial resources, do they make certain that their clothing is appropriate (clean, neat, appropriate for the weather) when meeting with the worker? Are they aware of the need to be well groomed in other social situations, including the workplace?

14. *Communication Skills:* Do clients use language in a clear and precise way? Is the language free of slang and inappropriate language? Do clients use language creatively by using words that are more complex or out of the ordinary? Is language used to convey feelings and inner thoughts and are clients able to use language to convey difficult and often angry or destructive emotions without the need to act out feelings that may result in destructive behavior?

15. *Prior Attempts to Resolve the Problem:* Have clients been able to manage or resolve similar problems in the past, with or without professional help? Do they have a good idea about why the prior problems took place or see connections between their current problems and prior life issues or experiences?

16. *Decision-making Skills:* Are decisions made usually thoughtful with positive outcomes? Are the outcomes likely to help them in their social and emotional lives? Are the decisions based on logical thinking or is the thinking disorganized or highly chaotic?

17. *Relationships with Significant Others:* Do clients have a positive, loving, and warm relationship with their extended family, a significant love interest in their life, or with close friends? Do they understand the concepts of love, intimacy, and commitment to family and friends? Are they faithful to their significant love interests? Can clients make emotional commitments to others, and do they maintain those commitments? Are they accountable to others for their behavior? Wolin and Wolin (1993) suggest that resilient people often seek positive relationships with significant others as a way of "filling the void" left by families who are too dysfunctional to turn to. Are clients able to "fill the void" by seeking healthy and constructive relationships?

18. *Level of Spirituality or Religiosity:* Do clients regularly attend religious services? Are they concerned with issues of spirituality (the meaning of life, the hereafter, their relationship to a higher being or order)? Do they have a strong moral code that derives from involvement with spiritual issues? Are they tolerant of other religious and philosophical beliefs even if their personal beliefs are very strong? Do they have close friends with different religious and spiritual beliefs? Are they able to plot paths that permit new information and knowledge to achieve further personal growth? Does that level of growth translate itself into becoming more socially responsible, trusting, and giving, and does it lead to an ability to be more intimate with others? Finding meaning in life traumas may provide people with a significant ability to cope with crisis and a more complete understanding of their lives. As Frankl (1955, 1969, 1975) notes, "Suffering is a potential springboard, both for having a need for meaning and for finding it" (Greenstein & Breitbart, 2000, p. 487).

19. *Healthy Personal Habits:* Are clients concerned about good diet, exercise, using the most recent information about food, drugs, and so forth to make changes in their lifestyle? Are they concerned about weight, abusing substances, good health, and a long life? Do they seek appropriate medical and psychological help when it is required?

20. *Using Alternative Approaches to Resolving Problems:* Are clients receptive to alternative approaches to health? Do they think that strong spiritual beliefs can help heal physical and emotional problems? Would they seek alternative approaches to problem solving if the need were great enough, and would they encourage others to do the same? While this may seem a bit overly "new aged" for some people, the search for alternative ways of healing suggests a proactive and energized person with a highly internal locus of control (Rotter, 1966).

21. *Locus of Control:* Do clients believe that they have the capacity to make life changes (an internal locus of control), or do they believe that all life issues are controlled by luck, chance, or fate (an external locus of control)? Do they continually blame others for their lack of success or unhappiness suggesting an external locus of control, or do they take responsibility for their current situations suggesting an internal locus of control? Do they look for new pathways to resolve problems, which suggests that they have some degree of control over life events?

22. *Orientation to the Present:* Do clients live their lives in the present or do they live more in the past or in the future? Do they think the problem will get better with some hard work in the present or do they feel the problem will magically go away in the future? Do they believe that because something happened in the past, that it will never get better regardless of what helpers and the clients do together?

23. *Self-Concept:* Do clients think positively about themselves? If you ask them to tell you what they like about themselves, do they get stuck, or are they able to provide a realistic list of positive attributes?

24. *Financial Intelligence:* Are clients able to manage finances with available resources? Even when finances are limited, are they charitable? Are clients able to manage finances when income is plentiful? Do they plan for the future by using available savings plans? Are they committed to supporting family even when finances are limited? Do they get joy from spending money on family members even when it might mean that they must go with less? Do they have a financial philosophy that discourages spending more than they earn, or is it their philosophy of money to get into debt beyond any realistic chance of ever paying the money back? Even when financial resources are limited, would they always correct mistakes in financial transactions that unfairly go in their favor? And conversely, would they challenge mistakes made by others that are financially costly to them? Do they use finances to enjoy life even when finances are limited? Would they responsibly take vacations or eat out if it gave them pleasure even when finances were limited? Conversely, would they deny themselves pleasurable experiences even if finances were plentiful?

25. *Emotional Intelligence:* Even though clients are bombarded by numerous problems, many of them not of their making, would they handle their lives with a great degree of natural intelligence? People with high emotional intelligence are able to discover solutions to problems that are often unconventional, but effective. They often keep families together on very limited incomes. They bring culture and enjoyment to children when finances are almost nonexistent. They provide good moral and ethical values for others, and are considered good role models by their communities because they have a way of coping with the world that tends to inspire others. Most of all, they are able to think problems through rationally and come up with solutions that are creative and have a synergizing effect on others.

26. *Creativity:* Do clients use a rich inner world to deal with life problems? Do they use art, writing, sculpting, gardening, car work, woodworking, house repairs, decorating, poetry writing, and other creative outlets to deal with life issues? Are they inspired by creative people? Do they experience joy at the thought of attending lectures, plays, exhibits, demonstrations of new ways of doing things, poetry readings, or other experiences that are meaningful and creative? Do they turn to creative pursuits when experiencing inner conflict and do they use those pursuits to problem-solve? Might they build or otherwise create something for a loved one as a sign of concern and affection? Can they use quiet moments in their lives to creatively think through problems?

27. *Uniqueness:* Do clients have a highly individualized and unique way of addressing the world? Although they may seem eccentric to others, they may tend to be helpful in coping with daily life issues.

28. *Curiosity:* Curiosity is the desire to learn new things about self, community, and others. Curious clients want to experiment with new ideas, behaviors, and life directions. Do clients have a sense of intellectual adventure? Are they willing to permit new life experiences to take place? Does they enjoy new places to visit, or, on a drive, are they compelled to stop and see interesting historical markers or vistas that they might otherwise miss if they stayed directly on the road? Do they share a sense of curiosity and adventure with significant others, particularly children? Does that sense of curiosity continue as they age?

29. *Intimacy:* Intimacy is the desire for physical and emotional closeness. Do clients long to be physically and emotionally close to mates, children, extended families, and friends? Are clients comfortable being touched, hugged, stroked, and praised? Do they seek responsible, mature love? Are they capable of reciprocating that love? Do they trust others with their feelings?

30. *The Desire to Be Autonomous and Independent:* Do clients feel comfortable with themselves and their decisions, or do they always defer to others? Do they enjoy time alone and do they value their observations and thoughts about their lives. Wolin and Wolin (1993) suggest that independence is the person's ability to physically and emotionally distance themselves from troubled situations that could cause emotional harm.

31. *Conviction:* Are clients able to maintain strong philosophical or political beliefs even in the midst of intense criticism and social pressure placed on them to change? Are those convictions parts of larger philosophical and moral stances? Do client convictions come after thoughtful analysis rather than appearing to be impulsive? Are those convictions prompted by external forces rather than introspection and careful thought and analysis?

32. *Flexibility:* When it is important for security or to compromise for the sake of a relationship, do clients possess the flexibility to moderate their views of people, situations, and events? Perhaps another way of putting this might be the ability to set aside strong beliefs, without changing them, for the sake of moving a particular issue, relationship, or situation in a more positive direction.

33. *Fun:* Do clients know how to laugh? Can they appreciate and/or tell jokes or stories, some of which may be self-deprecating? Can they use laughter to heal themselves in difficult situation? Do they enjoy the feeling of having fun in a way that approximates the feelings they experienced when they were having fun as children? Can they be playful with loved ones? Do they enjoy seeing or making other people laugh? Would others say they have a good sense of humor and that it helps them resolve interpersonal conflicts? Anderson (1997) says that humor "channels pain and discomfort in imaginative ways" (p. 597).

34. *Trust:* Do clients have the capacity to trust others? Not foolishly or without deference to the qualities of the other person, but when the right people offer advice or reach out to form relationships, do they have the wisdom to permit that person to influence them?

35. *Tolerance:* Are clients tolerant of other beliefs, cultures, races, and genders? Do they value a diverse society, or are they confused and apprehensive about diversity? Do they have close friends and acquaintances who demonstrate an appreciation of diversity? Do they allow themselves to have experiences in life that suggest a willingness to learn about diverse cultures, sexual orientations, ethnicities, religious beliefs, and political points of view?

36. *Risk Taking:* Are clients willing and able to take chances to improve their lives even when those risks may have negative consequences? Are they appropriately informed about the risks of new adventures, or do they take chances without information or consideration of the dangers? Do they consult others when they are about to embark on a chancy life event? Do they take into consideration the impact that event may have on them and on those for whom they have responsibility? Is the risk they take to better their life, or is primarily to run away from problems that will continue to follow them and will always remain unresolved? Do they take chances just for the stimulation it provides, or are the chances they take meant to enhance their lives and the lives of others?

37. *Resilience:* Are they able to deal with adversity, learn from their experiences, and then continue on with life with a minimum of emotional traumas? Are they able to come back from adversity even stronger than when the difficulty occurred? Anderson (1997) notes that resilient people have been described as being "socially, behaviorally, and academically competent despite" a number of social, economic, and environmental factors and hardships which they resolve without the help of treatment because "they find ways to be successful despite their troubled environments" (Anderson, 1997, p. 594).

38. *Passion:* Are clients passionate about many things? Passion is important in the lives of people and without it, they may have little hope for the future. Some people might liken this to having dreams for the future or a quest to do something meaningful or exciting.

39. *Persistence:* Are clients able to stay with work assignments, educational challenges, difficult but rewarding relationships, career expectations that require the ability to continue on without giving up, difficult family situations, and complex financial arrangements that require careful planning and time to complete? Persistence is one of the most important requirements for successful treatment. If clients are persistent in other areas of their lives, it's quite likely that persistence will define the way they approach treatment.

40. *Determination:* Determined clients have strong positive notions that they will be able to master most life situations. Clinicians may sometimes see this negatively, as in the case of people who are addicted to work and compulsively stay with assignments at the expense of their personal lives. In a positive sense, determination is the desire to master and complete assignments, life problems, and career requirements. Determination is the mindset that leads to persistence.

41. *Knowing the Difference between Being Needed and Being Wanted:* Unfortunately, many people confuse being needed with being wanted. This confusion often leads them to take jobs in which others fail to accept them but still need their expertise. It may also lead to personal relationships that are often defined as co-dependent. The confusion between need and want is fundamental to many of our clients and helping them distinguish one from the other may be a significant area of work using the strengths perspective.

42. *Introspection:* Are clients in touch with their inner world? Do they try and see connections between the present and the past? Do they think about quality of life issues, the meaning of life, and their role in the world? When in conflict, do they look at their own behavior and try to gauge its impact on the problem and their role in resolving that problem? Are they in touch with their emotions, and do they understand the origins of those emotions?

43. *Variety:* Do clients change patterns of behavior to prevent repetition and boredom? Are they willing to change long-held beliefs, political causes, work, or personal interests because to keep them without change might lead to rigidity, bitterness, and isolation? Conversely, can they hold on to long-held beliefs because they are important, while still considering the reason for those beliefs and the possibility that there are other points of view that might be interesting and stimulating?

44. *Internal Peace:* Even though clients may be experiencing a great deal of conflict and stress, do they normally enjoy inner peace and tranquility? Do they possess serenity and calm in the face of powerful external life forces?

45. *Insight:* This is the ability to see a situation as it really exists. Insightful people are able to understand that a situation of importance in their psychosocial development may actually differ from their memory and may "not [be] what it's supposed to be" (Wolin & Wolin, 1993, p. 73).

EVIDENCE OF THE RELATIONSHIP BETWEEN CLIENT STRENGTHS AND POSITIVE BEHAVIORS

This list of positive behaviors, while not all encompassing, does suggest a number of attributes that contribute to positive or negative social and emotional functioning. A low score on any of the attributes (less than 5.0, for example) might suggest problem areas. Many scores less than 5.0 would suggest a preponderance of negative behaviors, although in almost all clients, scores over 5.0 will probably outweigh the scores below 5.0. But let's consider the clients who would have traditionally had very troubled diagnoses on the DSM-IV and a GAF score below 40. Those diagnoses might suggest the existence of mental illness or personality disorders, implying considerable difficulty in treatment. If the client's negative behaviors outweigh the positives, would the strengths perspective be abandoned for more traditional approaches, perhaps those using the medical model? No, because even very troubled people have positive skills and behaviors that are transferable and can be used to cope with more serious problems. A number of chapters in this book are devoted to very troubled clients, but for now, let's consider some research findings to support the belief that the strengths perspective can be used with clients experiencing a considerable amount of psychosocial difficulty.

The Surgeon General's report on mental health (Satcher, 1999) notes that to be effective, treatment must be tailored to take into consideration the client's age, race, ethnicity, culture, gender, geographic area, and value system. The Surgeon General's report goes on to suggest that diagnosis and treatment must be individualized, and are most effective when they support existing client strengths. Those strengths include family, support groups, culture, religious and spiritual convictions, and past efforts to cope with serious emotional problems. The Surgeon General's report doesn't specify which approach is best but encourages practitioners to enlist the client and the client's family in the treatment process so that the services offered are supported by those receiving them. Ring-Kurtz, Sonnichsen, and Hoover-Dempsey (1995) indicate the value of using a child's positive attributes (strengths) when mental health services are offered in a school setting. Oswald et al. (2002) report, "Individual child strengths may mitigate the impact of serious psychiatric symptoms and risk, allowing children to remain in homelike settings successfully" (p. 9).

The Surgeon General's report on youth violence (Satcher, 2001) notes that children with many of the early signs of violent behavior change as a result of mentors and significant others who support and encourage positive change. Those positive changes are often the result of focusing on what's right about children and helping them see that they posses positive attributes that often significantly outweigh the negatives.

Stinnett and DeFrain (1985) studied the issue of why some families handle crisis and stressful experiences better than others. In their attempt to find common qualities of strong families in worldwide studies, the authors suggested six qualities that strong families across the world seem to share: (1) commitment to the family; (2) appreciation and affection for each other; (3) a positive communication pattern; (4) enjoyable time together; (5) a sense of spiritual well-being and connection; and (6) the ability to successfully manage stress. Each of these qualities mirrors qualities noted earlier in this chapter and suggests that positive family attributes reflecting a strengths orientation result in stronger families that are better able to deal with serious crises.

Yalom (1980) suggests that groups providing services to clients with cancer offer benefits that include a sense of universality among otherwise isolated people who may feel shunned because of their illness, a feeling of helping oneself by helping others, hopefulness fostered by seeing how others have coped successfully with difficult issues, and a general sense of belonging to a larger group. Greenstein and Breitbart (2000) note that there has been little work using Frankl's existentialist system of Logotherapy in a group context with ill participants (Lazer, 1984; Zuehlke, & Watkins, 1975). However, Zuehlke and Watkins (1975) used Logotherapy with patients with terminal cancer. Their objective was to help patients develop meaning from their illness. They did this in part by showing important life connections between the past, present, and the future. Patients who participated experienced a stronger feeling of purposefulness and meaningfulness than did those in the control group using the Purpose in Life Test (Crumbaugh, 1968). As Greenstein and Breitbart (2000) note in describing Frankl's belief in the importance of life meaning, "Having a feeling of purpose and meaning can also help alleviate the distress caused by these painful facts of life [terminal illness] in the first place" (p. 487).

Brady et al. (1999) found that patients who found a significant degree of meaning in their lives through the use of Logotherapy experienced considerably more enjoyment in life than did those who experienced a lesser sense of meaning, even when severe pain or fatigue were present. The ability to find meaning within traumatic events has also been correlated with an increased ability to cope with the events (Davis, Nolen-Hoeksma, & Larson, 1998; McIntosh, Silver, & Wortman, 1993). Wolin and Wolin (1993) noted that people who survive traumatic childhoods, including sexual abuse, have "enduring" strengths that developed as a way of protecting themselves against troubled families, and that they manage their traumatic experiences with little assistance from others. Wolin and Wolin identified seven strengths that highly relate to the ability of children to cope with childhood traumas: insight, independence, initiative, relationships, morality, creativity, and humor. And as Anderson (1997) notes in discussing children who have been sexually abused,

> The strengths perspective emphasizes the child's ability to cope with traumatic situations. The ability to live in the present depends on the child's ability to recognize and uncover their strengths (Barnard, 1994; Saleebey, 1997). Because the traumatic event may result in children losing sight of their strengths and abilities, the practitioner's role is to assist in recovering their submerged survival abilities (Barnard, 1994; Saleebey, 1997). (Anderson, p. 592)

EXPLAINING THE PURPOSE OF THE CRITICAL RESPONSE

One of the features of this book is to provide a critical response to material presented in each chapter. This is done to give the reader an alternative view and to stimulate critical thinking. A colleague or friend reviewed each chapter in this book, and the author wrote the critical responses from their comments to maintain consistency in the writing style. The following provides the essence of the feedback the author received for this chapter.

A CRITICAL RESPONSE

One can't argue with the list of positive behaviors. All clinicians should be lucky enough to have clients with a preponderance of positive attributes. However, many of our clients in public and nonprofit social and mental health agencies have long-term and very serious social and emotional problems. For these clients, the

DSM-IV is very helpful. The DSM-IV and its earlier versions were developed to provide practitioners with a more precise way of categorizing dysfunctional behavior: "The purpose of the DSM-IV is to provide clear descriptions of diagnostic categories in order to enable clinicians and investigators to diagnose, communicate about, study, and treat people with various mental disorders" (American Psychiatric Association, 1994, p. xxvii).

The DSM-IV was not meant to diagnose normal fluctuations in behavior or to make value judgments about behavior: "The clinical and scientific considerations involved in categorization of [certain conditions] as mental disorders may not be wholly relevant to legal judgments, for example, that take into account such issues as individual responsibility, disability determination, and competency" (American Psychiatric Association, 1994, p. xxvii). There is a great deal of difference between the situational crises seen by many clinicians in private practice and the severe emotional difficulties experienced by many of our clients in public and not-for-profit social and mental health agencies.

It appears that a straw man has been created out of the DSM-IV. First, it's described as pathology oriented, which it is, of course, and then because of its orientation, the criticism is that it does clients a disservice. How can a correct diagnosis do anyone a disservice? It's similar to saying that a medical diagnosis does a patient a disservice. A diagnosis is developed because it should lead to the most effective treatment possible. This is certainly the case in mental illness where a combination of drug and talking therapies may be very effective with certain types of problems. Would we want to give out powerful psychotropic medications without first having a diagnosis and then using treatments shown to be effective with that diagnosis? One certainly hopes not.

And Saleebey's (1994) criticism of the DSM-IV—that it leads to an obsession with emotional ills and that "victimhood has become big business as many adults, prodded by a variety of therapists, gurus, and ministers, go on the hunt for wounded inner children and the poisonous ecology of their family background" (p. 296)—just seems preposterous. How can the DSM-IV lead to a sense of victimhood? And his criticism that we have twice the number of categories of emotional difficulty than we had seven years after the publication of DSM-III shouldn't strike anyone as odd. The same can be said for diagnosis in the medical field and the advancement in many areas of life in America as we receive new knowledge.

Insurance companies are blamed for forcing clinicians to use incorrect diagnoses so that clients receive needed services. That's not the fault of the insurance companies; it's the fault of the helping professions in not showing a strong and compelling relationship between treatment effectiveness and psychotherapy. Why would insurers pay for expensive services that lack evidence of treatment effectiveness? Most insurers don't pay for homeopaths and yoga, not because either isn't sometimes helpful, but because the research on their effectiveness is nowhere as sophisticated and well documented as medical treatments. Even with fairly sophisticated research, insurance companies are questioning the choices in treatment made by doctors and are concluding that physicians often choose treatments, not because they necessarily work, but because the physicians feel comfortable with their choices. Sound familiar?

Getting back to the list of positive attributes, certainly we should have a positive view of our clients. Focusing on positives is a good idea, but not with all clients, many of whom only learn through negative reinforcement and punishment. Personality-disordered clients often manipulate clinicians who use positive feedback and support and do their best when there are strong negative reinforces for their harmful behavior. In the domestic violence field, arresting and incarcerating perpetrators has led to a substantial decline in reports of domestic violence (Sherman & Berk, 1984). In domestic violence perpetrator groups, there isn't compelling evidence yet that the treatment provided in perpetrator groups is as powerful a deterrent as the threat of prison, should the domestic violence continue. One could say the same about a number of categories of pathology. Not everyone accepts positive reinforcement well nor changes because the therapist is being nice. In fact, not everyone has a good inner life or positive feelings for others. Many clients are often troubled in very serious ways. They need the controls placed on them by others with better ego strength. It is these very strengths of the practitioner that keep our clients going and that model positive behavior. So unless we've limited this discussion to the fairly healthy people who come for treatment because they're unhappy, or because life isn't going well for them at the moment, most clients seen in the public or not-for-profit sectors are very troubled people who like to be treated well, naturally, but who often fail to change without immediate and sometimes forceful consequences.

This entire discussion is reminiscent of R.D. Laing (1959), the British psychiatrist who thought that mental illness was a special gift and that clinicians should view it as a beautiful journey. The clinician's job, according to Laing, was to help the client learn from that journey (Laing, 1959). Unfortunately, all too many of Laing's clients ended up in the emergency rooms of hospitals because, beautiful as their journeys may have been to Laing, to clients, they were full of delusions, hallucinations, paranoid and bizarre thoughts, voices, erratic behaviors, and unhappiness on a scale that most of us cannot imagine (Burstein, 1996). So, yes, high marks for the strengths perspective with clients who are fairly normal and who function well, most of the time. Middle marks for clients who are resilient but still experience episodic crises. And low marks for clients who are very troubled and require mental health or criminal justice intervention much of the time. And aside from the fairly well functioning clients seen in private practice, or the occasionally normal client seen in public and nonprofit settings, most of the clients in the helping professions consist of people with long-term, serious, debilitating, and difficult problems that suggest an absence of almost every strength identified in this chapter.

A final concern: A simplistic way of measuring strengths is included in this chapter. Isn't this the DSM-IV in reverse? If you have an absence of positive behaviors, doesn't that mean you have the presence of a great deal of pathology? However one frames it, clinicians make judgments about strengths and pathology. We use client strengths every day to promote change. We do not avoid discussion of pathology, because that's why the client has come to see us. If the pathology is great, we frequently direct our attention to ways of minimizing the dysfunctional behavior.

As a philosophy of treatment, the discussion in this chapter is interesting, but as a guide to understanding positive behavior, it feels terribly limiting. The people one sees in treatment, who survive the awful things that have been done to them early in life, do it in ways the author hasn't begun to mention. They steal, they lie, they manipulate, and they do it for the best of all reasons: to exist, to live, and to survive.

SUMMARY

In this chapter, a list of positive behaviors is presented to help clinicians look for the positive attributes in client behavior that might be recognized and used in treatment. Additionally, a simple Likert Scale is proposed as a way of measuring positive attributes. A criticism is made of the Scale, suggesting that it is DSM-IV in reverse, and opposing points of view about the material in this chapter are presented. Much of the criticism centers on the level of positive behavior in most clients seen for serious social and emotional problems. An observation is made that many of these clients do better with restraints that inhibit their negative behaviors than with support and encouragement.

INTEGRATIVE QUESTIONS

1. The list of positive attributes in this chapter could be endless. Do you feel the attributes listed were inclusive enough, or were there positive attributes you can think of that should have been added to this list?

2. The criticism of the Likert Scale as DSM-IV in reverse seems to be a valid criticism. Is it possible to evaluate client functioning without making judgments about the degree of client dysfunction?

3. The critical view of R.D. Laing seems very stilted. Laing did some very original and useful work. Perhaps you might find some of his writings and decide whether they make a positive contribution rather than merely accept the critical response offered in this chapter.

4. Many clinicians feel that the DSM-IV is overly positive about behavior and that its attempt to be fair makes it vague and inadequate as a diagnostic tool. Do you feel that Saleebey's criticisms of the DSM-IV are valid?

5. The attributes of positive behavior seem fine, but the definitions are troublesome. Can you find definitions of positive attributes provided in this chapter that are vague, poorly developed, or incorrect? How would you redefine them?

REFERENCES

American Psychiatric Association. (1994). Diagnostic and statistical manual of mental disorders (4th Ed.). Washington, DC: American Psychiatric Press.

Anderson, K.M. (November 1997). Uncovering survival abilities in children who have been sexually abused. *Families in Society: The Journal of Contemporary Human Services, 78,* 592–599.

Barnard, C. (1994). Resiliency: A shift in our perception? *American Journal of Family Therapy, 22,* 135–144.

Brady, M.J., Peterman, A.H., Fitchett, G., et al. (1999). A case for including spirituality in quality of life measurement in oncology. *Psycho-oncology, 8,* 417–428.

Burstein, D. (1996). *The wing of madness: The life and work of R.D. Laing.* Cambridge, MA: Harvard University Press.

Crumbaugh, J.C. (1968). Cross-validation of Purpose-in-Life Test based on Frankl's concepts. *Journal of Individual Psychology, 24,* 74–78.

Davis, C.G., Nolen-Hoeksma, S., and Larson, J. (1998). Making sense of loss and benefiting from the experience: Two construals of meaning. *Journal of Personality and Social Psychology, 75,* 561–574.

Farber, E., and Egeland, B. (1987). Invulnerability among abused and neglected children. In E.J. Anthony and B.J. Cohler (Eds.), *The invulnerable child* (pp. 289–314). New York: Guilford.

Frankl, V.E. (1955/1986). *The doctor and the soul.* New York: Random House.

Frankl, V.E. (1969/1988). *The will to meaning: Foundations and applications of logotherapy* (Expanded Edition). New York: Penguin Books.

Frankl, V.E. (1975/1997). *Man's search for ultimate meaning.* New York: Plenum Press.

Franklin, A.J. (1992). Therapy with African American men. *Families in society: The Journal of Contemporary Human Services,* 350–355.

Greenstein, M., and Breitbart, W. (Fall 2000). Cancer and the experience of meaning: A group psychotherapy program for people with cancer. *American Journal of Psychotherapy, 54,* 4, 486–500.

Laing, R.D. (1959/1965). The divided self: An existential study in sanity and madness. Tavistock, 1959; reprinted London: Pelican.

Lazer, E. (1984). Logotherapeutic support groups for cardiac patients. *International Forum for Logotherapy, 7,* 85–88.

Markowitz, F.E. (1998). The effects of stigma on the psychological well-being and life satisfaction of persons with mental illness. *Journal of Health and Social Behavior, 39*(4), 335–347.

McIntosh, D.N., Silver, R., and Wortman, C.B. (1993). Religion's role in adjustment to a negative life event: Coping with the loss of a child. *Journal of Personality and Social Psychology, 65,* 812–821.

Moxley, D.P., and Washington, O.G.M. (May/June 2001). Strengths-based recovery practice in chemical dependency: A transpersonal perspective. *Families in Society, 82* 251–262.

Oswald, D.P., Cohen, R., Best, A.M., et al. (September 2002). *Journal of Emotional and Behavioral Disorders.* Available online at: www.findarticles.com/cf_0/m0FCB/3_9/77865937/print.jhtml.

Ring-Kurtz, S.E., Sonnichsen, S., and Hoover-Dempsey, K.V. (1995). School-based mental health services for children. In L. Bickman and D. Rogs (Eds.), *Children's mental health services: Research, policy, and evaluation* (vol. 1, pp. 117–144). Thousand Oaks, CA. Sage.

Rotter, J.B.(1966). Generalized expectancies for internal versus external control of reinforcement. *Psychological Monographs, 80,* 1–28.

Saleebey, D. (1994). Culture, theory, and narrative: The intersection of meanings in practice. *Social Work, 39,* 352–359.

Saleebey, D. (May 1996). The strengths perspective in social work practice: Extensions and cautions. *Social Work, 41,* 3, 296–305.

Saleebey, D. (1997). The strengths approach to practice. In D. Saleebey (Ed.), *The strengths perspective in social work practice* (pp. 49–57). New York: Longman.

Satcher, D. (1999). Mental health: A Report of the U.S. Surgeon General: Chapter 8. Department of Health and Human Services, Office of the Surgeon General. Rockville, MD. Available online at: http://www.surgeongeneral.gov/library/mentalhealth/home.hmtl.

Satcher, D. (2001). *Youth violence: A report of the surgeon general.* Washington, DC: U.S. Department of Health and Human Services, Office of the U.S. Surgeon General. Available online at: http://surgeongeneral.gov/library/youthviolence/report.html.

Sherman, L.W., and Berk, R.A. (1984). The specific deterrent effects of arrest for domestic assault. *American Sociological Review,* 49, 261–272.

Stinnett, N., and DeFrain, J. (1985). *Secrets of strong families.* Boston: Little Brown.

Werner, E., and Smith, R. (1992). *Overcoming the odds: High-risk children from birth to adulthood.* Ithaca, NY: Cornell University Press.

Wolin, S., and Wolin, S. (1993). *The resilient self.* New York: Villard.

Yalom, I.D. (1980). *Existential psychotherapy.* New York: Basic Books.

Zuehlke, T.E., and Watkins, J.T. (1975). The use of psychotherapy with dying patients: An exploratory study. *Journal of Clinical Psychology,* 31, 729–732.

CHAPTER THREE

THE STRENGTHS PERSPECTIVE
Psychosocial Assessments

A psychosocial assessment is an attempt to place all of the relevant information we know about a client into a concise statement that permits another professional reader to understand the client and the client's problem(s) just as well as we understand them. Psychosocial assessments differ from DSM-IV diagnostic statements in that they provide brief historical information about the possible cause of the problem. Further, while they are problem focused, they also provide an evaluation of the client's strengths. The following case study is done using a strengths perspective approach to assessment as described in the following statement by Van Wormer (1999):

> At the heart of the strengths perspective is a belief in the basic goodness of humankind, a faith that individuals, however unfortunate their plight, can discover strengths in themselves that they never knew existed. No matter how little or how much may be expressed at one time, people often have a potential that is not commonly realized. The first step in promoting the client's well-being is through assessing the client's strengths. A belief in human potential is tied to the notion that people have untapped resources—physically, emotionally, socially, and spiritually—that they can mobilize in times of need. This is where professional helping comes into play—in tapping into the possibilities, into what can be, not what is. (p. 51)

CASE STUDY: MR. SOLOMON, THE CHILD OF HOLOCAUST SURVIVORS

This case study is presented to help show the way in which the strengths perspective might be used in assessing a client seeking help for depression. The outline used here is for illustrative purposes only. Under each heading, there is a description of the information one might include for that heading of the outline. The important thing to remember is that the assessment provides information to other professionals. Although it is framed in a positive way, it necessarily needs to include all the information relevant to the case. Some of that information might pertain to ongoing difficulties or previous life problems experienced by the client. Most importantly, however, it includes the positive and successful behavior that has permitted the client to function well in other areas of his or her life and the supports that consistently help in successful coping.

The Psychosocial Assessment Outline and Relevant Information Pertaining to Mr. Solomon

Brief Description of the Client and Problem   In this section of a psychosocial assessment, include the client's age, marital status, family composition, what the client is wearing, the client's level of verbal and nonverbal communication, the client's affect, and anything of interest that may have happened in the interview. Also include the defined problem(s) as stated by the client. Normally, don't make interpretations here; just report the relevant information. This is an example of how this section might be written from a strengths perspective:

> Harold Solomon is a 32-year-old entrepreneur whose presenting problem is a sense of unworthiness over earning more than a million dollars each year in the past 10 years of his work career. He says that the amount of money he's earned is considerably out of keeping with the degree of energy used and that compared with people who do "real work," it seems completely wrong for him to earn so much money.
>
> Mr. Solomon came to the interview on time, was appropriately dressed, is deeply tanned, and says that he is 6′ 1″ and weighs 165 pounds. He looks fit and athletic. He wore no rings or other jewelry but did have on a gold Rolex watch. Initially, he moved around a great deal in his chair, and his fingers continually tapped on the arm of his chair. In a short period of time, however, he slumped back in his chair and, from time to time, wiped tears from his eyes as he discussed the impact his career has had on his former marriage, his family life, and on issues of intimacy. He comes to treatment for help in resolving problems related to continuing feelings of unworthiness, depression, and guilt.

Historical Issues   This section includes any past issues of importance in understanding the client's current problems. Continuing with Mr. Solomon, these might be salient points to include in the historical section of the report:

> Mr. Solomon became an entrepreneur in the computer field after his sophomore year at Stanford University. He has not returned to finish his degree and says that his lack of formal education makes him feel insecure about his intellectual abilities. However, he reads a great deal and has tried to make up for his lack of formal education by reading books recommended by people he respects. Mr. Solomon comes from an intact family of an older brother (three years older) and a younger sister (four years younger).

His parents, both deceased, were very opposed to his decision to become a business-man. In his strict Orthodox Jewish family, this seemed to his parents to be a career that would take him away from the moral, religious, and spiritual beliefs of his Orthodox background. His father frequently told him that businessmen were the very people who most condoned anti-Semitism in Nazi Germany and who often do whatever is sit-uationally necessary to make money. His parents wanted Mr. Solomon to enter a ser-vice field and had hoped that he would become a scholar or a physician. Both parents were Holocaust survivors, and the client describes them as serious, hypervigilant, con-tinually fearful, and unaffectionate. When they died, he was not speaking to them be-cause of their opposition to his career and because he had married a non-Jewish woman. He has only a superficial relationship with his siblings, seldom seeing or call-ing them. He has no other contact with a small extended family consisting of an aunt and uncle and several cousins on his father's side of the family, all of whom live in the Midwest. Almost all of his extended family perished in Europe during the Holocaust.

Mr. Solomon and his ex-wife had severe problems because his business career re-quired him to continually be away from home. The couple often fought and, on sev-eral occasions, hit one another. Mr. Solomon believes that his wife was trying to make him jealous, and, in time, he discovered that she was having an affair with one of her university professors. As a result, the marriage ended in a bitter divorce two years ago, following five years of marriage. There were no children.

Mr. Solomon has experienced symptoms of depression since the divorce. The negative feelings about his career and the money he has made began about the time of the divorce, although one parent died shortly before and one shortly after the divorce. He feels guilty that he had stopped talking to them and said that he had a great deal of "unfinished business" with them when they died. The most important piece of unfin-ished business was that his parents performed the ancient Jewish ritual of reading him out of the family after his marriage and never tried to contact him after he became di-vorced. He said that in his most important hour of need, his parents were not there for him. He is proud to be Jewish but thinks it is a religion that often causes friction be-cause it can be so demanding and because it tends to isolate Jews from non-Jewish peo-ple. To help him deal with his ambivalent feelings about his religion, Mr. Solomon attends discussion groups, reads a great deal about Jewish history and traditions, and has tried to understand and resolve his confused relationship with Judaism. It is an at-tempt that isn't always successful, but he continues to try.

He describes an early life full of success and accomplishment because of his ability at business. His relationships with people, however, have always been diffi-cult, and he describes himself as shy and frequently withdrawn. He has few friends in the business world and feels very much alone because he is the only Jewish busi-nessman in a business area dominated by non-Jewish people. He has experienced a great deal of anti-Semitism in his work and says that the people with whom he is in competition can be very cruel in their continuing effort to try and "psych" him out by making rude and bigoted remarks about Jews in his presence. He reports just one other episode of depression or anxiety in his life and says that he is healthy, al-though he sometimes feels easily fatigued. He has no sleeping problems and has kept his weight fairly stable. He is not currently in a relationship and feels that his trust level for relationships is very low. He was on a tranquilizer several years ago because of anxiety and depression during the divorce but cannot remember the name of the medication. He said that it made him sleepy and that he discontinued its use be-cause it interfered with his work.

Diagnostic Statement   The diagnostic statement is a brief overview of what are considered the most relevant problems experienced by the client and their potential causation. In the diagnostic statement, combine material from the prior two sections and summarize the most relevant information in a brief statement. Continuing with Mr. Solomon, this might be an example of the diagnostic statement:

> Mr. Solomon is a 32-year-old divorced Jewish entrepreneur who seeks help for feelings of guilt and depression over the large amount of money he has made over the years in a career that he characterizes as "frivolous." He describes ongoing feelings of isolation and loneliness and is concerned about his inability to trust others. The onset of these feelings seems to have coincided with the death of his parents and the divorce from his wife as a result of her infidelity. These events took place within a few years of one another.
>
> Further issues that need exploration include his relationship with his deceased parents; his difficulty in handling the anti-Semitic behavior of his colleagues; problems in relating to people, particularly women; the degree to which an increasingly troublesome depression is interfering with his life; and feelings of guilt over his choice of a career that has earned him a large amount of money in work he considers frivolous.
>
> Mr. Solomon has a great many positive qualities that should be particularly helpful in his treatment. He is very successful at work, he has a strong value system, he is introspective and feels concern over his current emotional state, and he has a beginning degree of insight into the origins of his problems with his parents, siblings, and former wife. He appears to be highly motivated for change, and although he suffers from a steady degree of depression, he is still able to continue to work at a highly successful level. He longs for more intimacy and wants to form the types of caring relationships that have been so elusive in his life. He also values education and has made a conscious effort to improve his general level of knowledge in an attempt to make up for his early withdrawal from university. He also seeks more information about his religion and seems genuinely interested in finding out more about the history and the traditions of Judaism, information that he resisted earlier in his life.
>
> Currently, a beginning diagnostic impression appears to be that his depression and feelings of unworthiness may be related to his parent's opinion of his career. That they died before he could resolve serious problems with them, and that he then went through a divorce, seem to have reinforced a belief that he is being punished for a career at odds with his parent's notion of the serious and high-minded work they had in mind for him, work that might serve as a repayment for the fact that his parents both lived through the Holocaust. His choice of careers may have alienated his parents and indirectly contributed to his wife's infidelity. His depression may be a result of internalized guilt over the way his important relationships with his parents and his wife were affected by his career choice. Guilt over the money he has made may be related to an internalized belief that a frivolous career has somehow made him a frivolous person, and that work has destroyed his primary relationships.
>
> There is no obvious evidence at this point of any severe emotional problems that might result in further depression or suicide, but of course, enough information to fully make that judgment hasn't yet been gathered. He may be far more depressed than is evident, and only very careful discussion will reveal the depth of his depression and the potential for self-harm. He appears to think rationally, is highly motivated to change, is articulate and bright, speaks about his problems openly, and relates easily.

He has never been in therapy, and while fearful of the process, says that he is optimistic that it will help him. Although he complains of depression and fatigue, he continues to do well in his work and has wisely invested his large income for the future. He is an avid reader and has tried, over the years, to use available literature to understand and resolve many of his problems, sometimes effectively. The prognosis for improvement is very positive at this initial point in treatment.

Treatment Plan   The treatment plan describes the goals of treatment during a specific period of time and evolves from the agreement made between the worker and the client in the contractual phase of treatment. In this example, the client will be seen for 12 sessions over a three-month period.

The following goals of treatment are set to help Mr. Solomon resolve the problems described in the diagnostic statement. Because the worker is using the strengths perspective, the early sessions will primarily focus on developing the relationship. The goals will be nondirective, with the worker asking questions only when necessary to clarify issues. Mr. Solomon lacks relationships of intimacy, and the worker is offering him the opportunity to talk about intimate issues. It may be a revelation for Mr. Solomon to discover that someone can listen to his inner thoughts and not make judgments or jump to negative and critical conclusions. A contract has been developed that identifies the issues the client and the worker agree are areas to be worked on and resolved. Consistent with the strengths perspective, the way in which resolution of his current problems take place requires a focus on the positive efforts the client has used to problem-solve in the past. Using these successful problem-solving skills and the many other successes in his life, we will continue to focus on what works for him in life, helping him see that he has developed a large reservoir of successful coping strategies in many areas of his life. The problem areas the client and the worker have mutually agreed are essential to focus on during this initial three-month contract include the following:

(1) To help Mr. Solomon see important connections between his current feelings of depression and guilt and the consequences of his choice of careers; (2) to help him promote new relationships and to discuss issues of intimacy; (3) to help him work through confused feelings about his parents and his ex-wife that might still be affecting him; (4) to continue to evaluate the depression and to possibly ask for a psychiatric consult to consider medication to relieve lingering symptoms of depression; (5) to evaluate the issue of anti-Semitism in his business dealings and to help him develop better ways of coping with that problem; (6) to help him explore the possibility of continuing his education; and (7) to help him explore his ambivalent feelings about Judaism.

Contract   This is the agreement between the worker and the client. It specifies the problems to be worked on in treatment, the number of sessions agreed to, and other relevant rules related to time, payment, and the cancellation policies. Many workers have these rules in written form, with the client and the worker signing the contract. A contract with Mr. Solomon might be as follows:

Mr. Solomon has committed himself to 12 one-hour sessions to be held over the next three months. However, he understands that more sessions might be necessary. We have agreed to evaluate the effectiveness of what we have done after each session. After 12 sessions, we will evaluate the cumulative impact of treatment to date and renegotiate additional sessions, if required. He has signed the contractual agreement that spells out the other issues of the contract, including time, payment, and the cancellation policy.

Discussion

I have tried to show a connection between Mr. Solomon's early childhood experiences and his current behavior, but you may have a very different explanation. The strengths perspective doesn't suggest that one treatment perspective is superior to another. What it always tries to do is to understand the client's behavior in a way that focuses on nonjudgmental explanations. It also tries to view all of the participants in the client's current difficulty by framing them in the most positive and humane way possible. Often, this is very difficult to do when parents do unkind, even cruel things to their children. To achieve emotional health, the client needs to remember the positive behaviors and attributes of his or her parents while remembering the context in which the negative behaviors took place. One of the attributes of children who successfully cope with childhood abuse is their ability to frame the behavior of their parents in a nonblaming way that permits them to still feel loyalty to their parents. Henry (1999), for example, points out that children are willing to give parents many opportunities to correct their abusive behavior and can be very understanding and even sympathetic to parents whose behavior may be seen as emotionally damaging. Although clients need to see the harm done and to understand its impact, they benefit from a more complete view of their parents. This is the function of treatment: to help Mr. Solomon understand his parents as they would have explained and defended their behavior.

In this analysis, Mr. Solomon is still caught up in the confused and damaged family environment of two parents who endured the Holocaust. One cannot overstate the harmful consequences to normal family functioning that such an experience might have. In the children of survivors of genocide, one often finds hypervigilance, lack of trust, an inability to form relationships, very superficial notions of intimacy (if you can't trust anyone, your ability to have an intimate love relationship may be limited), confusion about identity, deep feelings of despair over what happened to their parents, and the children's impossible job of empathizing with the parents' early life traumas when parents are sometimes emotionally distant, critical, and have very high expectations (Hass, 1991, p. 97).

Children of survivors often feel an overwhelming sense of fragility in their parents, who sometimes suffer from serious physical and emotional problems because of their experiences. Survivors may have nightmares about the death camps, or they may have obsessive thoughts about real or imagined dangers that are transmitted to their children. They may see their home as a fortress and not permit anyone but a few trusted people inside. They may suffer from deep-seated and long-lasting depressions.

Their worldview may be cynical and pessimistic. And they may use their children as vehicles of self-protection against the potential dangers they always anticipate. In this type of environment, there is an absolute sense that children must obey their parents. If they fail to do so, horrible things might happen to the family. Shared stories reinforce the terror parents experienced in the camps, stories that often make their children frightened and distrustful (Baron et al., 1996). As Baron et al. report,

> Two hundred and eight children of Holocaust survivors who were born after their parents' Holocaust experience (children of survivors; COS) and 70 children of parents who left Europe after Hitler's rise to power in 1933 but managed to escape or avoid the Holocaust (children of escapees; COE) were recruited from various Jewish organizations. Research was conducted using questionnaires that were returned by mail. Measures of stress resilience, locus of control, and Jewish identity were administered to all participants. The Children of Survivors were found to have less resistance to stress and to identify less with feelings of being Jewish. (p. 513)

It is also important to remember that Mr. Solomon's parents had their lives disrupted in ways that are almost impossible to describe. Their attempts to toughen up their children and to stress obedience came from a deep reservoir of fear that what happened to them in the death camps of Europe could also happen to their children. Many survivors of genocide have problems with intimacy. For Jewish survivors of genocide, the people who are seen as threats to their continued safety and survival are non-Jewish. For Mr. Solomon's parents, the act of his marrying a non-Jewish woman might be seen as an act of betrayal, and not only betrayal, but a threat to the very beliefs that kept them functioning from the time of their incarceration in the death camps to their own deaths. This sense of betrayal by their son, although harsh for many of us, is a strongly felt belief among some Jewish survivors of the Holocaust, and if Bosnia and Cambodia can be used as a comparison, among many other victims and survivors of genocide.

Mr. Solomon's parents may have had a sense that their lives were saved by their religious beliefs. We might then understand that a child in conflict with those beliefs could cause disruption and pain to the parents. It is possible that his parents believed that nonobservant children would result in God withdrawing His protection and comfort. Along these same lines, the parents' sense of what would constitute acceptable work might be very limiting. For Mr. Solomon's parents, their son's career might have been seen as a way of providing contrition for their survival. Many survivors of genocide feel overwhelming guilt that they lived while others, whom they regarded as more worthy perhaps, did not. Consequently, professions for children to follow are sometimes those with high social worth: the helping professions, teaching, medicine, law, perhaps, but certainly not something as base and materialistic as business. Is this always the case? No. There are many survivors who see the accumulation of wealth as an ultimate form of self-protection. For Mr. Solomon's parents, however, business may not have been seen as a profession with dignity and would probably not please their God.

This may sound like rigid and irrational thinking to people unfamiliar with those who lived through the Holocaust, but it is an understandable rigidity when seen in the light of what happened to Mr. Solomon's parents. They believed that the people who did harm to them once, could do harm to them again, and that only through vigilance and self-protection would their family survive. How at variance this view is with that of the strengths perspective summarized here by the noted defense attorney Murray Richman, who wrote, "I learned that not all people were like me, yet they were no better or worse for it. I learned that human beings do things that other human beings do not understand. I learned that some people hurt others and yet, do not see themselves as hurters; that infliction of pain may indeed be a cry that pain is being inflicted on them" (Gourevitch, 2001, p. 164).

Mr. Solomon's case is an example of a survivor's child trying to gain his own identity and then being criticized and punished for that effort by his parents. The resulting impact on Mr. Solomon is guilt at having tried to establish his own life and parental rejection for his efforts. The result, not surprisingly, is Mr. Solomon's depression and sense of unworthiness. Is it a mild depression, or does it have potential to be more serious? One can only speculate that any depression has potential for serious consequences.

The dilemma for children of survivors, who grow up in an environment with very limited intimacy, is what Weiss (1961) calls an "existential crisis." An existential crisis is one without any apparent reason for its onset. It usually does not move into a prolonged clinical depression. Instead, the existentially depressed person loses a sense of desire for newness in life. They may be cynical about relationships and prone to isolation and withdrawal. Their goals in life may be limited by a sense of futility in even caring or trying. They may view the world as a place full of suffering and torment, and obsess about the negative events in the world around them. As Weiss (1961) notes in paraphrasing Karen Horney, "[I]t [an existential crisis] is a remoteness of the client in crisis from his own feelings, wishes, beliefs and energies. It is a loss of feeling of being an active, determining force in his own life [and results in] an alienation from the real self" (p. 464).

The approach used in the strengths perspective to treat Mr. Solomon is to utilize his many positive attributes. Decidedly, Mr. Solomon is a good man. He may be confused and unclear about the early-life events that shaped him, but he has great potential for change. As a child, Mr. Solomon had to establish his own identity in a family in which autonomy issues became confused with pleasing and protecting his parents. Mr. Solomon chose to become independent and to put his considerable talents and abilities into the process of becoming highly successful. Most families would applaud Mr. Solomon for his efforts. That his parents rejected him because of his independence and success is very confusing to Mr. Solomon. He thinks that what he did was healthy and necessary for his own survival. He cannot see that his parents needed children to serve as vehicles of thanks for being saved in the Holocaust. The very thought of a career in business, with its attempt to make a profit, probably felt wrong to his highly religious parents. Why is this even an issue? Because the parents felt that they had a debt to pay for being saved. That debt would be paid through the work of their children.

Mr. Solomon does not understand that many of the coping skills he developed that helped make him successful at business also make relationships difficult. This function of parents to give children the ability to succeed and survive but to deny them the ability to love and achieve intimacy is a common problem in families that experience genocide. To survive, one must be single-minded and tough. Career and security always overshadow personal happiness. Perhaps Mr. Solomon's parents never actually projected personal examples or models of happiness or intimacy, replacing messages of intimacy with those related to hard work, determination, persistence, and religious observance. Mr. Solomon could admire his parents' will to survive, while failing to recognize that he had all too little preparation for intimacy. This recognition now comes in adulthood as the financially successful client realizes how unhappy he is in his personal life and perhaps has come to believe that his parents were right all along about his choice of careers. Business, he may believe, has led to unhappiness, and it has become just as unfulfilling as his parents had predicted.

USING THE STRENGTHS PERSPECTIVE
WITH MR. SOLOMON

Most of Mr. Solomon's values, behaviors, and beliefs are very positive. His determination, persistence, financial success, and introspection bode well for treatment. Unfortunately, the one thing that he lacks is any operative understanding of relationships and intimacy. These are no small issues to work with in treatment. Applying his many strengths to deal more effectively with relationships might work, but still he needs to experience a relationship that models emotional intimacy. This is where the practitioner's role is most significant. The practitioner must approach Mr. Solomon on the assumption that as much as he craves closeness, intimate emotional relationships also cause Mr. Solomon confusion and discomfort. He will probably see in the worker the good parent he lacked in childhood. However, his idea of the good parent may be so unrealistic and fantasized that what we end up with is Mr. Solomon's confused view of someone who doesn't realistically represent anyone's good parent. Consequently, the clinician must be patient. She must receive her cues about Mr. Solomon's notion of the good parent from Mr. Solomon. She must be mindful that Mr. Solomon's expectation of the good parent will create expectations that, in a sense, she must fulfill. Completely? No, but certainly to a large extent.

Let's explore what this might mean in realistic terms. It means that the worker must be very empathic and that she will have to listen with a third ear, see with a third eye, and feel with a second heart. It also means that the worker must be aware of the subtle signs of discontent that may signal Mr. Solomon's disapproval of the worker at any given moment. It means positive acceptance of the client, and, as is always true of the strengths perspective, it also means that even when Mr. Solomon is off track or using coping mechanisms that distance him from the helper and the problems at hand, the strengths perspective "obligates us to understand . . . to believe that everyone (no exceptions here) has external and internal assets, competencies and resources" (Saleebey, 2000, p. 128), and that these resources, regardless of how dormant or untested, are able to provide the wise helper with the ability to facilitate the relationship in a way that permits the client to work through relationship concerns and discomforts.

Mr. Solomon, as a novice in the area of relationships, will feel discomfort as he begins to awaken from a life with very little emotional intimacy. Fear of intimacy may release feelings of jealousy, anger, and distrust. In a sense, Mr. Solomon is using the relationship to test feelings, albeit somewhat confused feelings, about intimacy, trust, and confidence in others.

The book will have much more to say about relationships and the strengths perspective, but in reading this case, a practicing psychologist in the high-tech area of Austin, Texas, said,

> Like all too many successful people in our society, and much like the successful clients I see who work in the technology field, Mr. Solomon has incredible technical skill, but his ability to relate to others is at a very infantile level. Increasingly, the problems in relationships lead clients like Mr. Solomon to business-related problems and to feelings of unhappiness and self-deprecation. Many of my clients are very successful people, but as we begin to touch one another, as we begin to form a bond together, it is so moving to them, so touching and powerful that sometimes they break down and cry. It is as if the crying they did as infants never achieved a response from their parents and now they cry, out of some deep sense of gratitude, that someone senses their needs and responds accordingly.
>
> I think the Freudian notion of transference isn't compatible with what really happens in treatment. In my view, what happens is that the client develops a sense of joy. Frequently, you'll witness a period of regression as the client begins to joke and become playful in treatment. One of my clients told me that his daughter, commenting on this new side of her father, said that he had the "best mind ever to stay in sixth grade." It is the most promising of signs because it tells us that as clients experience the playful intimacy they missed in childhood, they'll move ahead into adult notions of intimacy. For this, we have the client-therapist relationship to thank. It is the mechanism that promotes the ability of clients like Mr. Solomon to progress into the world of feelings and the sensitivity to others that comes with intimacy.
>
> I think of what happens in treatment as a journey into life, and that we, as helping people, are the privileged ones who are allowed to go along on that journey. It is a journey that makes all of us more keenly aware of our own humanity, and it can be very humbling. I see my clients as brave fighters, and I marvel at how each of them copes so well when so much harm has been done to them.

In describing a similar experience with clients in existential crisis, Weiss (1961) wrote,

> To defrost, to open up, to experience and to accept himself becomes possible for the patient only in a warm, mutually trusting relationship in which, often for the first time in his life, he feels truly accepted as he is, accepted with those aspects of himself which early in life he had felt compelled to reject or repress. (p. 474)

Weiss goes on to note that as treatment progresses, the client who may appear so devoid of self-awareness and who seems emotionally lacking in feeling and introspection will "begin to reveal surprising aliveness and depth, passionate longings, and strong feelings of loss" (p. 475).

A CRITICAL RESPONSE

Mr. Solomon's is an excellent case. It has many elements that would intrigue most clinicians. It's also clear how the strengths perspective will probably work with Mr. Solomon. He has numerous life skills and has achieved at a highly sophisticated level. To be sure, he also has some serious problems. However, it's important to keep in mind that the therapy research isn't completely clear on the effectiveness of alternative treatment approaches, including the strengths perspective. Take, for example, the work of Wampold et al. (1997), who found that there were no real differences in treatment outcomes between more traditional therapies and newer forms of therapy that are highly flexible and tend to be seen as client-centered. In evaluating the literature on the effectiveness of certain types of approaches to client problems, Chambless and Ollendick (2001) found that not all problems respond well to all types of treatment. Certain types of therapy are more effective with certain types of problems. They also note the importance of accurate diagnosis so that the treatment approach with the most research support might be used. However, this is clearly a very interesting case, with a good prognosis using the strengths perspective as an alternative form of treatment. The importance of the worker-client relationship cannot be overstated with a client like Mr. Solomon.

SUMMARY

In summary, the psychosocial assessment is a way of determining areas of difficulty and areas of strength. Used correctly, it can provide the practitioner with an understanding of the connecting elements that have created the current crisis in a client's life. The psychosocial assessment, using a strengths perspective, can help us develop strategies that may move the client in directions that create changes in the client that are both significant and elegant.

INTEGRATIVE QUESTIONS

1. Do you have an alternative theory about why Mr. Solomon is currently depressed and seeking help?

2. There are many children of Holocaust survivors who do not fit the description of Mr. Solomon and who do well in life. Isn't it possible that stereotypes of the children of survivors are being used in this case, and do not apply to the majority of children of survivors?

3. Question 2 might be asked about the *survivors* of genocide. Many survivors don't have the dour and rigid ideas about their children as those described here. Isn't it possible that these stereotypes of survivors provide misinformation that mislead practitioners in treatment?

4. While the strengths perspective is critical of the DSM-IV because it fails to individualize clients, doesn't a psychosocial assessment essentially do the same thing? The format seems a bit rigid. Think of some alternative ways of assessing client behavior that really individualize the client and his or her experience.

5. This case uses an intelligent, well-read, and highly successful client. Would the strengths perspective work as well with someone who had none of these positive attributes?

REFERENCES

Baron, L., Eisman, H., Scuello, M., Veyzer, A. and Lieberman, M. (September 1996). Stress resilience, locus of control, and religion in children of Holocaust victims. *Journal of Psychology*, 130, 513–525.

Chambless, D.L., and Ollendick, T.H. (2001). Empirically supported psychological interventions: Controversies and evidence. *Annual Review of Psychology*, 52, 685–716.

Gourevitch, P. (2001). The crime lover. *The New Yorker*, February 19 and 26, 2001, pp. 160–173.

Hass, A. (1991). *In the shadow of the Holocaust: The second generation*. London: I.B. Tauris.

Henry, D.L. (September 1999). Resilience in maltreated children: Implications for special needs adoptions. *Child Welfare*, 78, 519–540.

Saleebey, D. (Fall 2000). Power to the people: Strength and hope. *Advancements in Social Work*, 1, 127–136.

Van Wormer, K. (June 1999). The strengths perspective: A paradigm for correctional counseling. *Federal Probation*, 63, 51–58.

Wampold, B.E, Mondin, G.W., Moody, M., Stich, F., Benson, K. et al. (1997). A meta-analysis of outcome studies comparing bona fide psychotherapies: Empirically, "All must have the prize." *Psychological Bulletin*, 122, 203–215.

Weiss, F.M. (1961). The existential crisis. In E. Josephson and M. Josephson, *Man alone* (pp. 463–479). New York: Laurel.

CHAPTER FOUR

THE STRENGTHS PERSPECTIVE AND THE CLIENT–WORKER RELATIONSHIP

OVERVIEW OF THE IMPORTANCE OF THERAPEUTIC RELATIONSHIPS

Many professionals believe that the quality of the relationship between the helper and the client is more important than the system of therapy used. Carl Rogers (1951) believed that it took a very objective and giving person to be a therapist, and that the therapist had to be free of biases and prejudice that might negatively affect the client. He also believed that the client–worker relationship was the key element in the helping process. The strengths perspective would go one step further. It would maintain that the relationship requires the worker to frame most of the client's behavior in a positive way. Behavior that is self-destructive, abusive, or harmful to others? No, certainly not. But when discussing a client's negative behavior, it is well to remember that even hurtful behavior has a reason for existing and that those reasons can be used to better understand the client and to help the client develop change strategies.

In an assessment of a study done using *Consumer Reports* data on the effectiveness of psychotherapy, Seligman (1995) suggests that clients have the wisdom to "shop around" for therapists who meet their own particular needs. The types of therapy they receive are far less important than the intangible aspects of whether they like the therapist and think that he or she will be able to help. Seligman writes, "Patients in psychotherapy in the field often get there by active shopping, entering a kind of treatment they actively sought with a therapist they screened and chose" (p. 970).

Weiss, Sampson, and O'Connor (1995) suggest that the client is in control of the relationship and that highly motivated clients order the importance of the problem(s) they wish to resolve and then actively "coach" the worker for the purpose of "guiding them, so that they may provide the experiences, display the capacities, or convey the knowledge that patients need to disconfirm from their pathogenic beliefs" (pp. 1–2). Commenting further on the importance of the therapeutic relationship in the change process, Warren (2001) writes, "The relationship between the quality of the patient–therapist relationship and the outcome of treatment has been one of the most consistently cited findings in the empirical search for the basis of psychotherapeutic efficacy" (p. 357). Holmes and Lindley (1989) consider the central feature of psychotherapy to be "the use of a relationship between therapist and patient . . . to produce changes in cognition, feelings and behavior" (p. 97). However, Gelso and Hayes (1998) wonder if we have a clear understanding of what is meant by the worker–client relationship, and write, "Because the therapy relationship has been given such a central place in our field, one might expect that many definitions of the relationship have been put forth. In fact, there has been little definitional work" (p. 5).

In describing the key elements of the relationship, Bisman (1994) calls the therapeutic relationship a form of "belief bonding" between the worker and the client, and that both parties need to believe that, "the worker has something applicable for the client, the worker is competent, and that the client is worthwhile and has the capacities to change" (p. 77). Gordon Hamilton (1940) suggests that bonding takes place when the clinician and client work together and that, "treatment starts when mutual confidence is established, only when the client accepts your interest in him and, conversely, feels an interest in you" (pp. 189–190). Alan Keith-Lucas (1972) defines the relationship as, "The medium which is offered to people in trouble and through which they are given an opportunity to make choices, both about taking help and the use they will make of it" (p. 47). Keith-Lucas says that the key elements of the helping relationship are "mutuality, reality, feeling, knowledge, concern for the other person, purpose, the fact that it takes place in the here and now, its ability to offer something new, and its nonjudgmental nature" (p. 48).

The Freudian notions of transference and countertransference provide little direction in describing a therapeutically effective relationship. While one can appreciate Carl Rogers' description of a positive therapeutic relationship as one in which the worker approaches the client with warmth, genuineness, and empathy, if it were as simple as avoiding transference and countertransference or developing the attributes of the facilitatively effective therapist, we should be much further along in our understanding of what takes place between two people that promotes, or fails to promote, change. To further understand the importance of the relationship in practice, this chapter describes how the therapeutic relationship is used in the strengths perspective to promote positive client change.

RELATIONSHIPS AND THE STRENGTHS PERSPECTIVE

A cooperative relationship must first exist between the worker and the client in which the goals of treatment have been clearly agreed on by both parties. Power differential between the helper and the client must be removed to enable the client to work independently and to seek new information that may help in resolving the problem. "Social workers must engage individuals as equals. They must be willing to meet them eye-to-eye and to engage in dialogue and a mutual sharing of knowledge, tools, concerns, aspirations, and respect" (Saleebey, 1996, p. 303). The information shared by the client with the worker may be personal, or it may come from other sources including literature searches, discussions with friends and families about the origins of the client's problems, or independent consultations with other professionals. The worker's function is to facilitate the process by explaining that he or she has some expertise in helping people gather relevant information about a problem and then discussing that information so that the client may experience it in a deeply felt way. The nature of that discussion may be surprising to both the client and the worker. To help in communicating important information, the worker is always searching for new information to use in treatment which will be shared with the client for the purpose of promoting change. In a sense, the worker is a sharer of knowledge and encourages the client to independently search for additional information about his or her problem so that it might help in the process of change.

While the client provides the worker with information about a problem and its possible origins, the helper tries to organize and understand that information by asking for clarification and feedback. Once the client provides relevant information, the worker and the client begin a process of knowledge gathering to promote successful resolution of the problem. The knowledge that is gathered may be found in the available research literature, or it may be a more concise and accurate social history with the client providing more specific information about life events that may be affecting the client. In this process of gathering and assimilating information, it is important to remember that the client must know as much as the helper. The helper cannot hold back information hoping to find a correct moment in time to share it. The information shared with the client must be based on the evidence at hand. This does not permit wild leaps of faith or interpretations that come from nowhere just to see how the client reacts.

It is important that the client understands that the helper has no prescriptions or quick fixes for resolving a problem. The helper may have ideas to promote discussion, or they may have some thoughts about the information shared by the client. Otherwise, the helper's role is to keep the discussion open so that it's possible for the client to talk about anything. The atmosphere during the discussion is one of acceptance and mutual respect. The partnership formed in the helping process may lead to quick and significant change, or it may lead to gradual change. This is a function of how well the two people work together.

Definition of the Therapeutic Relationship from the Strengths Perspective

The therapeutic relationship is the bond developed between two or more people for the purpose of helping resolve social and emotional difficulties. The bond derives its purpose from the belief that establishing a caring partnership where power differences are eliminated and the helper and the client communicate in a way that is comfortable, sincere, and honest will lead to positive change. The positive elements of the client's prior and present behavior promote a belief that the client can use these elements of strength to resolve current life problems.

TWELVE ELEMENTS OF THE HELPING RELATIONSHIP IN THE STRENGTHS PERSPECTIVE

Following are the twelve primary elements of the helping relationship in the strengths perspective:

1. *No Power Differentials:* There are no power differentials between clients and helpers. This applies to all clients, including children, involuntary clients, and clients diagnosed with what we so easily call "diminished capacity" in this society, a euphemism that seems humane but is in reality cruel and dehumanizing. The absence of a power differential is the driving force of the strengths perspective. Beginning the relationship with the assumption that we know less than clients about their problems is humbling. We need information from clients that only they can provide if we are to be helpful.

2. *Know What the Client Wants of Us:* It is important to know what clients want from workers and, if possible, to honor that request. It is not OK for workers to believe that they know what's best for clients or that they always act in the clients' best interest. Harm can be done when we bypass the clients' wishes and provide information, opinions, and judgments they haven't asked for and may not want. This need to know what the clients want should be spelled out immediately in the very first client contact, even if the client is an involuntary client and sees us in an adversarial role. The purpose of the work we are to do together should be specified by developing a contract between the client and the worker that frames the issues to be resolved and the therapeutic processes required. As one client said,

   It's so frustrating. You go to see someone for a personal problem, and it's hard to get up the energy and courage to see him or her in the first place. You come full of what you want to say and how you think the therapist can help, but before you know it, the therapist is asking questions and leading you in a different direction. The story you wanted to tell doesn't get told, and you leave with this sad feeling that the therapist hasn't heard a word you've said. It makes you feel that the therapist isn't interested in your point of view, and isn't going to take much of what you say, or want, into consideration. It's very frustrating.

3. *Early Rapport Is Essential:* It is important to establish an early rapport with clients. Rapport has been defined in many ways, but it is simply the level of comfort a client feels with a worker. There is no particular trick to establishing rapport, but it is often thought to be a process in which the worker helps

the client feel comfortable with the worker and the process of change. If the worker is relaxed and confident, those conditions may be quickly felt by the client and often promote immediate client involvement. Some workers use part of an initial session to help clients overcome the "stage fright" they may initially experience. Small talk may be used or the workers may talk a little about the helping process, asking the clients to share their feelings about what has been said. As Bisman (1994) notes in her concept of "belief bonding" between the worker and client, the initial contact with the client establishes whether the worker and the client will be able to work together. The developing relationship, based on the comfort level between the helper and client, defines whether the degree of belief bonding will be adequate to help resolve the client's problem. The mutuality of beliefs, according to Bisman, and the level of comfort felt in approaching the problem, will determine whether the problem will be resolved.

Rapport is established, or not established, almost immediately. The contributing factors in establishing rapport are the helper's level of warmth, the helper's comfort level, the similarity of the contact with the client's usual social interactions, the warmth and comfort of the physical setting, the lighting, the comfort of the seating arrangements, and the clothing worn by the helper. The client immediately takes all of these factors in and a judgment is made about whether the worker can be trusted and how much of a commitment the client will make to treatment. As one client said,

I went for therapy over the loss of my job, and I was feeling very distrustful of people at the moment. The woman I went to had come very highly recommended. She had a very nice voice. In the first minute or two, as I was sizing her up and trying to get my thoughts together so I could tell her what was wrong with me, I couldn't help notice that she was wearing suede shoes and that a little piece of suede was missing. Maybe other people would have seen it differently, but to me it was endearing. I thought to myself, this is a regular human being who has flaws and she'll be easy on me and I can trust her. And the fact was that she was excellent and she *did* help. I came to that conclusion in the first minute or two I was in her office.

4. *Active and Attentive Listening:* A core ingredient of the strengths perspective is the ability of workers to help clients clearly communicate the nature of their problems and the impact the problems are having on their lives. For this to happen, workers need to allow clients to tell their stories unfettered by questions or observations until it is clear to both parties what the problems are and what the clients would like the workers to do about them. This process of active and attentive listening requires patience, time, and a considerable willingness to let clients tell their stories in a way that feels right to them. At some point in time, if we listen well enough, are nonjudgmental, and keep interpretations of the material from entering into our thinking, we will accurately know the clients' versions of the problems. Think about an experience you've had with a physician who made a diagnosis before you'd completed your description of the symp-

toms, and recall how unwilling you were to use the treatment recommended by the physician. This same level of disenchantment affects clients as they try and tell their stories logically, only to be frequently interrupted by the worker. The result is a disrupted story and incomplete information that the client believes is vital to being helped.

5. *Evidence-based Practice:* To assist in the process of communication, workers must be able to access and share information from the research literature that might lead to change. This means that workers must know the sources of empirical information, be able to explain those sources to their clients, and help clients consult those sources by encouraging independent reading, thinking, and evaluation of the information. Clients need to know what helpers know. The purpose of the strengths perspective is to empower clients to use their own resources to understand the complex nature of their current situations and to process those situations in ways that lead to client-directed change. Gambrill (1999) suggests the creative option of providing clients with research information and writes, "One option is to prepare books for clients critically reviewing the literature in relation to key areas of concern in social work (e.g., child welfare) that describe what has been tested to what effect and what has not been tested (see, for example, Enkin et al., 1995)" (p. 358).

6. *Encouraging Independent Client Solutions:* Clients are encouraged to gain knowledge by reading the materials available to the workers and by coming to their own conclusions about what it may mean, even if it differs from the perceptions of the workers. The same process is used when clients explore past life experiences through the encouragement of workers who hope that clients will begin a process of self-discovery about their cultural and social roots, family origins, and significant conflicts, failures, and successes. Through this process, clients begin to have a more accurate view of their own histories. The ability to clearly see one's history is a powerful tool for change because it prompts feelings the clients may have had during earlier life experiences and helps tie current feelings to relevant prior life events.

As one client said, "The therapist suggested that I keep a journal of my past history and jot down the things that happened to me that might be related to a depression I was going through. As I was driving to work one day, I remembered having this terrible argument with my father about my boyfriend in which he told me that my boyfriend was an indication of how poorly I thought of myself, and that if I was a healthy person, I'd be going out with healthier guys. And I mean he used to say that about everyone I dated. Here I am in my forties and I have the same troubled feeling that the men I date are all inferior and that I'm an unhealthy person. It's not true, any of it, but I sure got in touch with what I've been feeling lately just by being encouraged to think about my past history. And what was so good about it is that the therapist started the sessions by asking me about any insights I'd gained through my journal writing. She was really interested and encouraged me to talk about my thoughts and feelings until I felt I'd learned a lot about developing my own awareness of why I feel the way I do. It was very empowering, really."

7. *The Worker May Share Opinions:* Workers may share opinions, but these opinions need to be explained in a way that utilizes the clients' ability to comprehend and process them, and to disagree when they seem incorrect. The strengths perspective believes, as does evidence-based practice, that change comes from knowledge, and that the function of treatment is to help clients critically evaluate information. The strengths aspect of this approach is the recognition that clients have inner resources, critical thinking competencies, and the ability to rationally determine what is best for them. The workers' opinions are just that. They aren't truth nor are they carved in granite.

8. *Focusing on the Positives:* Helpers always promote the clients' understanding that they have used successful approaches to problem solving in other areas of their lives that may be transferable to their current life difficulties. Just as clients consult automobile reports before purchasing a car or look up histories of companies before buying a stock, these similar problem-solving skills can be used with personal problems. It is the workers' role to help clients reflect on the clients' prior use of gathering rational and informed information before making a decision so that the same process can be applied to the task of resolving current personal problems.

9. *Humility as a Key to Helping:* In the real world, people expect helpers to do just that—help them. Clients want the helpers to be nice about it, but, more to the point, they expect honesty and humility from them. It is a privilege to help someone. The privilege is from the clients opening up their hearts, baring their internal conflicts and pain, and trusting helpers with private and often distressing information. That process should promote a sense of humility and deeply felt respect for the brave and often painfully troubled people who place their pain and the expectation that their suffering will end in the helpers' hands.

10. *Clients Need to Understand Our Work:* Clients have the right to know what helpers are doing. Our work is not mysterious. It's a process between two people that constantly needs to be explained, discussed, and evaluated. If clients don't know what we are doing and why, it only serves to confuse them and impact negatively on the relationship. The worker who asks a client to do a role-play very soon into treatment, but doesn't explain its purpose, is going to have a client who feels confused and discounted. The insights from the role-play will be diminished, and the exercise will end with the client feeling that the helper is playing games. Some clients hate role-plays and some of the other techniques of the profession. It is the helper's obligation to search for the techniques of treatment that promote the most comfort in a client and come closest to the client's usual way of problem solving. This is a very important rule to remember, particularly for the client who is new to treatment and is anxious to please the helper, but is confused about what the helper is doing. Clients should never be confused about the worker's approaches or the techniques of practice they are using. Informed clients who are in cooperative relationships with workers will have a sense of empowerment in knowing they can ask questions, disagree with the workers, and provide feedback to achieve a successful outcome in treatment.

11. *Working with Transference:* Freud believed that clients tended to see workers as substitutes for the loved ones they never had in their lives. The loved ones they

want the workers to represent can be parents, siblings, friends, or others to fill a void in their lives left by the absence of suitable parental or adult love relationships. Freud believed that it was inevitable that clients experienced a transference relationship with workers, because the workers, particularly if they were kind, empathic, and concerned, would represent something so unusual in the clients' lives that the workers could easily be placed in a role of intimacy that might help or hinder treatment.

A positive example of transference might be when the worker is seen as the good parent and the client wants to please the worker by gaining his or her acceptance and love through hard work and improvement. An example of transference that could be problematic is when the client sees the worker as the representation of the adult love object the client fantasizes having but has thus far not experienced. A client who place a worker in this role often becomes jealous, demanding, and inquisitive about the worker's private life, and creates hoops for the worker to jump through that are inconsistent with the worker's role. The client might actually profess love for the worker and expect the worker to reciprocate. How the worker resolves the transference relationship, according to Freud, determines whether treatment will be effective.

From a strengths perspective point of view, transference occurs when workers subtly encourage clients to place workers in roles of importance they should not hold. This is not to say that clients don't develop strong positive feelings for their helpers or that these feelings may not become intense. It is to note that the strengths perspective constantly evaluates the effectiveness of the therapeutic work. If clients are beginning to develop strongly emotionally charged feelings for their workers that could create problems in treatment, the feelings would be dealt with immediately, not after they've become entrenched. The intimate questions about the worker, the desire to increasingly know whether the worker values the client above all other clients, the hurt if the worker has to change an appointment time or cancel an appointment, all of these indications of transference can be avoided by observation, immediate reflection back to the purpose of the work, and, finally, evaluating whether this increasing interest in the worker is helpful to the client. This can be done in a positive and gentle way, of course, but it must be done as early as possible to avoid the dependency problems associated with transference.

A client described his experience with a female therapist and how the worker dealt with it. "I was seeing a therapist regarding a problem I was having with my love relationship. My therapist wasn't particularly attractive, but she was very warm and kind, two qualities lacking in my girlfriend. I started writing short stories and showing them to her during our therapy sessions. I'd dress extra well and I'd notice what she was wearing and comment to her about it. She was very professional and she accepted each gesture objectively. It was driving me crazy. It wasn't that I wanted to see her outside of the office or to be involved with her physically; I just wanted her to love me beyond any love she'd ever felt. I even wrote her a short story comparing her to my love relationship and describing all of the things I loved about her but didn't love about my lady friend. It was a bit more complicated than that, but she remained objective, said very little to encourage these feelings, although a few times, I got irrationally angry at her for discounting me, but, in time, I felt how safe I was in working through the feelings I had for her when she was always very professional. I still like her a lot, appreciate the help she gave me, and am thankful, in a curious sort of way, that she didn't fall for my baloney, since it was the same stuff I was using in my love relationship and it was ruining any chance I had for the relationship to work."

12. *Writing Summaries of the Work after Each Session:* One of the techniques that some workers describe as effective is having clients write summaries after each session and sharing those summaries with the workers so that issues to explore during the next session might be identified. A colleague who had just begun therapy with a therapist he liked very much used this technique. After nine sessions, just as they were beginning to progress in treatment, my colleague accepted a new job in a small community thousands of miles away. Because of the absence of therapists in the new community, the original therapist and my colleague decided to continue treatment by telephone. The day after the first telephone session, my colleague began to send the therapist a fax outlining what he'd learned during the telephone session, what he intended to do about it, and the issues(s) he wanted to discuss during the next session. He said that, in many ways, the work they did together on the phone was much more powerful and relevant than the work he had done with the therapist in person. "First of all," he said, "it *is* possible to do therapy on the phone. I had to be very focused, but since I was in a room with no distractions, that was easy. Then, we had to have a sense of where we wanted each session to go or we would misuse the time. Therapy seemed to last longer on the phone, because, I suppose, there were no distractions. In my prior sessions, we must have spent a lot of time warming up, because I'd leave feeling sort of half done. On the phone, I felt as if we'd covered the material in a much more concise and usable way. The day after the first telephone session, I wrote about a page of what I'd gotten from the session, what I was doing about it, and what I wanted to talk about during next session. Then I'd fax it to my therapist. It started a process I found extraordinarily helpful. Of course, the therapist was terrific, and after a session or two, I think we both knew that something pretty special was taking place. The other thing our phone calls did was that I took a more proactive role in my treatment. I began to read everything I could find about mid-life depression and loneliness. What I found was a very strong literature that was really helpful. I discussed medication with my therapist and then went to see my physician about it. In the end, they didn't recommend medication because of the side effects, but my goodness, I felt as if I was being consulted and cared for in an extraordinary way even though my therapist was thousands of miles away.

"I should add," he said, "that one of my sessions was held on the day of the World Trade Center bombings. We were both in such a troubled state of mind because of the horrible loss of life that the session was electric. I still can't quite believe how powerful it was or how touched I was that my therapist was in her office waiting for my call when she had family members in New York who may have been harmed by the bombings."

TEN GUIDELINES FOR ESTABLISHING RAPPORT

Following is a brief list of suggested guidelines for establishing rapport with clients. The guidelines relate primarily to early contacts with the client and to warm-up experiences at the beginning of each session.

1. *Self-Disclosure Takes Time:* Many clients will not self-disclose easily. Warm-up periods and false starts are likely to take place initially, because people often believe that therapy will make them worse. They also believe that therapists can read their minds—not literally, of course—but they do think that their darkest secrets will be revealed and that the therapists will think badly of them. Letting clients talk about anything will help them get to the issue they want to discuss. Warm-up periods are always necessary, even when the clients have been seen many times before.

2. *Treatment May Require an Indirect Approach:* Treatment may require a less direct path, with considerable opportunity given the clients to brag, tell self-aggrandizing tales, and deny culpability in any problem. In time and with patience, however, most clients reach a point at which they are willing to self-disclose and work on change. Pollack (1990) says that therapists must learn to reach out to clients, mindful of the clients' need to "save face" in the process of self-disclosure and intimacy.

3. *Intimacy Takes Time:* Many clients, particularly men and clients from very traditional cultures, may not bond with their therapists easily and are generally suspicious of attempts to form relationships before they are emotionally ready. Do not assume an intimate therapeutic relationship, even when clients suggest that one exists. Many clients are fearful of getting hurt by those they must trust the most.

4. *Denial of Pain:* The level of pain in clients and the parallel denial of that pain should never be minimized. Clients often have few outlets to discuss emotional difficulty, so it tends to build inside without an opportunity for release. Clients often believe that it is best to deny emotional difficulties, because many people with whom they share intimate feelings may give insensitive or antagonistic responses.

5. *Clients Feel Weak in Treatment:* Many clients feel weak when they are forced to admit to being in pain, particularly emotional pain. Asking clients to admit that they hurt will often be met by denial, because some clients have been taught that succumbing to pain may lead to a complete breakdown in functioning. This is particularly true of men, especially "traditional" men.

6. *Don't Be Distracted by Manipulation:* Clients often try to manipulate workers they admire or feel attracted to, but in the process, they may also work hard to please and may make significant gain as a result. As with all of us, clients want to be liked. To increase the probability of being liked by the workers, they may not tell workers everything workers need to know, or the clients may be untruthful. Don't take this as a sign of manipulation; accept it as the course clients often take to gain trust and to self-disclose when ready.

7. *Let Clients Talk:* Although many clients may not want to talk about their emotional distress, most people love to talk about themselves. Let them talk about anything, even things that may seem insignificant. In time, and when they are ready, they will often indirectly bring up important issues in their lives for discussion. If self-disclosure isn't taking place, and a significant amount of time has gone by, you might say, "I wonder if we might talk a bit about [the issue that brought you here]."

8. *Structure Treatment:* Many clients need order in their lives. Structure therapy carefully so that it has a logical set of steps to achieve a result, with a predictable point at which it will end. Most clients want to know how long it will take to resolve a problem. They don't approach treatment as a lifelong process but as a short-term, immediate step to reduce stress, unhappiness, and anxiety. Suggest that a client's symptom may be much better in a specific period of time (three months, for example) if the worker and client follow the contract they've developed to guide their work together.

9. *Use Praise:* Praise clients for their accomplishments. Keep the discussion focused on the clients' positive behaviors, because clients are often reluctant to discuss negatives issues unless they feel they are operating from a position of emotional strength. Praise should be honest. If it's not genuine, clients will know it and will resent workers for using such an obvious and demeaning strategy.

10. *Don't Label:* Most clients do not like to be categorized. Never use diagnostic terms with negative implications or clients may feel demeaned and resentful. This is particularly true of men and clients from traditional cultures who view labels as attempts to narrowly view them as people. As Saleebey (1996) reminds us, "Many alienated people have been named by others—labeled and diagnosed—in a kind of total discourse. The power to name oneself and one's situation and condition is the beginning of real empowerment" (p. 303).

A CRITICAL RESPONSE

There is such emphasis in the literature on the importance of the therapeutic relationship, and so little research data to suggest what that means, that one tends to be a little skeptical. If Seligman (1995) is correct that we shop around for someone who makes us feel comfortable in treatment, then the definition of a relationship is limited to someone with whom we feel comfortable. That person could be an ogre or someone who is incompetent. One can hardly think that either would be helpful to a needy client. And if Gelso and Hayes (1998) are correct about the lack of solid and behaviorally oriented definitions of the therapeutic relationship, one tends to wonder what the fuss is about. In reality, we know all too little about why people change. Does it have to do with the system of treatment, worker experience, the discipline of the worker, the ethnic or social class and educational fit between worker and client? We still don't know. To manage the lack of knowledge about why clients change, we've put a great deal of emphasis on the relationship without really knowing what that means.

One suspects that it means something different for just about every client who works with a therapist.

What is particularly troublesome is the emphasis in the strengths perspective on the relationship. Our emphasis should be on results and determining why people get better. The lack of evidence about why people improve just confirms that placing a great deal of emphasis on the importance of the relationship is a way of saying we don't really know why people change, but we fervently believe that it's because of the therapeutic relationship. In fact, in an attempt to determine the most effective approaches to treatment, assuming that clinicians might use empirically based studies that suggest treatment approaches for use with a specific type of problem, not once in their work do Chambless and Ollendick (2001) mention the word *relationship*. Either they decided that it was too difficult to quantify and measure, or they believe it's not relevant for effective treatment. Interestingly, in reviewing the effectiveness of over 75 approaches to therapy, the authors found little evidence that one approach worked better than another, although in arguing for a more rational approach to treatment, they did find treatment protocols that seemed more effective with certain types of problems, but not with all clients. However, Gambrill (1999), responding to the following claims in a social work publication, finds little in the way of support made for any of them—first the statement made by a social work publication and then Gambrill's response:

[Statement]
Professional social workers possess the specialized knowledge necessary for an effective social services delivery system. Social work education provides a unique combination of knowledge, values, skills, and professional ethics which cannot be obtained through other degree programs or by on-the-job training. Further, social work education adequately equips its individuals with skills to help clients solve problems that bring them to social services departments and human services agencies (NASW News, March 1999, p. 14). (Gambrill, p. 342)

[Gambrill's Response]
To my knowledge, there is no evidence for any of these claims. In fact, there is counterevidence. In Dawes' (1994) review of hundreds of studies, he concluded that there is no evidence that licenses, experience, and training are related to helping clients. If social work is a profession based on claimed rather than demonstrated effectiveness in helping clients attain hoped-for outcomes, how is this embarrassing situation handled? One strategy has been to ignore the contradiction between claims and reality and to censor related data by not sharing this with students. (Gambrill, p. 342)

One can hardly think, given Gambrill's response, that we know very much about why people change. Her statement about claimed rather than demonstrated effectiveness appears to be another way of saying that we have developed a hierarchy of beliefs that we passionately defend without much evidence that these beliefs are correct. While it's easy to understand the arguments in favor of the importance of the relationship, much more research needs to be done to determine the particular characteristics of the relationship that appear to work best with different populations of clients and, importantly, *why* they appear to work well.

SUMMARY

This chapter discusses the importance of the relationship in work with clients. From a strengths perspective point of view, the relationship is the most important single aspect of effective therapeutic work. A critical response to this belief argues an opposing point of view suggesting that the belief in the importance of the relationship is more philosophical than empirical. Much more evidence is needed about relationships to match clients with workers and to achieve maximum gain in treatment.

INTEGRATIVE QUESTIONS

1. Considering yourself, how would you describe the way you relate to other people? Based on their interactions with you, how do you think people view your communication style?

2. You've been provided with a critical response to the issue of how important the relationship is in helping people change their behavior. After reading both sides of the argument, what is your conclusion about relationships and their impact on client change?

3. Can you conceive of a treatment approach that doesn't use the helping relationship between worker and client? If so, what would it be like in practice?

4. When Seligman says that clients shop around for the worker with whom they feel most comfortable, do you think he's talking about emotional comfort or comfort with the expertise of the worker?

5. Aren't there people who need to be treated with condescension and arrogance just to get across the fact that their behavior is harmful? Isn't this a possible way to change very unwanted behavior in clients, such as violence, abuse, and criminal behavior?

REFERENCES

Bisman, C. (1994). *Social work practice: Cases and principles*. Belmont, CA: Brooks/Cole.

Chambless, D.L., and Ollendick, T.H. (2001). Empirically supported psychological interventions: Controversies and evidence. *Annual Review of Psychology*, 52, 685–716.

Dawes, R.M. (1994). *House of cards: Psychology and psychotherapy built on myth*. New York: Free Press.

Enkin, M., Keirse, M.J.N., Renfrew, M., and Neilson, J. (1995). *A guide to effective care in pregnancy and childbirth* (2nd Ed.). New York: Oxford University Press.

Gambrill, E. (July 1999). Evidence-based practice: An alternative to authority-based practice. *Journal of Contemporary Human Services*, 80, 341–350.

Gelso, J., and Hayes, J.A. (1998). *The psychotherapy relationship: Theory, research and practice*. New York: John Wiley & Sons.

Gibbs, L., and Gambrill, E. (1999). *Critical thinking for social workers: Exercises for the helping professions* (2nd Ed.). Thousand Oaks, CA: Pine Forge Press.

Hamilton, G. (1940). *Social casework.* New York: Columbia University Press.

Holmes, J., and Lindley, R. (1989). *The values of psychotherapy.* London: Oxford University Press.

Keith-Lucas, A. (1972). *Giving and taking help.* Chapel Hill: University of North Carolina Press.

National Association of Social Workers. (March 1999). *NASW news.* Washington, DC: National Association of Social Workers.

Pollack, W. (Fall 1990). Men's development and psychotherapy. *Psychotherapy, 27,* 63–72.

Rogers, C. (1951). *Client-centered therapy, its current practice, implications and theory.* Boston: Houghton Mifflin.

Saleebey, D. (May 1996). The strengths perspective in social work practice: Extensions and cautions. *Social Work, 41,* 296–305.

Seligman, M.E.P. (1995). The effectiveness of psychotherapy: The *Consumer Reports* study. *American Psychologist, 50*(12), 965–974.

Warren, C.S. (2001). Book review of *Negotiating the therapeutic alliance: A relational treatment guide. Psychotherapy Research, 11*(3), 357–359.

Weiss, J., Sampson, H., and O'Connor, L. (Spring 1995). How psychotherapy works. *Bulletin of the Psychoanalytic Research Society, 4,* 5–27.

THE PHILOSOPHICAL UNDERPINNINGS OF THE STRENGTHS PERSPECTIVE

Part II includes material on spirituality and religious beliefs, resilience, and natural helping. These three subjects capture several of the major themes of the strengths perspective that guide its approach to treatment. Several other important concepts, including natural healing, are discussed in the chapters on substance abuse and mental illness. One of the core beliefs in the strengths perspective is that religion and spirituality offer clients a great deal of solace and support and are used by many people in times of crisis. Chapter 5 looks at a number of health and mental health studies that suggest the positive impact of religious beliefs and spirituality. Chapter 5 also considers complex questions related to training mental health professionals to deal knowledgeably and sensitively with religious and spiritual material. Chapter 6 discusses the increasingly important subject of resilience, which suggests that many children who have been traumatized are able to cope with their experiences and lead reasonably normal lives. This concept does not try to negate the real damage done to children by adults, nor does it suggest that everyone who has been traumatized will escape the experience without lingering social and emotional problems. We know too well that this isn't true. Research on resilience provides us with information about the positive coping strategies people use to deal with trauma and may eventually help us know more about the treatment approaches to use with children and adults who deal less well with trauma. Chapter 7 covers material related to the natural helping process, including self-help groups, which play an increasingly important part of the helping process in the United States. Data presented in Chapter 7 suggest that self-help groups may be as effective, if not more effective, than professional help in the treatment of addictions and in recovery from serious illness. As the health care crisis deepens in America and mental health services are severely reduced to many of those who need them the most, some people believe that self-help groups will assume many of the responsibilities of professional mental health services.

CHAPTER FIVE

SPIRITUAL AND RELIGIOUS BELIEFS

WITH LIZA FRASER

The helping professions have often discounted the relevance of religion and spirituality as important factors in the ability of people to cope with life problems. But as Frankl notes (Loewenberg, 1988), "Man lives in three dimensions; the somatic, the mental, and the spiritual. The spiritual dimension cannot be ignored, for it is what makes us human" (p. ix).

A number of findings suggest the need to recognize the importance of spirituality and religiosity in people's lives. As examples, the majority of Americans indicate that they believe in God (Yntema, 1999), and 7 out of 10 say they attend church or synagogue (Loewenberg, 1988). Religion is regarded as highly important in the lives of older Americans (McFadden, 2000), while active religious and spiritual participation has been shown to positively influence overall health (Ellison & Levin, 1998).

DEFINITIONS OF SPIRITUALITY AND RELIGIOUS BELIEFS

Some confusion exists over the appropriate definitions of spirituality and religious belief. We have defined each as follows: *Spirituality* is defined as the means by which one finds wholeness, meaning, and purpose in life. It arises from an innate longing for fulfillment through the establishment of loving relationships with self and the community. Spirituality suggests harmony with self, others, and the world. Spirituality includes issues that help us search for meaning in our lives (Canda, 1989; Dudley & Helfgott, 1990). Spirituality also may be thought of as the intrapsychic dimension of human development in which we move toward connectedness and well-being (Derezotes, 1995). It is our way of finding meaning in the social and cultural forces and relationships that affect our lives. It is also a way of seeing ourselves in relationship to others against a background of shared meaning and purpose (Fowler, 1981). Canda (1989) notes, "All human beings possess spiritual needs for a sense of meaning and purpose in life, including expressions both within and without formal religious institutions" (p. 36). Manheimer (1994) uses a broader definition of spirituality when he writes, "Spirituality, while certainly overlapping with church or synagogue affiliation, refers to a psychological and personal inward experience that may be totally independent of institutional membership" (p. 72).

More easily conceptualized than spirituality, *religious involvement* is defined by Derezotes (1995) as "a system of beliefs, rituals, and behaviors, usually shared by individuals within an institutionalized structure. It is an external expression of faith" (p. 1). Siporin (1985) writes, "Religion usually has an institutional structure of communal denominations and congregations, in which people become members and take on religious roles, identities, and relationships with one another" (p. 211). In the lives of most Americans, the "spiritual dimension" is practiced as part of one's religious observance (Loewenberg, 1988), but as Derezotes (1995) notes, "The spirituality and religiosity of clients and practitioners may be one of the most neglected dimensions of social work practice" (p. 2).

THE SIGNIFICANCE OF SPIRITUALITY AND RELIGIOUS BELIEFS IN PRACTICE

To reinforce the importance of spirituality and religious involvement, there is a beginning literature suggesting that individuals who are involved in spiritual and/or religious practices cope better with life stressors and, as a result, experience improved health and enhanced quality of life. This may occur through increased social supports and by providing people with positive views of themselves. Religious involvement also may discourage behavior that increases health risks, including the use of tobacco and abuse of alcohol and other drugs (Ellison & Levin, 1998).

Spirituality and religious involvement are of particular significance in the lives of older adults. Spirituality, community, and the last stage of life are interrelated. Simmons (1998) writes, "The last years of life cannot be adequately described without attention to a struggle to keep the human spirit from being overwhelmed by frailty, which is described as a spiritual struggle" (p. 73). Involvement in spiritual and religious practices is particularly helpful in coping with physical and emotional losses associated with aging. Mitka (1998) notes that spirituality and religious involvement are particularly helpful after physical and emotional traumas.

Research on the relationship between spirituality and physical, mental, and social health suggests a positive link. One study conducted by the National Institutes of Health in 1998, as reported by Mitka (1998), found that people who attend religious services and read the Bible regularly have consistently lower blood pressure than those who do so less frequently. Another study reported by Mitka (1998) found that the more religious patients are, the more quickly they recover from depression. Elderly people who regularly attend church were found to have healthier immune systems than those who did not attend on a regular basis (Mitka, 1998). A study reported by Riley, Perna, and Tate (1998) examined religious, existential, and nonspiritual patients suffering from chronic illness or disability. The study considered the overall physical health, quality of life, and life satisfaction of the participants. Individuals in both the religious and existential groups experienced better quality of life than those in the nonspiritual group. According to Mitka (1998), studies suggest that medically ill older adults who participate in a religious community use hospital services less and that spirituality and religion may have a positive impact on physical health.

In a study reported by Berthold (1989), it was noted that approximately one-third of all adult Puerto Ricans consult spiritist mediums for help at some point in their lives. Berthold provides two examples of spiritist traditions, one involving reincarnated spirits and the other, saints. In both religious practices, spirits attach themselves to human beings and "exert a profound influence on human affairs" (p. 503). Among a Puerto Rican population in New York, these two traditions of spiritism are often blended. It seems apparent, from this example and others, that practitioners should be aware of "alternative models of healing and criteria of pathology" (Berthold, 1989, p. 502). A practitioner's knowledge base should therefore extend into notions of spirituality and religiosity that are culturally relevant to a broad base of clients.

Religion plays a significant part in the lives of many rural people. Meystedt (1984) reports that 75 percent of the people sampled in rural areas feel confidence in organized religion. Burnett (1979) writes, "Religion is a way of life, and understanding one's religion is essential to a full understanding of the person" (p. 220).

Winkler (1986) studied 20 Orthodox Jewish clients receiving outpatient mental health services to determine their attitudes toward therapy. The study found that Orthodox Jewish clients entered therapy as a last resort and only after all other resources had been exhausted. The Orthodox participants voiced their desire for a practitioner, of no particular faith, who would be sensitive to their reluctance to enter treatment and the cultural risks they took in seeking treatment. Although the sample was small, the feelings expressed certainly suggest the reluctance of some highly religious people to seek treatment. This reluctance may be partially explained by a sense that religious observance should negate the need for mental health interventions. It may also indicate a belief that helping professionals may be critical, if not antagonistic, toward strong religious convictions, a concern that may be valid.

A study analyzing the social service needs of Dominican immigrant elders in the United States revealed a strong belief in spirituality as a way of coping with stressful events (Paulino, 1998). Another study, designed to determine the importance of religion in the lives of older adults, revealed that the majority of older persons (76 percent nationwide) regard religion as highly important in their lives (McFadden, 2000). The same study revealed that 52 percent of all older adults attend weekly religious services (McFadden, 2000). A generally high level of religious activity among older adults suggests that practitioners need to understand the dimensions of religiosity in later life. McFadden (2000) believes that understanding religiosity and spirituality helps us comprehend the concept of "aging well."

The relationship of spirituality to emotional and physical health among 131 chronically ill elders was the subject of a study by Burke (1999), who found a very significant relationship between good mental health and feelings of "closeness to God." He also described the importance of spirituality while coping with pain associated with chronic illness. These findings suggest that spirituality may be an important component in coping with disease, disability, and pain. Dying summons basic spiritual questions. Dudley and Helfgott (1990) suggest that techniques involving rituals, meditation, prayer, or readings of religious texts may be appropriate interventions in helping dying clients.

Research conducted by Gallup and Castelli in 1989 (as cited in Sheridan, Wilmer, & Atcheson, 1994) found that religion and spirituality continue to be important factors in the lives of most Americans. The survey revealed that 74 percent of the respondents stated that their primary mechanism for coping with stress was prayer. A more recent study reinforces these figures. A majority of Americans believe in God, and those ages 55 to 64 were found to be the most devout (Yntema, 1999). Seventy-two percent of the respondents said that, without a doubt, they believe in God. Manheimer (1994) reports that church membership plays a significant role for ethnic and racial minorities. Religious participation, according to Manheimer, is a good predictor of happiness among older African Americans, with social activities related to church attendance significantly contributing to their life satisfaction and personal adjustment. As Haight (1998) notes in her study of the spirituality of African American children,

> Available empirical evidence suggests a relationship between socialization experiences emanating from the African American church and a number of positive developmental outcomes. For example, Brown and Gary (1991) found that self-reports of church involvement were positively related to educational attainment among African American adults. In an interview study of African American urban male adolescents, Zimmerman and Maton (1992) found that youths who left high school before graduation and were not employed, but who attended church, had relatively low levels of alcohol and drug abuse. In a questionnaire administered to African American adults (Seaborn-Thompson & Ensminger, 1989), 74 percent responded "very often" or "often" to the statement, "The religious beliefs I learned when I was young still help me." On the basis of data from the 1979–80 National Survey of Black Americans, Ellison (1993) argued that participation in church communities is positively related to self-esteem in African American adults. (p. 215)

■ ■ ■ ■ ■ ▬▬▬▬▬▬▬▬▬▬▬▬▬▬▬▬▬▬▬▬▬▬▬▬▬▬▬▬▬▬▬▬▬▬▬▬▬

SAM AND ED: A CASE STUDY

Sam is a 46-year-old lawyer who recently discovered that he has advanced prostate cancer that has metabolized to his bladder and kidneys. Sam has been told that his chances of living much more than a year are unlikely. Sam was born a Catholic and lived in a religiously observant family who received great spiritual joy for their religious involvement. However, Sam found Catholicism overly restricting and slowly moved away from his religious background, seeking, instead, secular explanations of life. He was highly active in political and civic affairs before his illness and had been cited on many occasions for his positive contributions to the community. Sam's personal life, however, has been highly chaotic. He was married and divorced three times. He often drank to excess and admits to using drugs to stay alert. He has three children whom he seldom sees and whom he thinks dislike him. "I've been a lousy father," he told the hospital psychologist, "What can I say?"

Sam is afraid of dying and is deeply angry at God for letting this happen to him at such an early age. He frequently vents his anger at the hospital chaplin who tries to console him. On several occasions, Sam has thrown pillows or vases at the chaplin, who sadly walks away discouraged and hurt that Sam has such anger at God. One of Sam's roommates in the hospital is an older man named Ed who studied for the priesthood but didn't complete his ordination because he had serious doubts about the nature of his beliefs. Like Sam, he is also angry at God. Together, they rail against religious beliefs and fill one another with feelings of anguish and despair.

And yet, as they try to cope with their terminal illnesses, a rapport has developed between them. Late in the evenings, the hospital psychologist comes by to say good night and often finds them deep in conversation about the meaning of life and the finality of death. Frequently he sits and listens to the two men and feels a remarkable calmness come over both of them. During the day, they are as cantankerous as ever, but at night, during the quiet of the evening when the hospital is still and they are left alone, both men discuss their lives and search for meaning.

A transformation has begun to come over them. They seem to be developing a joy in life and a sudden acceptance of death. Visiting one evening the psychologist remarked about the changes in both men. Sam said that he had a lot of unfinished business before he died and felt intent on "squaring" things with his kids and his ex-wives. "I was a shit most of my life," he said, "and I regret it. The only thing I can do now is to apologize with all of my heart." Ed nodded appreciatively and wondered if the staff connived to place both men together and then realized that hospitals never run that efficiently and thought that maybe some things were divinely inspired. "You put two fallen away Catholics together," he said, "and you either blow the place up or you start looking for contrition and absolution. Death has a way of bringing out the important questions about life and Sam here helped me at a time when I was so full of bile and hatred, I couldn't feel anything but sorry for myself."

Both men lived the next year having frequent contact with one another. They died at roughly the same times and didn't live longer than they were expected to live. The hospital psychologist, wondering if there were other beneficial effects of their search for meaning, asked the hospital staff. Both men were much easier to work with, the staff told him, and both became very giving people. A nurse who knew them told the psychologist, "The amazing thing about our Sam and the Rev., as we called him, was that almost to the end of their lives, neither used pain medication to any extent. I mean the pain must have been severe, but both men said that they had an inner pharmacy and that it was much better than any medication we could give them."

In trying to understand the change in Sam and Ed from antagonism toward recognition of the spiritual and the religious in their lives, an interview by Eric Gamalinda (2002) with the noted poet, Agha Shahid Ali, himself dying of a terminal brain tumor, might be instructive. Commenting on his deep sense of spirituality as he approached his own death, the poet said, "Where do you turn to in the hour of uncertainty? You turn to the realm that goes beyond the rational or undercuts the rational. And that's where religion, or spiritual elements of religion can help. . . . People have been finding in medical history that many people respond to treatment if they also have a deep spiritual base" (p. 50).

TRAINING HELPING PROFESSIONALS TO USE SPIRITUALITY AND RELIGION IN PRACTICE

The literature cited thus far indicates that religiosity and spirituality aid in overall coping and healing. However, as an example of the internal conflict within some of the helping professions, schools of social work often exclude the religious and spiritual elements of client care in their curricula. In a report of 53 social work faculty members, Dudley and Helfgott (1990) revealed that those opposed to a course on spirituality were concerned with conflict in three areas: (1) the mission of social work, (2) problems stemming from the separation of church and state, and (3) concerns that religious and spiritual material added to the curriculum would conflict with their own beliefs.

The absence of professional training in understanding spirituality and religion in the helping professions causes some authors to be critical of the void. Amato-von Hemert (1994) writes, "Just as we train and evaluate how workers address issues of class, gender, and race, we must maintain our professionalism by training workers to deal with religious issues" (p. 16).

The opinions of educators are clear on the subject of inclusion of spirituality and religion in social work education. In one study by Sheridan, Wilmer, and Atcheson, (1994), educators from 25 schools of social work were surveyed regarding inclusion of religious and spiritual content in social work programs. Results showed that the majority (82.5 percent) supported inclusion of a specialized course, primarily as an elective. However, their opinions were not reflected in the formation of curriculum. In a another study, by Sheridan et al. (1992), of 328 social work practitioners surveyed, 83 percent of the respondents stated that they received little or no training in the area of religion and spirituality during their graduate studies. The same practitioners also reported that a third of their clients presented religious or spiritual concerns during the course of their work with them.

Spirituality is a basic dimension of human development but one that has been given little attention by the helping professions (Dudley & Helfgott, 1990). Helpers should be prepared to respond to their clients' spiritual needs, just as they should respond to other needs. However, as Dudley and Helfgott (1990) note, "Social workers cannot respond effectively without professional preparation" (p. 287). The discussion of spirituality has, for the most part, been absent from the curricula in most of the helping professions. More recently, however, specialized courses on spirituality and religion have been included in some schools. Other schools are including some related content through integration into existing courses (Russel, 2000). According to Canda and Furman (as cited in Sheridan, 2000), a national survey of 1,069 social workers in 1999 revealed that over 50 percent of the respondents utilized spiritually based interventions with their clients. The majority of the respondents also believed that integrating religion and spirituality into practice was not only appropriate, but consistent with professional values.

Recognizing the difficulty in providing clear descriptions of what the integration of the spiritual and the religious would look like in practice, Boorstein (2000) reported a study by Lajoie and Shapiro (1992) that provided more than 200 definitions of transpersonal (spiritual) psychology. The authors concluded that transpersonal psychology is "concerned with the study of humanity's highest potential, and with the recognition, understanding, and realization of intuitive, spiritual, and transcendent states of consciousness" (p. 91). Boorstein further noted the difference between traditional psychotherapy and spiritually based psychotherapy:

> I believe that traditional psychotherapy is basically pessimistic (though called "realistic") in its outlook. There is the oft-quoted line attributed to Freud that psychoanalysis attempts to convert "neurotic misery to ordinary misery." Transpersonal psychotherapy attempts to open awareness to this and to other psychic realms where joy, love, serenity, and even ecstasy are present. As I have stated, without a basic belief in and/or experience of these transpersonal or spiritual realms, I do not think one can be a transpersonal or spiritual psychotherapist. (p. 413)

Canda (1988) believes that the helping professions have largely separated themselves from sectarian institutions and ideologies, but that many workers express a need for a renewal of commitment to include spiritual issues in practice. "Most discussions of spirituality and social work," he notes, "are based upon separate issues of religion or philosophical belief systems, without reference to how one affects the other. Despite repeated calls for professionals to focus on spiritual issues in practice, researchers agree that this area has been neglected" (p. 238).

The decision to discuss religion or spirituality with clients is a value issue. Even to suggest discussion of value-free issues is a value-laden position (Perlman, 1976): "Religious beliefs and practices reflect assumptions about the basic nature and purpose of human existence" (Canda, 1989, p. 38). Furthermore, a value-free discussion of religion would reduce it to facts and beliefs, ignoring the more philosophical questions about truth and the meaning of life, according to Canda (1989).

Three areas of content for teaching general and specific aspects of religion using a value-free approach were suggested by Canda (1989): (1) "Religion as a Universal Aspect of Experience," (2) "Religious Diversity," and (3) "Meta-Comparison" (pp. 17–18). These content themes would allow the educator to serve as a facilitator and a model of value accommodation. A continuous shifting between perspectives would utilize a symbolic interactionist approach with the facilitator taking on each role (Canda, 1989). According to Canda (1989), to be effective facilitators, it is imperative that educators personally and professionally come to terms with their own religious and spiritual issues.

Dudley and Helfgott (1990) explored the relevance of spirituality to social work practice in a small sample ($n = 53$) of full-time social work faculty in four schools of social work located in the eastern United States. The authors studied the perspectives of faculty who indicated an understanding of the spirituality of certain ethnic groups and the importance of spirituality for those working in the mental health field, particularly work with terminally ill patients. Although there may be considerable support for introducing spirituality content into social work programs, this study suggested that divisions existed among faculty members. The greatest concern expressed by 6 of 13 Jewish faculty, 4 of 21 Christian faculty, and 1 of 12 agnostic/atheist faculty was the conflict of separation of church and state. Other concerns noted by Dudley and Helfgott were that the views of one religious group might take dominance over another. Concerns regarding women's right to abortion, prayer in public schools, and the general introduction of more traditional and conservative views in the classroom were also expressed. However, the majority of the faculty in this study believed that spiritual content should be included in social work education.

Dudley and Helfgott (1990) urged educators to emphasize only coursework pertinent to social work practice and to "focus on practice-related religious and spiritual issues appropriate to understanding the cultural, social, and individual aspects of client groups and field settings with which students will be involved" (p. 293). To avoid one instructor's views taking precedence over another's, the authors recommended that a team of faculty, possessing differing spiritual and religious beliefs, teach the course.

Sheridan and Amato-von Hemert (1999) studied 208 students from two schools of social work regarding their experiences with religion and spirituality in education and practice. The sample comprised 86.4 percent women and 13.6 percent men, with an average age of 28.19 years. Eighty percent of the sample was white. Questions were asked concerning personal, religious, and/or spiritual affiliations and beliefs; views of the role of religion and spirituality in social work practice; use of religious or spiritually oriented interventions with clients; and previous training in religion and spirituality. In addition, the subjects were asked to assess which courses, if any, presented content on religion and spirituality. Results of the study indicated that student respondents generally had a strong, personal connection to religion and spirituality. Many of the respondents had very traditional belief systems and indicated a positive position toward the role of religion and spirituality in social work practice. Although most respondents had limited exposure to content on religion and spirituality in their social work courses, over 30 percent of the respondents had used four of the specific spiritual or religiously based interventions listed in the questionnaire in their work with clients. Results also indicated that students wanted instruction in dealing with issues of spirituality and religiosity with clients.

An exploratory study by Joseph (1988) identified the need for the examination of religious and spiritual issues in social work practice. The sample consisted of 53 master's degree field instructors working with students from a church-related school of social work in Washington, D.C. Questions were designed to elicit information regarding the way respondents felt about the importance of institutionalized religion as a resource for clients, and how important the respondents felt it was to wait for the client to bring up religious issues. Additional questions were asked to determine the types of resources or collaborative efforts used in handling religious issues with clients. The respondents were predominately women (81 percent), ages 20 to 68 years, with a median age of 41 years. Slightly more than 80 percent were white. The clinicians in this survey had considerable experience as supervisors, family therapists, direct practitioners, and administrators. Nearly two-thirds worked in settings that were not religiously oriented, but 7 percent worked in church-related agencies. The study found that respondents believed that the religious dimension of clients had been ignored. The practitioners in this study viewed religious and spiritual concerns, particularly as they pertained to life cycle and ecological issues, as being very important in social work practice. They also expressed the desire for more training in this area.

Tobias and colleagues (1995) believe there is also a need for knowledge and sensitivity to diverse religious beliefs. Ethical and practical demands require workers to respond to religious diversity and to understand diversity in all of its forms. According to Tobias and colleagues, "Today's multiethnic America encompasses a wide-ranging spiritual orientation that is, if anything, diverse" (p. 1).

To better understand how social workers utilize client spirituality and religion in practice, a study by Sheridan (2000) asked social workers a variety of questions regarding spirituality and religion. The results indicated that 73 percent of the respondents had generally positive attitudes toward religion and spirituality in practice. Respondents noted that over one-third of their clients discussed religious or spiritual issues, and that 73.6 percent of the practitioners considered the religious and spiritual practices of their clients in their assessments of client functioning (Sheridan, 2000). In the same study, respondents were asked to separately rank-order their perceptions of the role of spirituality and religion in the lives of their clients. On average, 43 percent of the respondents reported that religion played a beneficial role in the lives of their clients, while 62 percent stated that spirituality played a beneficial role. Spirituality was reported to play a detrimental role in their clients' lives only 12 percent of the time, while religion was reported detrimental to client functioning 21 percent of the time (Sheridan, 2000). A majority of the respondents reported that they had utilized a number of spiritual and religiously based interventions with clients. Respondents in the Sheridan study (2000) were also asked to answer questions regarding their educational and training experiences in the areas of religion and spirituality; 84 percent reported little or no instruction in this area, but over half of the respondents reported attending workshops and conferences that addressed religion and spirituality as part of their posteducational experience.

In a study reported by Canda (1988), social workers with varying personal philosophical perspectives were interviewed to determine the diversity of their religious orientations. Social workers with Christian, existentialist, Jewish, shamanist, and Zen Buddhist perspectives exhibited common qualities, including compassionate concern for the well-being of individuals and social and economic justice in the broader society. All of the respondents agreed that a good helping relationship should be sensitive to the spiritual and religious needs of the client.

Dudley and Helfgott (1990) suggest that a practitioner must be familiar with religious and spiritual diversity. "Understanding spirituality," they state, "is essential to understanding the culture of numerous ethnic groups that social workers help" (p. 288).

In summary, there is compelling evidence that many clients have strong religious and spiritual beliefs that play an important role in the way they cope with social, emotional, and physical difficulties. Although many practitioners understand and value the importance of religious and spiritual beliefs, few feel prepared to work with either issue, and most feel that professional education should include content related to understanding and applying knowledge of spirituality and religious beliefs. Concerns, however, were raised when faculty were asked how material would be taught, and differences of opinion suggest that the diverse nature of faculties in the helping profession make additional discussion necessary before courses can be offered.

A CRITICAL RESPONSE

It is almost heresy to criticize religious and spiritual issues in the helping professions. They touch deep chords in our collective belief systems. However, not a few of our clients come to us for help because the religions of their families are overly critical and dogmatic. What can one say about religions that consider homosexuality to be evil? How could such a religious conviction be helpful to gay clients coping with social and family rejection? Similarly, some religions still practice forms of exclusion and excommunication for behaviors commonly accepted in our society. How can contentious divorces be anything other than more contentious when an additional layer of conflict is added to the process because some religions require religious divorce procedures that sometimes antagonize couples and families?

And what should one make of certain spiritual beliefs? We assume that anything spiritual is a blessing, but some beliefs can be dangerous. Practicing certain common meditation approaches, while certainly beneficial, should not be used as a replacement for needed medical care. Are we ready for new religious movements on the horizon that might preach hatred and bigotry? We've had historical moments in our country when this has happened during times of national crisis.

The issue of teaching material related to religious and spiritual beliefs is troubling. One can see this done by instructors whose areas of expertise are religious and spiritual beliefs and practices, but these folks are usually not on faculties in the helping professions. How could the material they teach be linked to what we do in clinical practice? The issue of a helping professional teaching the material, while a rational idea, forgoes the heated disagreements that often occur along ideological grounds among faculties in the helping professions.

Although one applauds the material in this chapter and we have all seen the power of religious conviction and spirituality aide in the healing process, we need much more solid research to be done before we teach about religious or spiritual convictions and link either to better social functioning.

SUMMARY

Religious and spiritual issues frequently affect clients seen in the helping professions. Personal beliefs aside, there is a strong need for helping professionals to understand religious and spiritual issues and to treat them with sensitivity. Informed helpers are more likely to touch the lives of clients and to respect the religious and spiritual beliefs that often help clients cope with difficult life problems. It is helpful that the Council of Social Work Education, in its newest accreditation standards (2003), requires all social work programs to include content on religion. This acceptance of the importance of religious and spiritual differences in our clients is a step closer to accepting the diverse world in which we live and accommodating that diversity with sensitive and knowledgeable responses to our clients and the diverse beliefs that guide their lives.

INTEGRATIVE QUESTIONS

1. Although it may be true that many clients have deep religious and spiritual beliefs, isn't it also true that many of our clients have had negative experiences and have turned away from their religious beliefs? What should we do to help clients cope with feelings about religion that are often negative?

2. *Spirituality* is a vague term. Isn't it important to have clients define and explain their degree of spirituality before we assume they are spiritual? And once they define their spirituality, what would we do with definitions that seem incorrect or suggest harmful behavior?

3. Many people who grow up in religious families move away from the religious beliefs of their families. Is it our task to reconnect them with those beliefs?

4. Clients who believe that luck, chance, and fate dominate their lives often practice forms of religion that reinforce those beliefs. How do we move people toward a belief system that focuses on their ability to control most life events without interfering with their religious beliefs?

5. Concerns about the meaning of life are often important issues when clients are dealing with life-threatening events. How can we help clients grapple with meaning-of-life issues without our belief systems dominating the discussion?

REFERENCES

Amato-von Hemert, K. (1994). Point/counterpoint. Should social work education address religious issues? Yes! *Journal of Social Work Education*, 30, 7–11.

Berthold, M. (1989). Spiritism as a form of psychotherapy: Implications for social work practice. *Social casework*, 70, 502–509.

Boorstein, S. (Summer 2000). Transpersonal psychotherapy. *American Journal of Psychotherapy*, 54, 408–423.

Brown, D.R., and Gary, L.E. (1991). Religious socialization and educational attainment among African Americans: An empirical assessment. *Journal of Negro Education*, 3, 411–426.

Burke, K.J. (1999). Health, mental health, and spirituality in chronically ill elders. *Social Work Abstracts*, 44, 141–164.

Burnett, D.W. (1979). Religion, personality, and clinical assessment. *Journal of Religion and Health*, 18, 308–312.

Canda, E.R. (1988). Spirituality, religious diversity, and social work practice. *Social Casework*, 69, 238–247.

Canda, E.R. (1989). Religious content in social work education: A comparative approach. *Journal of Social Work Education*, 25(36), 15–24.

Council on Social Work Education. (2003). Educational policies and accreditation standards. Washington, DC: Council on Social Work Education. Found at: www.cswe.org/.

Derezotes, D.S. (1995). Spirituality and religiosity: Neglected factors in social work practice. *Arête*, 20(1), 1–15.

Dudley, J.R., and Helfgott, C. (1990). Exploring a place for spirituality in the social work curriculum. *Journal of Social Work Education*, 26(3), 287–294.

Ellison, C. (1993). Religious involvement and self-perception among black Americans. *Social Forces*, 71, 1027–1055.

Ellison, C.G., and Levin, J.S. (1998). The religion–health connection: Evidence, theory, and future directions. *Health, Education, and Behavior*, 25(6), 700–720.

Fowler, J.W. (1981). *Stages of faith*. San Francisco: Harper and Row.

Gamalinda, E. (March/April 2002). Agha Shahid Ali. *Poets and Writers*, 30(2), 44–51.

Haight, W.L. (May 1998). "Gathering the spirit" at First Baptist Church: Spirituality as a protective factor in the lives of African American children. *Social Work*, 43, 213–223.

Joseph, M.V. (1988). Religion and social work practice. *Social Casework*, 69, 443–452.

Lajoie, D.H., and Shapiro, S.Y. (1992). Definitions of transpersonal psychology: The first twenty-three years. *Journal of Transpersonal Psychology*, 24(1), 79–98.

Loewenberg, J. (1988). *Caring and responsibility: Crossroads between holistic practices and traditional medicine*. Philadelphia: University of Pennsylvania Press.

Manheimer, R.J. (Ed.). (1994). *Older Americans almanac*. Detroit: Gale Research.

McFadden, S. (2000). Retrieved April 9, 2000, from the World Wide Web: www.lutersem.edu/cars/newsletters/ARTUS.HTM.

Meystedt, D.M. (1984). Religion and the rural population: Implications for social work. *Social Casework*, 65, 219–226.

Mitka, M. (1998). Getting religion seen as help in being well. *Journal of the American Medical Association*, 280, 1896–1897.

Paulino, A. (1998). Dominican immigrant elders: Social service needs, utilization patterns, and challenges. *Journal of Gerontological Social Work*, 30(1/2), 61–74.

Perlman, H.H. (1976). Believing and doing: Values in social work education. *Social Casework*, 57, 381–390.

Riley B.B., Perna, R., and Tate, D.G. (1998). Spiritual patients have a better quality of life than those who aren't. *Modern Medicine*, 66(5), 45–48.

Russel, R. (2000). The development of social work courses with spiritual or religious focus. (unpublished manuscript)

Seaborn-Thompson, M., and Ensminger, M.E. (1989). Psychological well-being among mothers with school age children: Evolving family structures. *Social Forces*, 67, 715–730.

Sheridan, M.J. (2000). The use of spiritually-derived interventions in social work practice. Forty-sixth Annual Program Meeting of the Council on Social Work Education, 1–22 Washington, DC: Council on Social Work Education.

Sheridan, M.J., and Amato-von Hemert, K. (1999). The role of religion and spirituality in social work education and practice: A survey of student views and experiences. *Journal of Social Work Education*, 15(1), 125–141.

Sheridan, M.J., Bullis, R.K., Adcock, C.R., Berlin, S.D., and Miller, P.C. (1992). Practitioners' personal and professional attitudes and behaviors toward religion and spirituality: Issues for social work education and practice. *Journal of Social Work Education*, 28, 190–203.

Sheridan, M.J., Wilmer, C.M., and Atcheson, L. (1994). Inclusion of content on religion and spirituality in the social work curriculum. *Journal of Social Work Education*, 30(3), 363–377.

Simmons, H.C. (1998). Spirituality and community in the last stage of life. *Journal of Gerontological Social Work*, 29(2/3), 73–91.

Siporin, M. (1985). *Social work practice*. New York: McMillan Publishers.

Tobias, M., Morrison, J., and Gray, B. (Eds.). (1995). *A parliament of souls*. San Francisco: KQED Books.

Winkler, M. (1986). Pathways to treatment: How orthodox Jews enter treatment. *Social Casework*, 67, 113–118.

Yntema, S. (Ed.). (1999). *Americans 55 and older* (2nd Ed.). New York: New Strategist Publications.

Zimmerman, M.A., and Maton, K.I. (1992). Life-style and substance use among male African American urban adolescents: A cluster analytic approach. *American Journal of Community Psychology*, 20, 121–138.

- - - - -

CHAPTER SIX

RESILIENCE AND THE STRENGTHS PERSPECTIVE

The concepts of strengths and resilience are sometimes confused. *Strengths* refer to those sets of attributes that people possess that help them cope with life issues. *Resilience* refers to the ability to cope with serious traumas and stressors and not be significantly affected by them. Henry (1999) suggests that the notion of resilience was created to help explain why some children do well under very troubled circumstances (Baldwin et al., 1993). Resilience describes children who grow up in highly unfavorable conditions without showing negative consequences (Masten, 1989; Okun, Parker, & Levendosky, 1994; Radke-Yarrow & Brown, 1993; Werner, 1993). Henry (1999) defines resilience as "the capacity for successful adaptation, positive functioning, or competence despite high risk, chronic stress, or prolonged or severe trauma" (p. 521). In a further definition of resilience, Abrams (2001) says that it may be seen as the ability to readily recover from illness, depression, and adversity. Walsh (1998) defines resilience in families as the "capacity to rebound from adversity, strengthened and more resourceful" (p. 4). She continues in her definition by saying, "We cope with crisis and adversity by making meaning of our experience: linking it to our social world, to our cultural and religious beliefs, to our multigenerational past, and to our hopes and dreams for the future" (p. 45).

ATTRIBUTES OF RESILIENT PEOPLE

Werner and Smith (1982) identified protective factors that tend to counteract the risk for stress as genetic (for example, an easygoing disposition), strong self-esteem, and a sense of identity, intelligence, physical attractiveness, and supportive caregivers. Garmezy, Masten, and Tellegen (1964) noted three protective factors in resilient children: dispositional attributes of the child, family cohesion and warmth, and availability and use of external support systems by parents and children. Seligman (1992) stated that resilience exists when people are optimistic; have a sense of adventure, courage, and self-understanding; use humor in their lives; have a capacity for hard work; and possess the ability to cope with and find outlets for emotions. Luthar and

Zigler (1991) found that resilient children are active, humorous, confident, competent, prepared to take risks, flexible, and, as a result of repeated successful coping experiences, confident in both their inner and outer resources. Luthar (1993) suggested that resilient children have considerable intellectual maturity. Garmezy (1991), however, found that more intelligent children are often highly sensitive to their situations and are more likely to experience stress when compared with less intelligent children experiencing the same situations.

Other factors associated with resilience include the finding by Arend, Gove, and Sroufe (1979) that very curious children are more resilient. Radke-Yarrow and Brown (1993) associated resilience with children who have more positive self-perceptions. Egeland, Carlson, and Sroufe (1993) and Baldwin et al. (1993) found a relationship between assertiveness and independence, and a support network of neighbors, peers, family, and elders. In their 32-year longitudinal study, Werner and Smith (1982) found a strong relationship among problem-solving abilities, communication skills, and an internal locus of control in resilient children, and as Henry (1999) noted, "Resilient children often acquire faith that their lives have meaning and that they have control over their own fates" (p. 522).

Henry (1999) suggested five major themes that stem from the research she conducted on resilient children: loyalty to parents, normalizing the abusive environment, the invisibility of the child to the abuser, self-value, and future vision. Perhaps two themes should be clarified. Loyalty to parents suggests that even though parents are maltreating the child, there is an attempt by the child to understand the reasons for the abuse so that he or she might continue to feel loyalty and love for the abusing parent. The invisibility of the child refers to the child's attempt to vacate the home or to hide when the parent(s) become abusive. In this way, the child is able to negate the brunt of the abuse and to feel control over it.

Anderson (1997) states that the recognition of resilience as an important factor in the mental health of traumatized children came from concerns that children at risk might develop adult pathologies (Byrd, 1994). Anderson (1997) indicates that the term *resilient* originally referred to children who were thought to be "stress resistant" or "invulnerable" because they not only coped with adverse childhood traumas, but also seemed to thrive under very dysfunctional and stressful situations (Kauffman et al., 1979).

Resiliency research originally tried to discover the characteristics of at–risk children who coped well with stress (Werner, 1989). Over time, however, resiliency research has focused less on the attributes of resilient children and more on the processes of resilience. This new emphasis in the research suggests that rather than avoiding risk, resilient children take substantial risks to cope with stressors, leading to what Cohler (1987) calls adaptation and competence.

In a review of the factors associated with resilience to stressful life events, Tiet, Bird, and Davies (1998), note that higher IQ, quality of parenting, connection to other competent adults, an internal locus of control, and social skills have been identified as protective factors that allow children to cope with stressful events. Protective factors, according to Tiet and colleagues (1998), are primary buffers between the traumatic event and the child's response. However, the authors note that even resilient children respond inconsistently to stressful events, and that another way to look at resilience is to show the relationship between the specific traumatic event and the response. For example, in many of the maltreated children studied for resilience, school-based outcomes have been used that include grades, deportment, and the degree of involvement in school activities. Luthar and Zigler (1991) note that although resilient children do well on many school-based outcomes, many of these children suffer from depression. Interestingly, however, even though many of the maltreated children studied show signs of depression, they still did well on behaviorally oriented outcomes measures such as grades and school conduct (Luthar & Zigler, 1991).

In summarizing their work on resilient youth who have experienced serious life traumas, including maltreatment, Tiet, Bird, and Davies (1998) wrote,

> In conclusion, resilient youth tend to live in higher-functioning families and receive more guidance and supervision by their parents and other adults in the family. Higher educational aspiration may also provide high-risk youth with a sense of direction and hope. Although IQ had no impact in youth at low risk, youth at high risk who have a higher IQ may cope better and therefore avert the harmful effects of adverse life events. (p. 1198)

■ ■ ■ ■ ■

BOBBY, A MALTREATED CHILD: A CASE STUDY

Bobby is a 13-year-old boy in foster care who has been physically abused and neglected from birth by his natural parents. He is currently being seen in treatment to evaluate the impact of this abuse and neglect.

Bobby is doing well in middle school and maintains an "A" average in all of his classes. He is outgoing, perceptive, and has a keen intelligence that he uses in his language to describe his home situation:

> My parents drank a lot, and when they drank, they could be very mean. Pretty early on I could tell when they were going to become mean and I'd try and hide, or go to a friend's house. When they weren't drunk, they could be very nice. My dad is an accountant and he's pretty smart, but when he drinks, something comes over him. I saw the same thing in his dad, my granddad, when I spent a summer at their cabin. He could be nice as anything, but when he drank, it was like, you'd better watch out. I figured that if my dad grew up with a dad like that, he'd probably have the same temper when *he* drank. So I got to be able to tell when he was drinking too much, and I'd be sure not to be around. Sometimes it didn't work, and I'd get beaten up pretty bad. I guess I was able to keep straight that he loved me, even when he hurt me. It sounds weird, but that's what I did. My mom was different. She was mean all the time, even when she wasn't drinking. I know she was abused as a girl because she told me the stories a lot. She was full of hate, but I guess that's what happens when you get abused and you're just a kid. The drinking made her crazy sometimes and when she wasn't hitting me, she'd hit my dad and they'd have these bad fights.
>
> I used to hide in the basement until they'd fall asleep. While I was down there, and I was just a little kid, I found these books with stories. There were hundreds of them, and I started to read. It was wonderful. The stories took me away from all the fighting and made me see a different world. One of my friend's dad was an English teacher, and when

(continued)

CONTINUED

he found out I was reading (he knew about my parents and I think he was trying to make up for what was going on in my home), he gave me more books to read, and we'd talk about them. He was a very smart man, and when we'd talk, I'd just want to read more stories. He asked me if I ever wrote things, and I said no, that I never did. And he encouraged me to write, and I began to write stories about my parents and the fighting and all. I guess they were pretty awful stories, because after reading one, maybe I was about 11, he called the welfare office and now I'm living with my friend and his mom and dad. It's wonderful at their house. They're real nice to me. I see my mom and dad a lot, and they still love me in their own way. I know I won't be able to live with them, but they're my parents and you have to love your parents, even if they do have problems. My dad has stopped drinking and lives by himself. There's some talk about my living with him, but the welfare lady said that we had to be sure that he'd stopped drinking for at least a year before we could consider me living with him. But we do a lot of things together and he's a very smart man. The last time I saw him, he started to cry about how awful he'd been as a father. I don't know, to me he always seemed like he was trying to be nice but he had a lot of demons inside of him, at least that's what I think.

DISCUSSION

Bobby is a resilient child who has used a combination of protective factors to cope with the physical and emotional abuse of his parents. He has learned to protect himself while still feeling loyalty for his parents. He sees the dysfunctional behavior of his parents in a rational way, noting the early harm done to both parents by their families, and he is forgiving. He knows it's unlikely that either parent has the emotional capacity to allow him to live with them, but he sees them often and has begun to have a good relationship with his father. He is endlessly optimistic while maintaining a realistic view of his family. He hopes for a lot, but expects little. He has dreams for the future and has found a supportive and intellectually stimulating family with whom to live. He does well in school and has goals for himself that provide a positive view of his abilities and the way they might be used in the future. These coping skills and the rational way he views his family come from inner resources that are apparent to anyone who has met him. Bobby is, by any standard, an unusually healthy, highly intelligent, and rational young man. He is someone who has experienced extreme adversity and yet has rebounded as an even stronger person. Will these strengths continue through adolescence and into adulthood? We can't say for certain, but the odds seem good that they will.

TREATING RESILIENT CHILDREN

Anderson (1997) suggests the benefits of the strengths perspective in assessing the positive qualities of children who have been sexually abused. She believes that the focus of work should not be on the damage done to the child, but on the survival abilities of the child to cope with the abuse. This means that practitioners must look for themes of resilience in the "survival stories" of abused children and help them recognize the active role they played in their ability to survive the abuse. Perhaps, as Anderson suggests, "The psychological scars will never disappear completely;

however, focusing on the child's strengths and resiliency can help limit the power of sexual abuse over the child" (p. 597).

Henry (1999) reports that practitioners often miss an essential point: The way children cope with their abuse is actually "the strength that enables them to survive in an unsafe environment" (p. 519). Henry points out that the behaviors children develop as they cope with the abuse provide important pieces of information that can assist practitioners in helping children. Rather than viewing coping behaviors as dysfunctional or pathological, workers should try to understand the children's ways of dealing with extraordinarily traumatic experiences and be supportive and positive with them for their efforts. From the children's point of view, these coping skills are heroic. Workers who view the abuse as necessarily damaging will look for dysfunctional ways of coping and focus on what the children are doing wrong. From the children's point of view, they are doing the best they can and should receive support for their efforts. The work we do with children who have been maltreated, according to Henry, should focus on problem solving rather than on finding fault with the children's adaptation to their maltreatment.

Anderson (1997) indicates that the professional literature often reports the association between child maltreatment and emotional problems. She gives as examples the observation that many maltreated children use wishful thinking or daydreaming to emotionally distance themselves from the abuse. Rather than seeing these coping mechanisms as dysfunctional, Anderson suggests that we recognize survival strategies as a way of understanding the way in which maltreated children cope. The children's coping strategies should be seen as strengths, not as impediments or dysfunctions.

Henry (1999) points out that children are willing to give parents many opportunities to correct their abusive behavior. Through their actions, play, and approach to problem solving, children provide many ideas about the way they survive cruel and abusive life events. By working with adults who care deeply about them, children find the sorrow and distresses they've endured validated and, from that pain and the sorrow of their lives, find meaning in their maltreatment and joy and comfort in the way they have persevered, survived, and become stronger. In further stressing the use of the strengths approach, Anderson (1997) writes,

> [I]t is essential to formulate specific and clear guidelines for treatment that center on survival abilities because gathering this information helps children to take pride in their accomplishments. Rebuilding self-esteem and pride is extremely important for children who have been sexually abused because the trauma permeates their identity and may leave them lacking in feelings of self-worth. (p. 593)

■ ■ ■ ■ ■

JANIE, A RESILIENT SEXUALLY MOLESTED CHILD IN TREATMENT: A CASE STUDY

Janie is an 11-year-old girl who was raped and beaten six months earlier on her way home from school. She is being seen in supportive treatment at the request of her parents, but is doing very well at home and at school, considering the deeply traumatic event in her life.

(continued)

CONTINUED

Janie spoke to her worker several months into treatment and shared the following information:

I don't like talking about what happened and I still have bad dreams about it. I guess what surprised me was how nice my parents have been. They never blamed me for anything. I was supposed to get a ride home from a friend, but I was doing a project at school and by the time I was done, it was getting dark. I knew my mom would be worried, so I took a shortcut through the park and that's when it happened. I don't remember a lot of it very well. I remember being in the hospital and not being able to talk, but a lot of it is a blank. And I remember the bruises on my face and how much I hurt, you know, down there (points to her vaginal area). It was pretty dumb of me to take that shortcut. Everybody knows that bad stuff goes on in that park, but I wasn't using my head.

My mom and dad have been so kind to me, sometimes it just makes me cry. I think they worry a lot about me and if I'm OK. And the thing is, I *am* OK. I have bad dreams a lot, and sometimes I get scared and I don't know why. I don't like being alone, and I have to have the light on when I sleep, but I'm OK. My grades at school are fine, and nobody really knows what happened to me since the police don't let anyone know the name of the girls who get hurt like I was. I think they caught the man who did this, but I'm not sure. I can't remember much about it. Maybe that's good, do you think? I still like boys, but I don't think I'd like to dance with them or anything right now. I don't like being touched either, but it's getting better. I guess the stuff I'm feeling is what a lot of girls feel when this happens. My aunt told me the same thing happened to her when she was a girl, but she didn't handle it very well and she has a lot of problems now. She can't stay married very long, and I know she drinks a lot because I've heard my mom and dad talk about it. She's also sad pretty often. You can tell by the way she looks.

I think this helps to come and talk. I know I'll be better, and I know that this won't be a bad thing for me like it was for my aunt. I have a lot of dreams about what I'll do when I grow up, and I still feel the very same way. Just because someone did something to me because they're sick doesn't mean that I have to be sick, too. If that happened, then they'd be happy about it and I don't think I'll let that happen. My mom had this talk with me about, you know, sex. She didn't think it was necessary to talk to me until I was older, but after this happened, I guess she did. Anyway, what she said was that what happens between a man and a woman is beautiful and that love is the most wonderful thing that can ever happen. And when she fell in love with my dad, the world changed. She said the same thing will happen to me, and I believe her.

I think it helps me to come here and talk, but I don't think I'll need to come for very long. My mom and dad are wonderful, and things are pretty much like they always were at home. I have lots of friends, and I believe in Jesus and I know he's watching out for me. I guess if something awful has to happen to people, it's good that it happens to someone who has a lot of love in their life like I do. If I didn't, I don't think I'd be so good at dealing with it. But right now, I feel like my mom and dad are my friends and that they want me to do well, and that I will. I guess that's what I wanted to say today.

DISCUSSION

It may be difficult for many readers to accept the way Janie is coping with her molestation and assault. For many of us, and I confess, for the author, a good deal more underlying pathology would be expected as a result of the trauma Janie suffered. Most of us have been trained to associate trauma with distress, and most of the literature would certainly indicate a long list of probable symptoms related to the trauma: eating problems, nightmares, fear of being alone, withdrawal, depression, anger, and shame and humiliation, but as Anderson (1997) notes in the use of the strengths perspective with resilient children who have been sexually abused,

> Therapeutic paradigms that operate from a pathology focus are less likely to tap into areas of resilience because "we can only see and know that which our paradigms allow us to see and know" (Barnard, 1994, p. 137). A pathology focus encourages practitioners to perceive clients as having some disorder or deficit that creates negative expectations about their potential to address the stressors in their lives (Barnard, 1994; Saleebey, 1997). Identifying and building on the positive aspects of the self that helped the child survive trauma open up creative ways to work with children who have been sexually abused. (p. 597)

Although Janie may still have residual symptoms of the molestation and the assault that affect her through childhood and into adulthood, it doesn't seem very likely, given her discussion of the event. Certainly, her parents are strong positive reasons for her ability to cope with the traumatic event. Their consistent, supportive treatment is unlike the blaming and belittling behavior many rape victims experience from parents, friends, and other loved ones after a sexual assault. Glicken and Sechrest (2003) note the usual symptoms of childhood sexual abuse:

> In addition to depression, victims of sexual trauma may feel isolated from friends, peers, and family members, believing that others won't understand their emotional pain or that they will blame the victim for what has happened. It is not unusual for close friends and family members to be hypercritical of the rape victim for the way they are coping with the rape and, ultimately, to blame the victim for the rape itself (Furey, 1993). (Glicken & Sechrest, p. 136)

One additional helping issue is that Janie can see what happened to her aunt and the severe trauma the sexual attack had on her that led her aunt to experience depression, drinking, and multiple relationships. Janie has a model of what can happen if she permits herself to feel defeated by the assault. It takes a very healthy child to use that model in a positive way. An argument could be made that many children would accept her aunt's behavior as the inevitable outcome of a childhood trauma. This, one suspects, is what differentiates resilient children from nonresilient children. They are able to understand traumatic situations, learn lessons from them, and then use those lessons to prompt different adaptations to the traumas. The mechanism they use to do this is still unclear, but the attributes of the resilient child, coupled with exceptional coping skills, may provide a clue. Might we be able to teach less resilient children the coping mechanisms used by resilient children to deal with traumas? The answer is yes, if we focus on the strengths of the child. Anderson (1997) provides an instructive reminder when she writes,

> Somehow as children, they not only endure the sexual abuse but find ways to go on with their lives. . . . Their capacity for self-repair takes tremendous energy, preventing them from accomplishing important developmental tasks. Because their survival abilities are overshadowed by the trauma, these strengths may be overlooked during treatment if the practitioner limits the definition of resiliency to the exhibition of competency. (p. 595)

(continued)

CONTINUED

Before we continue, a poem by Jason Michael MacLeod (1996, p. 43) follows as a reminder of the terrible consequences of sexual assault, lest, in this chapter on the resilience of children, we forget that sexual assault, sexual abuse, sexual molestation, and whatever homogenized term we use, does terrible damage to the mind and the soul of its victims.

THE TWO OF US
Jason Michael MacLeod

> *After six months,*
> *I'm told about the oily green basement couch,*
> *the muffled evening news upstairs,*
> *and the two hands grabbing the back of her head,*
> *forcing it down to his crotch.*
>
> *And I can't hear this.*
> *I just want to drink beer and talk*
> *about the weekend or Raymond Carver*
> *or any other damn thing, but here I sit*
> *feeling my fingers rake flesh from my thighs.*
>
> *She thought that if she just went along—*
> *if she could have just made herself want to—*
> *it wouldn't have been what it was. But no one*
> *pulls that off and after walking past her parents,*
> *she fell to her knees and vomited on their porch.*
>
> *Then her voice trails off and I start in.*
> *I stand up and say to her, say to her,*
> *because I'm not yelling yet, what's his name?*
> *But she shakes her head and she*
> *just wants to forget. Forget it all.*
>
> *We are not doing any forgetting tonight.*
> *I punch the bookcase, knocking novels and poetry*
> *to the floor. I take her arms so she can't ignore me*
> *and yell things at her that I won't remember later and*
> *I feel strong and goddammit, somebody is going to bleed.*
>
> *Her look sobers me.*
> *I shut up and let go.*
> *Softly, she picks up her keys and walks out,*
> *leaving me to melt deep into the cracks of the couch,*
> *pale and shaking,*
> *like him.*

A RESILIENT CHILD COPES WITH ADULTHOOD: A CASE STUDY

Lawrence is a 31-year-old adult man who was sexually abused as a child by his mother. Lawrence was remarkably resilient as a child, and in spite of the sexual abuse that went on until he was age 18 and left home for good, he maintained an excellent GPA in high school, had many friends, went on to get a doctorate in anthropology at a prestigious university, and has had remarkable success in his professional life. He has not done as well in his personal life. While he copes with a recurring depression, Lawrence has been able to use many of the strengths in his adult life that he used in childhood. However, those strengths seem less able to carry him thorough the increasingly complex adult world of intimate relationships, work, and relationships with colleagues in an often-contentious academic department filled with rivalries and academic politics. Lawrence provided his therapist with the following information after several sessions:

> When I was a kid, I learned to compartmentalize what was happening to me. I put it aside and didn't think it mattered. I knew my mother was terribly disturbed and that my father wouldn't help. He was probably glad that she was spending time with me instead of him. So I got on with my life and I made what was going on at home a forgettable nightmare. I left home as soon as I could, got some good therapy, and went on and finished my education. I'm proud of my achievements, and I know there's something special about me that's allowed me to cope with a pretty sick experience. However, the competition in the department and the level of animosity among my colleagues makes me very uncomfortable. I taught myself to be accommodating when I was growing up. If I wasn't, my mother would become psychotic and had to be sent to mental institutions for pretty long periods of time. So my role was to keep her from getting crazy, even if it involved things she did to me that repulsed me. In this crazy academic department, I can't be accommodating. Everyone expects me to choose sides. The more I try and not choose sides, the more critical people are of me. They think I'm weak and incapable of making decisions. In academia, it isn't what you do, it's the side you choose; so I'm doubtful that I'll get tenure.
>
> I've put sex out of my mind. I can't think of myself as someone who would want to have sex. It's a repulsive act to me and yet I crave companionship and love. The women I go out with can't understand why I won't have sex with them, and I don't want to tell them. It feels like all the things I did to get myself through childhood aren't working for me as an adult. I'm proud of myself. Most people who went through what I did would be pretty messed up. I don't think I am, but it certainly has made adulthood pretty difficult. I guess what I want in treatment is to use my intelligence and my abilities to deal with these problems in adulthood just as I used my abilities and intelligence to deal with childhood problems.

DISCUSSION

Few people in the literature believe that children who are resilient are necessarily completely problem-free as adults. Yet, resilient children often develop survival skills that are used successfully in adulthood. The issues that Lawrence wants to discuss are realistic and treatable issues. That he knows they will cause emotional harm if they're not resolved shows a remarkable capacity for survival. The clinician who worked with Lawrence talked about his work with Lawrence:

(continued)

CONTINUED

Lawrence, understands the harm that was done to him in childhood. He also knows that some of the coping strategies he used in childhood to deal with a highly disturbed situation are not going to work well in adulthood. Lawrence is a very intelligent and rational person. To deal with the discomfort of the academic politics in his department required a great deal of discussion about what he wants from an academic career. He knows that contentiousness is often a fact of life in the academy and is realistic enough to know that he will find many of the same problems elsewhere, should he seek another position. Using his ability to see and understand the dynamics of his department, we worked on survival strategies within the department and the university. Lawrence knows that he needs mentors and friends in both places and has begun to develop those relationships as a hedge against the possibility of losing his chance for tenure. He has completed a very well received book and has others in mind. His teaching is excellent, and he has begun to feel that he is much more likely to achieve tenure than he first thought. His last tenure review gave a very positive appraisal of his tenure chances.

The issues of intimacy and sex are much more complicated. He has a female friend for whom he has very warm and tender feelings. At my suggestion, he told his friend that he had been abused as a child (he didn't mention his mother and kept the discussion very nonspecific). Because of the abuse, sex was problematic for him, but he had warm feelings for his friend and wanted to have a relationship with her. As the relationship developed, they began to have very gentle contact that began with holding one another and proceeded to other more intimate behaviors, which led to a fully experienced sexual contact. Lawrence is pleased that it happened and thinks it's a very good sign that the problem can be resolved. The treatment has moved in the direction of helping Lawrence understand his feelings about his mother, adult intimacy, and adult relationships. It's a very difficult process, and Lawrence is often depressed and angry about his mother's behavior and his compliance. Nonetheless, he has discussed deeply guarded feelings and experiences about his mother that has often left him crying and highly emotional in treatment. With each therapeutic episode in which he discusses his mother's behavior and his response, he seems stronger. The need to understand and the ability to forgive are significant parts of Lawrence's resilience. As the weeks have gone by, Lawrence seems much more able to focus on his needs as a man and the pleasure he is having from the relationship with his friend. Will Lawrence feel completely free sexually? Time will tell, but at this moment in time, the prognosis is good. Lawrence, like many resilient people I've worked with, has an inner strength and rationality that are pretty amazing. He sees where I'm going before I do and is prepared to work on issues in a way that shows great motivation. Like many of the resilient people I've worked with, he is an amazingly competent person.

A CRITICAL RESPONSE

One is very taken by the study of how children cope with adversity. It appears to be a much more useful way of understanding human behavior than the pathology model that seems to focus on what is wrong with the children. There is something very heroic about the coping strategies of maltreated children that, after all, come from their own inner resources, for the most part. But the quality of the resiliency research is a problem. For one, resilient children are not necessarily resilient adults. When adult stressors begin, the earlier problems of childhood traumas may assert themselves, and it may not be true that resilient children become resilient adults. This isn't to say that trauma needs to indefinitely affect people, but one wonders if the pathology model, which tracks so many dysfunctional people who have experienced childhood maltreatment, is necessarily all wrong. One also wonders why resilient children aren't more angry, and whether the anger tends to be internalized as depression.

As Tiet, Bird, and Davies (1998) reported, we still aren't completely certain about the actual mechanism resilient children use to deal with life stressors, nor do we know why children with high IQs seem to be more resilient than maltreated children with lower IQs. In fact, the research on resilience appears to be very limited methodologically. By taking children who have been maltreated and trying to separate the resilient children from the nonresilient children and then noting the characteristics of both groups, we're prone to get very spurious results. Furthermore, the results we do get seem inordinately influenced by the biases of the researchers. When you consider the list of attributes of resilient children noted in this chapter, it's like a shopping list of the more than 40 strengths indicated in Chapter 2, any number of which may or may not have anything to do with resilience. Choosing just a few of the attributes of resilient children described in this chapter, resilient children have higher IQs, an internal locus of control, know how to make themselves invisible, have more friends, and are better communicators. Many of the authors quoted in this chapter come up with different attributes, some of them mutually exclusive. If the research is well done, there should be consistency in the findings, and the list should not include over 20 attributes of resilient children in this chapter alone. Teit, Bird, and Davies (1998) are absolutely correct: The attributes of resilient children do not explain the mechanism used to cope with traumatic events. All they do is to provide a shopping list of characteristics of resilient children that may or may not explain why resilient children cope with trauma.

The intriguing notions of resilience and the strengths approach that tries to understand the way children cope with maltreatment and use those coping mechanisms in a positive way are exciting ideas that should be tested and studied in more detail. These are refreshing new ideas for clinicians to think about as they treat the many maltreated children in America, ideas that offer us a possible new direction to take in our future work with clients who have experienced childhood traumas.

SUMMARY

This chapter on resilience covers the many factors that define resilience in maltreated children. The chapter provides several definitions of the term *resilience* as it applies to the helping professions and discusses the confusion some people have in understanding the differences between strengths and resilience. Several case studies describe clients who have experienced traumas but cope with them in highly effective ways. Concerns are raised that resilience research, to date, fails to provide the mechanisms by which resilient people cope with life stressors and instead offers a shopping list of strengths that aren't particularly useful to the clinician, and may just suggest researcher bias.

INTEGRATIVE QUESTIONS

1. Isn't it likely that people who are resilient cope with some life issues in a healthy way and others in a dysfunctional way? The term *resilient* seems to imply healthy behavior in all areas of life, something that seems unlikely. Do you agree?

2. More than 20 behaviors were associated with resilient children in this chapter alone. Is it possible that we haven't any idea why certain people are resilient and why others aren't, and that the answer lies in other avenues of research, perhaps biological research showing that resilient people are more biochemically able to cope with stress?

3. The case studies in this chapter show amazing people dealing with terrible traumas. In the real world, don't people who have been traumatized develop a number of dysfunctional behaviors as a result of the damage done to them? Might resilient people just be a statistical anomaly composed of a small cohort of people who have better coping skills than others, just as some people are stronger, or smarter, or more attractive?

4. How does one treat a resilient child? Isn't it a contradiction in terms to take a child who is coping well and provide interventions that might possibly interfere with the child's progress?

5. Is it possible that the children who have been identified as resilient really aren't resilient, but that on the limited measures used by researchers, they appear to be more resilient than they really are? Don't we need long-term longitudinal studies of maltreated children over the life span to determine whether children identified as resilient maintain their resilience as adults?

REFERENCES

Abrams, M.S. (2001). Resilience in ambiguous loss. *American Journal of Psychotherapy*, 55, 283–291.

Anderson, K.M. (November 1997). Uncovering survival abilities in children who have been sexually abused. *Families in Society: The Journal of Contemporary Human Services*, 78, 592–599.

Arend, R., Gove, F., and Sroufe, L. (1979). Continuity of individual adaptation from infancy to kindergarten: A predictive study of ego-resiliency and curiosity in preschoolers. *Child Development*, 50, 950–959.

Baldwin, A., Baldwin, C., Kasser, T., Zax, M., Sameroff, A., and Seifer, R. (1993). Contextual risk and resiliency during adolescence. *Development and Psychopathology*, 5, 741–761.

Barnard, C. (1994). Resiliency: A shift in our perception? *American Journal of Family Therapy*, 22, 135–144.

Byrd, R. (1994). Assessing resilience in victims of childhood maltreatment. Doctoral dissertation. Pepperdine University, Dissertation Abstracts, 5503. Malibu, CA: Pepperdine University.

Cohler, B. (1987). Adversity, resilience, and the study of lives. In E.J. Anthony and B.J. Cohler (Eds.), *The invulnerable child* (pp. 363–424). New York: Guilford.

Egeland, E., Carlson, E., and Sroufe, L. (1993). Resilience as process. *Development and Psychopathology*, 5, 517–528.

Furey, J.A. (1993). Unknown soldiers: Women veterans and PTSD. *Professional Counselor*, 7, 33–34.

Garmezy, N. (1991). Resiliency and vulnerability to adverse developmental outcomes associated with poverty. *American Behavioral Scientist*, 34, 416–430.

Garmezy, N., Masten, A., and Tellegen, A. (1964). The study of stress and competence in children: A building block for developmental psychopathology. *Child Development*, 55, 97–111.

Glicken, M.D., and Sechrest, D.K. (2003). *The role of the helping professions in treating the victims and perpetrators of violence.* Boston: Allyn & Bacon/Longman.

Henry, D.L. (September 1999). Resilience in maltreated children: Implications for special needs adoptions. *Child Welfare*, 78, 519–540.

Kauffman, C., Grunebaum, H., Cohler, B., and Gamer, E. (1979). Superkids: Competent children of psychotic mothers. *American Journal of Psychiatry*, 136, 1398–1402.

Luthar, S. (1993). Annotation: Methodology and conceptual issues in research on childhood resilience. *Journal of Child Psychology and Psychiatry*, 34, 441–453.

Luthar, S., and Zigler, E. (1991). Vulnerability and competence: A review of research on resilience in childhood. *American Journal of Orthopsychiatry*, 6, 6–22.

MacLeod, J.M. (1996). The two of us. *Grinnell Review*, 15, 43.

Masten, A. (1989). Resilience in development: Implications of the study of successful adaptation for developmental psychopathology. In D. Cicchetti (Ed.), *The emergence of a discipline: Rochester symposium on developmental psychopathology* (pp. 261–294). Hillsdale, NJ: Lawrence Erlbaum.

Okun, A., Parker, J., and Levendosky, A. (1994). Distinct and interactive contributions of physical abuse, socioeconomic disadvantage, and negative live events to children's social, cognitive, affective adjustment. *Development and Psychopathology*, 6, 77–98.

Radke-Yarrow, M., and Brown, E. (1993). Resilience and vulnerability in children of multiple-risk families. *Development and Psychopathology*, 5, 581–592.

Saleebey, D. (1997). The strengths approach to practice. In D. Saleebey (Ed.), *The strengths perspective in social work practice* (pp. 49–57). New York: Longman.

Seligman, M. (1992). *Learned optimism: How to change your mind and your life.* New York: Pocket Books.

Tiet, Q.Q., Bird, H., and Davies, M.R. (November 1998). Adverse life events and resilience. *Journal of the American Academy of Child and Adolescent Psychiatry*, 37, 1191–1200.

Walsh, F. (1998). *Strengthening family resilience.* New York: Guilford.

Werner, E. (1989). High-risk children in young adulthood: A longitudinal study from birth to 32 years. *American Orthopsychiatric Association*, 59, 72–81.

Werner, E. (1993). Risk, resilience, and recovery. Perspectives from the Kauai longitudinal study. *Development and Psychopathology*, 5, 503–515.

Werner, E., and Smith, R. (1982). *Vulnerable but invincible.* New York: Adams, Bannister & Cox.

CHAPTER SEVEN

THE NATURAL HELPING IMPULSE OF THE COMMUNITY

This chapter looks at the community as a source of indigenous or natural helpers who often assist people in need before and after they see a professional helper. Natural helpers are often the individuals who are sought out by others for their wise and compassionate advice, but they are also the people who organize, develop, and then voluntarily lead self-help groups. Many indigenous helpers are volunteers, mentors, and the people in more traditional cultures that act as a bridge between the community and professional helpers. In the Latino culture, such people are called *promotoras* and are considered to be the people of wisdom who are also asked to help settle disputes.

SELF-HELP GROUPS

Wituk et al. (2000) write, "Self-help groups consist of individuals who share the same problem or concern. Members provide emotional support to one another, learn ways to cope, discover strategies for improving their condition, and help others while helping themselves" (p. 157). Kessler et al. (1997) indicate that an estimated 25 million Americans have been involved in self-help groups at some point during their lives. Positive outcomes have been found in groups treating substance abuse (Humphreys & Moos, 1996), bereavement (Caserta & Lund, 1993), care giving (McCallion & Toseland, 1995), diabetes (Gilden et al., 1992), and depression (Kurtz, 1988).

Riessman (1997) suggests that the following principles help define the function and purpose of self-help groups: (1) Members of a self-help group share a similar condition and understand each other as others can't. (2) The members of the group determine activities and processes, making self-help groups highly democratic and self-determining. (3) Helping others is often therapeutic. (4) Self-help groups are built on the strengths of the individual members, the group, and the community. (5) Self-help groups usually charge no fee and are not commercialized or sold as a product. (6) The social support that exists in self-help groups allows participants to cope with traumas because self-help is based on the notion of supportive relationships between members. (7) Self-help groups have values that help define the group meaning to its members. (8) Self-help groups use the abilities of the members to help others. (9) Seeking assistance from a self-help group is not stigmatizing as it may be when seeking assistance from a health or mental health professional. (10) Self-help groups use strengths perspective notions of self-determination, inner strength, self-healing, and resilience.

Although research is scant on the subject of the effectiveness of self-help groups, Seligman (1995) notes that in an evaluation of a larger report by *Consumer Reports* on the effectiveness of psychotherapy that "Alcoholics Anonymous (AA) did especially well, . . . significantly bettering mental health professionals [in the treatment of alcohol and drug-related problems]" (p. 10).

In a review of over 40 self-help group effectiveness studies, several of which are summarized here, Kyrouz and Humphreys (1997) reported the following research studies related to the effectiveness of self-help groups with a variety of health-related and emotional problems:

Edmunson and Bedell (1982) reported that after 10 months of participation in a patient-led, professionally supervised social network enhancement group, one-half as many former psychiatric inpatients (n = 40) required rehospitalization as did nonparticipants (n = 40). Participants in the patient-led network also had much shorter average hospital stays (7 days versus 25 days), and a higher percentage of members than nonmembers could function with no contact with the mental health system (53 percent versus 23 percent).

Vachon and Lyall (1980) studied 162 women over a two-year period whose husbands had passed away. Half of the women were assigned to participate in a "widow-to-widow" program. After six months in the program, participants were more likely than nonparticipants to feel healthier and less likely to anticipate a difficult adjustment to widowhood. After 12 months, participants were more likely than nonparticipants to feel "much better," to have made new friends, to have begun new activities, and were less likely to feel constantly anxious, or to feel the need to hide their true emotions.

Kurtz (1988) found that 82 percent of 129 members of the Manic Depressive and Depressive Association reported coping better with their illness since joining the self-help group. The longer they were members and the more intensely they were involved with the group, the more their coping skills improved. Furthermore, the percentage of members reporting being admitted to a psychiatric hospital before joining the group was 82 percent, but after joining, those requiring hospitalization fell to only 33 percent.

Humphreys, Mavis, and Stoffelmayr (1994) reported that one year after being admitted to a public substance abuse treatment agency, Caucasian and African American members were attending mutual help (Narcotics Anonymous, Alcoholics Anonymous) groups at the same rate. African American participants (n = 253) in Narcotics Anonymous and Alcoholics Anonymous showed significant improvements over 12 months in six problem areas (employment, alcohol, drug, legal, psychological, and family). African American self-help group participants had significantly more improvement in their medical, alcohol, and drug problems than did African American patients who did not participate in self-help groups after treatment.

Humphreys and Moos (1996) found that over a period of three years, alcoholics who initially chose to attend AA and were compared with those who initially sought help from a professional outpatient treatment provider (total n = 201) had a 45 percent ($1,826) lower average per-person treatment cost than did those who initially chose professional treatment. AA participants also experienced reduced alcohol consumption, dependence symptoms, adverse consequences, days intoxicated, and depression. These additional outcomes did not differ significantly from those of alcoholics who chose professional treatment and were true one year and three years after the start of the study.

Spiegel et al. (1989) studied 86 women undergoing treatment for metastatic breast cancer. Fifty of the 86 women were randomly assigned to have their medical care supplemented with a weekly support group co-lead by a therapist who had breast cancer in remission and a psychiatrist or social worker. The sessions focused on topics related to health, communications, expressing grief, and coping with pain. The support group participants lived twice as long as those in the control group, an average of almost 18 months longer.

Hinrichsen and Revenson (1985) studied adults with scoliosis who had bracing, surgery, and were members of a Scoliosis Association self-help group (n = 33). When compared with adults with similar treatment who did not participate in the group (n = 67), group participants reported a more optimistic outlook on life, greater satisfaction with their medical care, fewer psychosomatic symptoms, more self-esteem, and fewer feelings of estrangement.

■ ■ ■ ■ ■ ▬▬▬▬▬▬▬▬▬▬▬▬▬▬▬▬▬▬▬▬▬▬▬▬▬▬▬▬▬▬▬▬▬▬▬

A SELF-HELP GROUP EXPERIENCE: A CASE STUDY

The author was privileged to attend several support group meetings of a cancer recovery group of patients undergoing proton/radiation treatment at Loma Linda Medical Center in California. Most of the people were being treated for life-threatening malignancies in the brain, the eyes, and the prostate, malignancies that are difficult to remove surgically and are frequently terminal.

The group had no assigned leader and began with dinner at a restaurant near the hospital. At a point within the first hour of the support group meeting, everyone stopped eating and people stood up and began talking about their treatments, their fears of death, and their deep belief that their conditions would improve medically. There was a surge of emotion from the group when people described their optimism. The experience was very emotional to this observer, but the group members had a look of contentment and serenity on their faces. The author noticed that many of the support group members were also active participants at the Loma Linda University Wellness Center (the author was a member as well) where people in treatment can swim, play tennis, or use the facilities to stay in shape. Following are some statements from the people attending this particular self-help group.

Bernie, a 71-year-old psychiatrist from Alabama with advanced prostate cancer, said,

I've been a therapist and helper most of my life, but you put people in a group where all of us are fighting a common disease and the amount of unconditional love you feel is astonishing. It makes you think, even when inside you feel little hope, that you're going to make it. Many of these folks are terminal and everyone knows it, but for another year or two or three, they may extend their lives and live pretty normal lives without too much pain. I think much of my sense of optimism comes from the other patients who are remarkable and resilient. We get a sour puss once in a while, but they usually don't want to come to the groups. They want to feel sorry for themselves. I don't see them making it at all. But these tough and resilient people who go through some really awful medical procedures so they can live a little longer and be with their families and loved ones, my hat is off to them. Not only do they give to themselves, but also they give to the rest of us. What more can you ask for in a human being?

Greta, a 41-year-old accountant from Germany, said,

I know I'm going to die, but being around my fellow patients, sometimes I think I'm going to live to be a very old woman. My tumor in the brain isn't getting smaller, and I can tell from the technicians who do the proton treatment that I'm not getting better. But all the time I've been here, in my social contacts, in the dinners we go to, in the plays we see in Los Angeles, the feeling I get from the other people is that I'm going to be fine. It's begun a quiet determination inside of me to make it, to live.

Edgar, a clothing salesman from San Francisco, says that he has no doubt that he'll be fine. After tennis one day, he said,

I'm around a lot of other prostate cancer patients with much worse tumors than I have and they're all optimistic. It's infectious. I go to the dinners and the plays where we talk and get to know each other, and the bravery of the patients and their families is inspiring to me. You can't think very much about not getting better. It's always about getting better and staying better.

This recognition of the power of self-help has encouraged a number of clinicians to use group members to help facilitate the group experience. Many diversion projects for spousal abuse and domestic violence use mandatory groups to treat clients in jeopardy of doing time in jail. In these groups, members who have successfully stopped their abusive behaviors are often used as group facilitators. The use of people with similar life problems to facilitate groups, or to act as co-leaders with a professional, often provides ballast and hope to people in serious physical and emotional difficulty.

SELF-HELP PHILOSOPHIES

In considering the literature from individual self-help groups and from interviewing group leaders and participants, the following seem to be the recurring themes that are consistently suggested in the philosophies of self-help groups:

1. *Don't Blame Others for Life Difficulties:* Most self-help groups teach their clients not to blame other people for life problems. Never assume, they suggest, that because something was done to a client when they were younger that it must forever continue to affect them as adults. Blaming others for our problems doesn't make the problem go away.
2. *Never See Yourself as a Victim*: Calling yourself a victim or defining yourself as someone in recovery is a great excuse for not dealing with life problems. You

might be a victim and you might be in recovery, but defining yourself in these ways serves to keep your attention off change and on what was done to you. If you view yourself as someone in recovery, you never get on with your life. Instead, you focus endlessly on the event you are getting over. You may have an alcoholic addiction, but you still need to have a life, and you can't use your drinking problem as an excuse for not getting on with it. You define yourself by what is right about you, what works, and what you are most proud of in yourself.

3. *Therapy Isn't for Life:* Therapy is not forever. Neither is therapy a substitute for doing the day-to-day work that must be done to change one's life. Some people substitute therapy for a social life. They use therapists or support groups as substitutes for the friends and loved ones they should be developing on their own. Therapy is to be used for the emotional blocks we cannot remove by ourselves. Therapy is hard, unsettling work. Its purpose is to help us see connections between our life decisions and our past and current behavior. Often, it results in insights and perceptions of life that may be upsetting and troubling. The impulse to seek help when things go badly is a good one. Using therapists to fill a void in our social lives is not what therapy is about.

4. *No One Ever Said That Life Would Always Be Sweet:* Sometimes life is awful. You ride out the storms without criticizing yourself for the times that aren't so great.

5. *Try Not to Let Negative Feedback Affect You:* Many people in our lives tend to give us negative messages. Try not to listen to them and, certainly, try not to believe them. This is particularly true of friends, parents, children, spouses, and boyfriends and girlfriends. If they give you messages that are particularly negative, try to understand their reasons, but limit your contact with them. No one needs to continually be around others who say or do hurtful things to us.

6. *Be True to Your Goals in Life:* Have your own goals in life. Be certain of them and then stick to them regardless of what other people say to try and dissuade you. Most of the time, that is. If your goals are off-center, getting you into trouble, impractical, or pie in the sky dreams, have the foresight and strength to change them. But in this society, in which support and encouragement are often lost in the rush to compete and to win at any cost, many of our closest friends are also the ones who urge caution and inertia when we have dreams and ideas that need to be tested and activated.

7. *The Past Isn't Relevant Anymore:* It's not what's happened to us in life that may cause us to be unhappy, it's how we view those life occurrences. The Greek Stoic philosophers believed that people had the ability to control their emotions by what they said to themselves about an event. That is why people who go through really unfortunate life problems often come out of the events stronger than they were before the events took place. Their perception of the problems lead to positive life outcomes.

8. *Use Your Time Well:* In the end, it isn't the college degree you have, or the amount of money you've accumulated, or the successes that you've had in life; it's the way you've accumulated experiences, the knowledge you've gained, and the way you've used your life. Everything else may just be "ground noise" that

neither leads to happiness nor life satisfaction. To be sure, there are people who gloat over the money they've accumulated or the titles and degrees they've achieved. Most of us, however, get that glow of good feelings when we consider what we've have done with our lives. The better we've used our time and the more life experiences we've had, the more likely we are to give ourselves high marks for leading successful lives.

NATURAL HELPERS

Lewis and Suarez (1995) suggest three primary functions of natural helpers: (1) buffers between individuals and sources of stress; (2) providers of social support; and (3) information and referral sources and lay consultants. Patterson and Marsiglia (2000) note remarkable similarities in the characteristics of two cohorts of natural helpers coming from two distinct geographic locations in the United States:

> [M]ost helpers, irrespective of recipient type (relatives, friends, or neighbors), offered assistance before they were asked for help. The outcome of help for most helpers focused on eliminating or alleviating the source of stress associated with the recipient's problems. Helpers assisted friends in strengthening their coping capacities more frequently than relatives or neighbors. (p. 25)

Waller and Patterson (2002) believe that natural helping strengthens the social bond that holds communities together and that it promotes resilience in individuals and communities. Civic responsibility, according to Waller and Patterson, is "inextricably intertwined" with the well-being of individuals and communities.

Robert Bly (1986) believes that we seek others in the community, our close family, or people in our work environment for advice and support. He calls these natural helpers "People of Wisdom" because they listen well, are empathic and sensitive, and are known for their expertise in solving certain types of problems. We gravitate to these people because they help us in unobtrusive and informal ways that are often profoundly subtle. The lack of formal training by natural helpers is offset by their kindness, patience, common sense, and good judgment. The reasons people use natural helpers are summarized from a study done by the author (Glicken, 1991, p. 27).

1. People feel safe going to natural helpers. There is no fear regarding confidentiality, and they know that the advice given will not harm them. Frequently, the advice they get from natural helpers is to seek professional help. This advice, coming from someone they trust, makes it easier for them to seek professional help and to break down any resistance they might have to treatment.

2. Natural helpers use helping processes with which most people are comfortable. They listen, give common sense advice, and are usually gentle people. As one person interviewed said, "I went for professional therapy and the therapist, right away, had me talking to my dead mother who was supposed to be sitting in an empty chair opposite me. It felt really strange. I was having marital problems,

but I was supposed to talk to my dead mother? I just couldn't see it. Jim, who is a friend and a very good listener, sat with me at coffee and let me pour my heart out for two hours. He didn't interrupt, was very supportive and calm, and just said that my marriage had come to a point where it was so difficult for me to make a decision that I needed professional help. He was right, of course, but I would have never sought someone out if it weren't for him and, ultimately, after a few false starts, like the one I mentioned, I found a good counselor and it saved my marriage."

3. Natural helpers are wise people who have the ability to share advice that makes sense and is reasonable. Often, the advice offered is so compelling, it may prevent a crisis.

4. Natural helpers are optimistic. People who seek help from natural helpers often feel accepted, respected, and affirmed. Many people who seek help from natural helpers immediately feel more confident in their ability to resolve a problem, because the natural helper has defined it in a positive and solvable way.

5. Natural helpers usually learn their helping skills by observing parents or significant adults in childhood. They describe themselves as resilient and rational people who have always been able to resolve their own life problems without needing additional help. Natural helpers are usually able to use their own advice and to lead productive and exemplary lives. It is the healthy lives of the natural helpers that almost always encourages people to seek their company.

6. Natural helpers believe in a positive view of people. Most people who use natural helpers suggest that the optimistic way natural helpers frame problems is what makes them so helpful.

7. Because natural helpers have no formal training, the approach they use with others is very gentle and fluid. It often feels as if they are talking to a dear friend over coffee.

Examples of Natural Helpers

Natural Helper 1.   Sharon Miller works in a law firm in San Antonio, Texas, and gave this example of a natural helper in her office.

> I work in a highly competitive law office. You can't trust anyone. If you share anything personal, it gets all over the office and it's used against you in every way imaginable. You can never let people think that you're vulnerable or pretty soon you're considered weak. We have a wonderful paralegal who is everyone's friend. She's a great listener, she's honest, and she'd never break a confidence. Everyone shares personal and work-related information with her. She's the office safety valve. If it weren't for her, the place would explode.

Ms. Miller's selection of a natural helper was asked to share her experiences. She said,

> I never thought of myself as anything as grand as a therapist, but it's true that people have been coming to me for advice since I was a child. I've learned over the years that

listening well, keeping a confidence, and occasionally making suggestions when people ask for them can have a good effect on people's lives. I don't think of myself as a therapist or anything like that. I guess I just see myself as a good friend who has something to offer. Lots of times, the problems people ask me to listen too are so serious that it's clear they need professional help. I'm always sure to suggest that if it's warranted. Other times, people just need a kind person to listen and to remind them that they're good people. It's amazing how seldom we seem to let others know that they're really OK people. Folks just get down on themselves sometimes, and they need someone to help them see another path.

Natural Helper 2.   Oscar Anderson has been involved in the union movement in Kansas City for over 50 years as a teamster. He believes in reaching out to his co-workers and helping them in times of need. His weekends, when many of the men in the union drink to excess, are often spent helping the men who come to his home to discuss their serious personal problems. Oscar is a nonbeliever in counseling and psychotherapy, but what he does looks very much like therapy, in a rough and unorthodox way. He listens well, offers advice when it's needed, and knows where men can get specialized help. He can be supportive and encouraging, as well as confrontational and very directive. Now semiretired, Oscar had the following to say about helping people on the job:

> Most counselors I know never tell people that a lot of what they've done in their lives is good. They never praise people for their hard work or their support for families. They never use humor. All they do is criticize. I see a lot of immature young people at work. It's taken them a long time to grow up. You can't help people grow up overnight, it takes time. You've got to listen carefully to what they say, praise them for what they do well, and offer some advice and support for what they don't do so well.

Natural Helper 3.   Sam Goldfarb, another natural helper, is a retired manager of a large accounting firm. Sam is originally from Russia but has lived in Minneapolis for 40 years. His synagogue suggested a talk with Sam because he's spent his working years informally helping his co-workers, as well as the members of his synagogue. When Sam was interviewed, he was helping to transport an elderly member of the congregation to a doctor's office. Sam is 83 years old.

> You don't go around with a sign on your face that says to come see you if anyone wants to talk, but you let yourself be around the people who are in trouble. You can tell from their faces and the way they're acting that they're in some trouble in their life. Pretty soon they talk. People love to talk, but only if they feel you won't criticize them. I just listen . . . an old man with an ear and a heart to offer. And when they're done talking, I give them advice, an old man's advice. Sometimes they take it, sometimes they don't. That's life. But most of the time they're grateful to get their problems off their chest.

Natural Helper 4.   A colleague is a man of wisdom. He teaches history at a local university but has no training in counseling. A crisis in his family life sent him to a therapist several years ago, and since then, he's been on a quest to help other men. This is what he told me about the experience.

Most mornings I go to a local cafe for coffee. It's a sort of ritual for me. Sometimes I write checks for bills I owe while other times I try and organize my day. The local men often walk by my table and nod in recognition. Sometimes they stop and talk to me about my articles in the local papers about men. They are the workingmen of America; the plumbers and construction workers, the common laborers and retired railroad workers, the illegal immigrants from Mexico. Their trucks and beat-up old cars line the parking lot outside of the restaurant.

I have come to value my conversations with these men. Many of them have done badly by women and children, and readily admit it. Some of them are extraordinary people who have done better than most of us. And there are always the men who sit in the back of the restaurant and talk in whispered tones about women. They sound like abusers. Worse, they sound like children in adult bodies.

I've learned a lot from talking and listening to the men I meet in the coffee shop. Academics can be pretty disassociated from life, but these men talk like real people; people with flaws, people we all know in our daily lives. When the wives and kids of these men talk to me, you get a very sad picture of their behavior. They talk about abuse and neglect, about put-downs, and absences, and mean drinking, and, sometimes, about abandonment. They often describe the impact of insensitive behavior on the women and children who are trying so hard to love their men.

Sometimes I get a chance to sit with the men and women and listen to them talk about the gender wars they have fought. The men usually sit with their mouths open and, often as not say, "Was I that bad?" Everybody nods their heads. The men have mellowed a lot so it isn't easy for them to imagine that they've acted so badly in the past.

Sometimes the men hang around, after the women leave, to assure me that they weren't *that* bad, but there is an emptiness to their denial that rings hollow. Many times they walk away shaking their head, angry at me for making them hear so much bad information about behavior they'd rather forget. These men who interrupt me as I try and drink my coffee are ordinary men: Men who have had troubles in their lives; men who drink too much and who can be mean and petty; men who regret their past and have done a thing or two that leave them in the night sweats when they wake up from bad dreams; normal men who have made mistakes; decent guys who cared for the baby at night and have provided for families when it was nearly impossible.

Sensitive men? Probably not. Romantic men? I doubt it. Men who sweep women off their feet with the power and concentration of their lovemaking? It doesn't seem very likely. These men are just regular "Joes" who need the guidance and the sweet and tender love of a woman: Men who are better when a woman is in their life than when they are alone; men who can hardly navigate the complexities of life and depend on women in ways that seem childlike at times. Men like Roger, a plumber who joins the early morning construction gang at the coffee shop. He sees me sitting in the back reading the paper and comes over to sit with me. Today he complains about his wife. She's too fat, he says. He's lost interest in her. I look over at Roger who is perhaps 60 or 70 pounds overweight, and I ask if he's looked in the mirror lately. Does he know that his obesity is as off-putting to his wife as hers is to him? He mumbles something derogatory about my mother, but I see him everyday and he looks somehow, thinner. When I see him with his wife, they look nice together. Warm, maybe even tender in the way mature men and women can be with one another. He doesn't thank me for my advice or say how much his life has improved because of my simple advice. All he does is bring his wife over, an attractive woman in her forties, while I drink my coffee and try to read the paper. He beams at me. See how great my wife looks, his smile says?

See what a hunk I must be to attract such a great looking lady? It is thanks enough and I smile at their happiness.

Another guy, Richard, one of the few African American men who sit in the cafe, morning after morning, complains to me about the way his wife spends his money. "She's a shopping junky," he says. "There's no way she can spend so much money." He brings her in one morning, a nice, soft-spoken young woman. She talks to me about how difficult it is for a African American family to make ends meet but Richard is a good husband and father and they make the money go a little further. Richard wants to buy me breakfast. He feels like dancing in the cafe. His wife has touched a part of his heart with love seeds.

Denise sometimes comes for coffee and sits with a group of middle-aged women. Sometime ago, she and some of the other women at the table began asking me questions about men. I'd listen and, occasionally, I'd offer a suggestion or two. Denise would come back later and tell me how much better her husband was when she'd try little pieces of the advice I'd give her. The ladies were suspicious but, after a while, all of them asked for suggestions about how to understand the men in their lives. Without fail, enough of the suggestions worked so well that I often felt like I was doing therapy in the back seat of the coffee shop. Ladies would come up to me and ask every manner of question.

For example, Betty Sue wanted to know why her husband had lost interest in sex. I pointed out a few possible reasons like fatigue from work, or anxiety over finances. "He's a good man," she said, "and we used to have a great love life." All of the women in the group raised their eyes in disbelief and said, "Sure, sure," but Betty Sue persisted. There was something really wrong, she thought. So I said to her, why not just say to him something like, "Honey, it sure used to be nice how we'd spend our time in bed. It would be nice to have that again." Then, I said, see what he says.

The next day she came back with a big smile on her face. All the ladies at the table were ribbing her. Finally, someone motioned for me to join them. "He thought I wasn't interested anymore," she said. "He thought maybe I was seeing another man, and it was making him crazy."

I don't know if I'm doing any good. I'm just a historian, after all, and all I know about therapy is what I've observed in my own therapy and what I've learned in life. It just feels right to reach out to people. The more I think about it, the more I think it makes me the happiest I've ever been to help others. It's what my mother used to call a "mitzvah" or doing a good deed. Since I've been doing "mitzvahs," I'm a lot happier as a person, I can say that for sure.

A CRITICAL RESPONSE

It's interesting to note that the renewed interest in self-help groups and natural helpers comes at a time when health and mental health care are undergoing a crisis in America. A number of articles noted in this chapter suggest this notion explicitly. As health and mental health care become too expensive for most insurance policies to adequately cover, self-help groups are being urged to pick up the slack. Or, in a more veiled suggestion, professionals are being urged to work cooperatively with self-help groups for the benefit of the client. But who is that client if not the citizen whose health care plan doesn't provide sufficient professional help? And who does this leave receiving professional care but the more affluent person who can purchase adequate insurance or pay for health care through their own funds? As an example of this trend tying self-help groups to reduced health care resources, Humphreys (1998) wrote,

> Professional substance abuse treatment in the United States grew extensively through the 1970s and 1980s, becoming literally a billion-dollar annual enterprise. In recent years, however, the professional treatment network has contracted due to the arrival of managed health care and to recent public sector disinvestments. Clinicians and health policy planners now face the difficult challenge of attempting to care for addicted individuals within increasingly tight fiscal constraints. But there is a potential bright spot in the current gloomy addiction care picture—the possibility that self-help/mutual aid organizations can help substance abusers recover, while at the same time lowering demand for scarce formal health care resources. (p. 13)

In another article urging cooperation between self-help groups and the professional community, Humphreys and Ribisl (1999) asked, "Why should public health and medical professionals be interested in collaborating with a grassroots movement of untrained citizens?" (p. 326). Their answer is that money for health care is being reduced and that "self-help groups can provide benefits that the best health care often does not: identification with other sufferers, long-term support and companionship, and a sense of competence and empowerment" (p. 326).

The question then becomes, why should an affluent country like the United States not have universal medical care for everyone? And if we become dependent on self-help groups to provide a range of services, what is the assurance that these services will be effective? And, finally, is it ethical in a democracy to eliminate professional services to the less affluent among us who desperately need them, and will less affluent citizens use self-help groups? As Kessler, Mickelson, and Zhao (1997) discovered, people who use self-help groups for addiction treatment are more likely than people who don't use self-help groups to also use a professional. Doesn't this suggest that self-help attendees, at least those who have addiction problems, are more sophisticated in the use of the medical system and will use both professionals and self-help groups, while those who are less sophisticated in health care will probably not use self-help groups in the absence of professional help?

Finally, the argument is continually made that self-help groups are more down to earth, that they respond to diversity in ways that professionals don't, and that they are more user friendly. If that's true, what does it say about professionals, their training, and their levels of competence? Certainly, no one can be happy with professional help if these arguments in favor of self-help groups are true.

This isn't to criticize natural helpers or self-help groups. They serve a very important purpose and, according to the research in this chapter, often provide effective services for a range of physical and emotional problems. However, professional experience would make many of us a little less certain that natural helpers are the kind, sweet people depicted in this chapter. Like some professionals, self-help group leaders can be rigid and off-putting in they way they run and control groups. Self-help groups often become obsessed with slogans and catchy phrases that make them unattractive to many people. Conversations with newly immigrated people from more traditional cultures suggest that they trust modern American approaches to health and mental health much more than the traditional healing approaches used in their countries, approaches with minimal success, in their view.

Still, there is an idealism about people helping other people that surely bodes well for our society. Being weaned away from use of professionals may not be such a bad thing as more and more people consult with one another on solutions to problems. That, it seems clear, can only help bring us closer together as a people.

SUMMARY

This chapter deals with the natural helping approaches found in self-help groups and in the people who informally help one another: the natural or indigenous helpers we turn to in time of crisis. Research is provided showing the effectiveness of self-help groups with a variety of serious health and mental health problems, and examples are given of natural helpers and their philosophy of helping. The critical response cautions that self-help groups may be asked to fill the gap left by the lack of professional services being created by a health care crisis in America. The reliance on self-help groups may force less affluent people to use self-help groups or go without services. Concerns about the use of self-help groups as a forced alternative to professional help should not diminish the real service they provide, or the fact that they suggest a desire by people to strengthen communities by helping one another.

INTEGRATIVE QUESTIONS

1. The argument was made that we have a health care crisis in the United States that discriminates against less affluent Americans. Given this argument, do you believe that self-help groups will become an alternative for many health and mental health services now provided by professionals?

2. Self-help groups have been criticized for being overly controlling and requiring people to accept a philosophy of life that might be uncomfortable for them. How might a self-help group function so that group members do not experience these concerns?

3. The finding that self-help groups are often more effective than professional help appears to indicate the lack of effectiveness of professionals, or does it? Might there be legitimate reasons self-help groups work so well that doesn't suggest the inadequacy of professional helpers?

4. Natural helpers seem so appealing. Might there be situations and problems for which natural helpers should not be consulted and professional help should be sought immediately?

5. There is something very appealing about the self-help movement in America. Can you think of reasons self-help groups can have a unifying impact on communities?

REFERENCES

Bly, R. (1986). Men of wisdom. *Utne Reader,* April-May, 37–41.

Caserta, M.S., and Lund, D.A. (1993). Intrapersonal resources and the effectiveness of self-help groups for bereaved older adults. *Gerontologist,* 33, 619–629.

Edmunson, E.D., and Bedell, J.R. (1982). *Integrating skill building and peer support in mental health treatment: The early intervention and community network development projects.* New York: Plenum Press.

Gilden, J.L., Hendryx, A.S., Clar, S., Casia, F.P., and Singh, S.P. (1992). Diabetes support groups improve health care of older diabetic patients. *Journal of the American Geriatrics Society,* 40, 147–150.

Glicken, M.D. (July 7, 1991). Who to trust at work. *National Business Employment Weekly,* p. 27.

Glicken, M.D. (2002). In the lives of men. (Unpublished document)

Hinrichsen, G.A., and Revenson, T.A. (1985). Does self-help help? An empirical investigation of scoliosis peer support groups. *Journal of Social Issues,* 41(1), 65–87.

Humphreys, K. (1998). Can addiction-related self-help/mutual aid groups lower demand for professional substance abuse treatment? *Social Policy,* 29(2), 13–17.

Humphreys, K., and Moos, R.H. (1996). Reduced substance-abuse-related health care costs among voluntary participants in Alcoholics Anonymous. *Psychiatric Services,* 47, 709–713.

Humphreys, K., Mavis, B.E., and Stoffelmayr, B.E. (1994). Are twelve step programs appropriate for disenfranchised groups? Evidence from a study of post-treatment mutual help involvement. *Prevention in Human Services,* 11(1), 165–179.

Humphreys, K., and Ribisl, K.M. (1999). The case for partnership with self-help groups. *Public Health Reports,* 114(4), 322–329.

Kessler, R.C., Mickelson, K.D., and Zhao, S. (1997). Patterns and correlates of self-help group membership in the United States. *Social Policy,* 27, 27–46.

Kurtz, L.F. (1988). Mutual aid for affective disorders: The manic depressive and depressive association. *American Journal of Orthopsychiatry,* 58(1), 152–155.

Kyrouz, E.M., and Humphreys, K. (1997). A review of research on the effectiveness of self-help mutual aid groups [Online]. Retrieved October 13, 2002 from the World Wide Web: www.cmhc.com/articles/selfres.htm.

Lewis, E.A., and Suarez, Z.E. (1995). Natural helping networks. *Encyclopedia of Social Work* (19th Ed.) (pp. 1765–1772). Silver Spring, MD: National Association of Social Workers.

McCallion, P., and Toseland, R.W. (1995). Supportive group interventions with caregivers of frail older adults. *Social Work with Groups,* 18(1), 11–25.

Patterson, S.L., and Marsiglia, F.F. (2000). Mi casa es su casa: Beginning exploration of Mexican Americans' natural helping. *Families in Society,* 81, 22–31.

Riessman, F. (1997). Ten self-help principles. *Social Policy,* 27, 6–11.

Seligman, M.E.P. (1995). The effectiveness of psychotherapy: The *Consumer Report* study. *American Psychologist,* 50(12), 965–974.

Spiegel, D., Bloom, J.R., Kraemer, H.C., and Gottheil, E. (1989). Effect of psychosocial treatment on survival of patients with metastatic breast cancer. *Lancet,* October 14, 888–891.

Vachon, M.L.S., and Lyall, W.A.L. (1980). A controlled study of self-help intervention for widows. *American Journal of Psychiatry,* 137(11), 1380–1384.

Waller, M.A., and Patterson, S. (2002). Natural helping and resilience in a Dine (Navajo) community. *Society,* 81, 73–84.

Wituk, S., Shepherd, M.D., Slavich, S., Warren, M.L., and Meissen, G. (2000). A topography of self-help groups: An empirical analysis. *Social Work,* 45, 157–165.

PART III

THE IMPORTANCE
OF CULTURE:
TWO EXAMPLES

In the following two chapters, another important element of the strengths perspective is discussed: the beneficial impact of culture. Chapter 8 discusses traditional
Latino culture, and Chapter 9 describes the strengths perspective with ethnically
Asian clients. Both chapters focus on the client in crisis, and both chapters include
the importance of understanding the impact of cultural identity, in which the collective importance of extended family often overshadows the individuality of the
client. Chapter 8 offers some novel ideas about crisis work with traditionally Latino
clients and includes materials from interviews with therapists and social scientists
from Mexico. Chapter 9 develops Steven Ino's concept of the "collective self" as
the dominant focal point of work with ethnically Asian clients. The collective self
is a concept that stresses the importance of the extended family. Chapter 9 provides
case examples of clinical work, demonstrating how to incorporate the collective self
into treatment interventions with ethnically Asian clients. Both chapters provide information on two important ethnic groups in the United States and focus on the
use of the strengths perspective to demonstrate that the approach can be effective
with complex cultural and ethnic groups.

CHAPTER EIGHT

UTILIZING THE STRENGTHS PERSPECTIVE WITH THE CULTURALLY TRADITIONAL LATINO CLIENT IN CRISIS

WITH MINA A. GARZA

Newly immigrated and culturally traditional Latino clients increasingly seek assistance from social agencies for serious crisis-related problems. This chapter discusses the way they might best be helped through culturally relevant crisis intervention strategies using the strengths perspective.

The term *Latino* is used in this chapter to represent a group with a shared language and some similar customs and traditions. Hernandez (1990) notes that while three disparate groups of Latinos (Cubans, Puerto Ricans, and Mexicans) identify very different systems of beliefs related to political orientations, government involvement in their lives, and the extent of discrimination faced by each group in the United States, over 70 percent feel that all three groups are "very or somewhat similar."

THE LATINO WAY OF RESOLVING CRISIS

For the most part, newly immigrated and culturally traditional Latino clients often do not seek crisis treatment directly (Roger & Malgady, 1987) but may first discuss problems with extended family or *compadres*, the close friends who attend the baptisms of their children and who play such an important role in Latino culture. Latino clients also may seek help from clerics in the form of direct advice and suggestions. Elderly people, particularly women, represent wisdom in the Latino culture, and they also may be contacted before a professional is seen.

This chapter was presented in modified form to the *California Conference for Latino Social Workers*, Sacramento, October, 1996. (With Mina Garza)

When the problem becomes unsolvable and somatic complaints sometimes result, the client may seek help from the family doctor. Medication to relieve the crisis would be considered an acceptable form of treatment at this stage of coping with the crisis situation. Complaints at the emotional level might be confused, in the client's mind, with physical difficulties. Problems with anxiety, for example, might be thought to originate in the stomach, and the client might first attempt to seek medical relief for the stomach ailment. Depression or lack of energy might result in the client seeking medical help for a physical problem the client believes is the cause of the lethargy.

The family doctor plays a vital role in the treatment of clients in crisis. In many parts of Latin America and Mexico, the family doctor might prescribe antidepressive or antianxiety medications but tell the client that the medication is for the treatment of a physical ailment. This deception is not considered unethical, because it offers the client some relief and may decrease symptoms. Without counseling, however, the problem may cycle back and forth in severity. In this respect, the Latino client may experience an extremely long duration of the crisis.

Latinos have had a very troubled relationship with the power structures that have traditionally ruled Latin American countries. Often, these power structures have been autocratic and harsh and have subjected citizens to great harm. Consequently, the Latino client in crisis may have a dim view of any service provided by the state. In the client's mind, when the state is involved in the helping process, it may inevitably lead to legal problems, including loss of custodial rights to children, diversion projects that mandate unwanted treatment, and disruption of marriages and family life if abuse, alcohol, or drugs are involved. One might expect clients to resist state-sponsored services, because they are often equated with eventual harm.

CULTURALLY RELEVANT WORK WITH LATINO CLIENTS

Only with the recommendation of the family doctor is the client likely to seek specialized help from a crisis worker, and then it may be only when the client is in very severe crisis. Counseling and the idea of sharing confidential information with a therapist are not well-accepted ideas in Latino cultures. As Dr. Robert Snyder (1994), a United States–trained psychotherapist in Mexico, notes,

> Psychotherapy is poorly accepted and is often little understood in Mexico by any other than very affluent clients who are influenced by American trends. Any therapy used with Latino clients recently immigrated from Mexico or Central America must consider that the notion of going to a stranger to discuss highly personal issues is deeply at odds with prevailing ideas about the way Latinos resolve crisis. (Personal interview, July 1994)

As increasingly strict control of issues pertaining to child abuse, domestic violence, and substance abuse affects the Latino client, more and more newly immigrated Latinos find themselves involved in some form of treatment, often against their desire for help or their understanding of how the help will make a difference in their lives.

The following sections describe culturally relevant guidelines offered to help crisis workers assist the newly immigrated or culturally traditional Latino client.

Latino Clients Process Information Indirectly

The emotional problems related to a crisis are usually not discussed immediately by the client. Rather, there is a long period of talking around the problem. This is done partly as a way of gauging the worker's competence, but it also serves as a way of processing the problem in a manner that is familiar to the client. The crisis worker should be prepared for a longer and more indirect way of gathering vital information from the newly immigrated Latino client than is customary for the non-Hispanic white or more assimilated Latino client in crisis. The client also may be very suspicious of the worker's motives. Indirectness helps the client maintain control over the interview until the worker can be better evaluated for his or her competence and level of kindness.

Latino Clients Are Often Fatalistic

Many Latino clients are fatalistic and fearful about change. They have often been socialized to believe in the inevitability of luck, chance, and fate. There is a *dicho*, or wise saying, that sums up this belief: *Lo que dios mande*, or, "Whatever God wills." This fatalism is partly a result of the historical events that have shaped Latino culture. Hundreds of years of racial and ethnic animosities and subjugation by the conquistadors, as well as the revolutionary fervor of the twentieth century that pitted class and political orientation against one another, have resulted in a sometimes pessimistic and fatalistic orientation to life. Change, the client often believes, may take place, but it is usually related to fate rather than to anything the worker does in treatment or attempts at personal change made by the client. The worker needs to recognize that this sense of fatalism is not a dysfunction of the client but rests in prior socialization and life experience. To work with fatalism, the crisis worker needs to be positive, emphasizing the client's prior ability to change and the fact that one's luck may always improve.

Another way to help the client whose locus of control is very external is to ask the client questions such as, "How do you see yourself in 10 years?" Another is to use *dichos* in combination with story telling, or *cuento*. In this approach, the client takes a *dicho* and then tells a story around it to explain a belief system. From the story told, one can introduce ways to change a situation and explain how these changes might benefit the client's life.

The Importance of Strength in a Crisis

There is a considerable imperative on being strong, even in the midst of a crisis. The act of discussing feelings or complaining about inequities in life may make the client feel weak. This feeling of weakness in the midst of a crisis is complicated by its incompatibility with role expectations. Women, in particular, are expected to be strong, or the family may not function well without their guidance and direction. This emphasis on strength has its emotional impact on immigrant Latino women. Salgado (1990) found that immigrant Mexican women have a much higher level of generalized distress and psychological stress than do immigrant men. Salgado believes that immigrant Latino women are more likely to develop more long-term psychological problems, particularly depression and anxiety, than are non-Latino clients in crisis.

Speaking on the gender role differences among Hispanic men and women, Mae Brooks (1994), a Mexican journalist, noted:

> Hispanic women have been portrayed as being weak and ineffectual. It is not true. Hispanic women are the glue that binds the family together. They often work and care for large families. They manage the finances and set standards for the children. They keep going even while they are sick or emotionally drained. There is tremendous emphasis in Hispanic families for the mother to be above the commonplace crises of the day. She cannot get sick or emotionally down or the family may fall apart. Men may be given respect and admiration, but love is almost always the domain of the Hispanic woman. In a crisis, it is usually the woman who is the change agent for the family. But who takes care of her when she has a crisis? Why, she does. (Personal interview, July 1994)

Focusing on Positive Behavior

Latino clients, as with most of us, like to be admired for their accomplishments. One useful technique is to give praise for accomplishments, particularly those related to the extended family. Although clients, particularly female clients, may appear shy in the midst of such praise, it serves the purpose of building trust and gives the client confidence in their worker, as well as confidence in themselves.

Latino clients view the family as extensions of themselves. If children do well or do poorly, it reflects on them. One way to permit clients to discuss inner feelings is to pose the following question: "I know that you've experienced much heartache, and that you don't feel that your family appreciates you. How would you like your family to treat you differently?" This discussion might touch on core reasons for the crisis. Another useful question is to ask how clients taught their children to handle the issue of respect for a parent, because this issue is key to how parents view their children and, ultimately, how successful they have been with their children.

Many Latino clients, particularly male clients, have a strongly internalized belief that respect is the core of achievement in one's life. With respect, they are people of accomplishment and acceptance. Without respect, they are people of little consequence. When economic factors create underemployment or poverty, absence of respect from family is a sign of failure, and Latino clients may be more crises prone as a result. One widely misunderstood term to describe the need for respect is *machismo*. In describing the commonly defined way machismo is regarded, Baca Zinn (1980) wrote,

> The social science literature views machismo as a compensation for feelings of inadequacy and worthlessness. This interpretation is rooted in the application of psycho-

analytic concepts to explain both Mexican and Chicano gender roles. The widely accepted interpretation is that machismo is the male attempt to compensate for feelings of internalized inferiority by exaggerating masculinity. At the same time that machismo is an exaggeration of power, its origin is ironically linked to powerlessness and subordination. (p. 20)

Baca Zinn also notes that this traditional view of male roles in the Latino culture includes such exaggerated masculine behaviors as dominance, aggressiveness, an emphasis on physical prowess, and other highly stereotypic masculine behaviors that may be characteristic of many lower socioeconomic men. This view of machismo sometimes leads American workers to believe that Latino men are too proud to accept help in a crisis situation, but as Goff (1994), an American anthropologist who lives in Mexico, noted,

> Mexican men are often described as being very macho which, in the minds of some, translates into being stubborn and unwilling to accept help or advice from others. But we should understand that machismo is a way of providing men who have very little social esteem with self-importance and self-worth. There are bragging rights implied here. The best way to approach a Mexican male when help is needed in the family is to focus on his accomplishments, to praise him for his efforts to provide for the family, and to respect him for his hard work in difficult times. You will then get someone who is willing to work hard in treatment in the service of his family. (Personal interview, July 1994)

Respect for Educational Achievements

There is general respect in Latino culture for highly educated men and women. Wisdom and intellectual achievements are highly regarded and are generally considered to be attributes worthy of respect. Consequently, crisis work offered by men and women who fit these definitions of achievement and wisdom are likely to influence Latino clients. Placing professional certificates, licenses, and university degrees in public areas of an office and having resumes available that point to the achievements of the worker are important ways of influencing the clients because they help clients view the workers as persons of wisdom and respect. It should be noted, however, that some writers, such as Monsivais (1996), a Mexican journalist, caution that among many poverty-stricken Mexicans, there is an intrinsic hostility toward professionals and toward their degrees and licenses. Newly immigrated Latino clients in crisis may be less than enthusiastic about the notion of professionalism and achievement. Monsivais explains:

> Whether it is a by-product of a traditional Catholicism that fears reading because, "it poisons the soul," or whether it is rooted in the particular belief that *licenciados* (a professional with a degree) exist only to exploit the people, it is quite common for Mexican families to harbor anti-intellectual attitudes which in turn shape their responses toward education. (p. M2)

The Use of Therapeutic Metaphors or *Dichos*

In Latino culture, wise sayings, or *dichos*, assume considerable importance in guiding clients toward solutions to problems. An example of the use of a *dicho* concerns a client the co-authors heard about at a state hospital in California with a Spanish-speaking program for Latino clients.

A very depressed former butcher was to be released from a state psychiatric hospital to visit his family. Before he left, the therapist reminded him of a *dicho* that said that unless you keep your skills sharpened, they lose their usefulness. It was important for him, the therapist said, to return to his family or he might lose his ability to communicate with those whom he most loved. The butcher went back to his home and in his garage, found his old butcher knives, which were dull and rusted from lack of use. Remembering what the therapist had said, he took the advice literally, sharpened his knives, and immediately experienced the desire to return to work. Shortly thereafter, he was released from the hospital and is now working at his old trade.

The crisis worker seeing large numbers of Latino clients should have at his or her readiness common sayings that are well known in the culture. Zuniga (1992) notes that *dichos* are actually metaphors that have been traditionally used in treatment and comprise the following:

> 1) major stories that address complex clinical problems; 2) anecdotes or short stories focused on specific or limited goals; 3) analogies, similes or brief figurative statements or phrases that underscore specific points; 4) relationship metaphors, which can use one relationship as a metaphor for another; 5) tasks with metaphorical meanings that can be undertaken by clients between sessions; 6) artistic metaphors which can be paintings, drawings, clay models, or creations which symbolize something else. (p. 57)

The co-authors of this chapter have identified several *dichos* that may be commonly used in crisis intervention. *Sentir en el alma*, for example, translates literally to "Feel it in your soul," but the real translation means "to be terribly sorry." *Con la cuhara se le queman los frijoles* translates literally as "Even the best cook burns the beans," but, in reality, it means that everyone makes mistakes. *Entre azul y buenos noches* translates directly as "between blue and good night," but its popular meaning is "to be undecided." *A la buena de Dios* may translate literally as "as God would have it," but its common meaning is "as luck would have it." *No hay mal que por bien no venga*, for example, translates as "There is nothing bad from which good does not come," or "It is a blessing in disguise." Another *dicho* useful in crisis intervention is *La verdad no mata, pero incomoda*, which means, "The truth doesn't kill, but it can hurt." And yet another *dicho* with relevance for crisis work is *Al que no ha usado huaraches, las correas le sacan sangre*, which loosely translated means "he who has never worn sandals is easily cut by the straps," or "It's difficult to do things that one is not used to." And finally, as Zuniga notes for the client in a deteriorating relationship that might end in termination, the *dicho Mejor sola que mal acompanada* might help. Roughly translated, this *dicho* means that it's better to be alone or unmarried than to be in a bad relationship.

The Importance of Feelings

Feelings are highly valued in Latino culture. One approach to making feelings part of the therapeutic relationship is to tell the client that you will communicate with them, *de corazon a corazon*, or heart to heart. In Mexico, this concept of a close personal relationship in which true feelings can be communicated has various levels of meaning. It is sometimes associated with the process called *el desague de las penas*, or unburdening oneself. It is what North American therapists might call "venting." It also may be a part of the process of opening one's soul to a *compadre* or a close personal friend so that the friend can see inside a person's heart, and, therefore, feel his or her sorrow and despair. Allowing Latino clients to unburden themselves may significantly improve the quality of crisis work with the reluctant client in crisis.

The Importance of Dreams

Considerable credence is given to the significance of dreams in Latino culture. Dreams are considered omens or predictors of the future. Dreams provide answers to problems. Crisis workers should listen carefully to the dreams Latino clients discuss in treatment. They should not, however, ascribe specific meaning or interpretations to the dreams but should, instead, ask clients for their own interpretations. It may also be permissible to ask clients to suggest ways to complete specific dreams that may terminate before a clear message is given. This technique requires clients to finish their dreams as if they had control over the endings. In this way, the dreams become the clients' property, and they are no longer chance occurrences that may imply bad luck over which the clients have no control. In a sense, this is an empowerment technique that helps redirect the clients' sense of personal control.

Achievement May Alienate Family

As with other groups and cultures, some families in the Latino culture discourage any achievement by a child that may surpasses that of the parents. Children who share achievement wishes with parents or with extended family may be subjected to discouragement. Similarly, children who do well in school may be discouraged from doing so, particularly if parents did badly in school or need children to enter the workplace before school is completed. This dynamic of not overachieving is also a way to keep children close to the family. If children go on to complete their education, it is sometimes felt that they may stray from family or consider themselves superior to family members. Achievement in the face of family opposition may lead to estrangement of the children from their families, but in Mexico and in Latin America, it may also lead to rejection of children by their families, a rejection that may be irreversible.

In understanding this dynamic of family life, it is important to remember that one of the processes used in the subjugation of the Latin American people by the conquistadors and, later, the landed rich, who still control much of Mexico and Central and South America, is not to go beyond your current station in life if you are poor and without resources, but to accept the inevitability of your life. Monsivais (1996) describes this dynamic as follows:

> Many studies have shown that poor Mexican families see little intrinsic value in acquiring education. Furthermore, a recent Rand study on how immigrants fare in the U.S. education system shows the low academic aspirations of Mexican immigrant children as compared to other immigrant groups. Even more disturbing, the study found that the academic aspirations of subsequent generations of the children of Mexican immigrants, weakened. (p. M2)

Adding to Monsivais's concerns, Latino USA (2002) provides the following data on the problems facing Latino students:

> The dropout rate for Latinos in this country is above 30 percent. That is twice the rate for African Americans and almost four times the rate for Anglo students. Behind the numbers are many stories; poverty interfering with learning, overwhelmed teachers coping with large classes, and schools that promote children to the next grade despite gaps in their knowledge.

GENERAL PRINCIPLES OF LATINO CRISIS INTERVENTION

Ewing's work on crisis intervention as a form of brief psychotherapy provides some general principles for crisis work with Latino clients (1978, 1990). Ewing (1990) summarized the general principles of crisis intervention as (1) readily available and brief or time-limited; (2) dealing not only with the individual in crisis, but also with his or her significant family and social network; (3) addressing a broad rather than narrowly defined range of critical human problems; (4) focusing on present-time or current problems; (5) not only dealing with the current problem and on symptom relief, but also assisting the client in developing new coping skills; (6) reality-oriented and reality-focused; (7) requiring the crisis worker to assume nontraditional therapist role responsibilities (e.g., directive, active, advocating, pragmatic, etc.); and (8) serving a preparatory function for possible future mental health treatment (pp. 281–284).

Although Ewing's model offers direction for work with the Latino client in crisis, it is important to remember that Latino clients may need a longer period of time to discuss their problems and to develop a relationship with workers than may be common in typical short-term crisis work with non-Latino clients. Latino clients also may have more limitations on what they can actually do to change their crises without some adverse affect on others. And, finally, feelings and inner forces may be more complex and require more discussion than Ewing's model suggests. Consequently, it might be better to think of crisis intervention with Latino clients as a form of therapy that focuses more on feelings and emotions than on cognition and the process of change.

Adding to Ewing's work, Congress (1990) noted that the following elements are necessary ingredients of crisis intervention with Latino clients:

1. *Confianza:* Developing trust of the worker by the client
2. *Personalismo:* The positive way the client responds to treatment when the worker personalizes and focuses on what the client wishes to discuss at the moment
3. *Respecto:* The belief that respect is crucial in all interactions and that it forms a significant aspect of all crisis work with the Latino client. Without respect by the worker, the client will probably leave treatment.

THE LANDSCAPE OF LATINO CRISIS

It is important to remember that many crisis situations experienced by newly immigrated Latinos are created by feelings of not being welcome in this country, even when they have a legal right to be here. This immediate sense of alienation and the unfamiliar rules and regulations common to American life often place clients in situations that lead to crisis. Unfamiliar child care laws, expectations that drivers should not drink, and arguments within families that sometimes become loud and spill onto the streets may bring clients into immediate contact with the judicial system. Prevention of these unnecessary situations can be made by a process of socialization to the country, a necessary but often neglected function of the social and educational institutions of the United States. Emphasizing this sense of alienation, Gonzalez (2000) noted that Latinos are the largest minority group in America and that

> mental health problems of Hispanics living in poverty and undocumented Hispanic immigrants are often exacerbated by socioeconomic stressors, racism, and political oppression. Effective mental health treatment for this segment of the Hispanic population must encompass case advocacy, community outreach, and the mediating of complex social systems. Mental health clinicians who treat poor and/or undocumented Hispanics should be skilled in the implementation of multiple interventive roles such as that of advocate, mediator, broker, and teacher.

Commenting on the xenophobia that often exists among North Americans toward Hispanics, Brooks notes that:

> Mexican immigrants come to the United States to work and to help their families. What meets them is hesitant acceptance of their need to be in the country and cultural stereotypes that they are lazy, even when they work hard at cruel and dangerous jobs. If the United States wants the best of its neighbor's labor and the commitment to good citizenship, it should recognize the Latino as a worthy and proud person capable of grace and beauty. (Personal interview, July 1994)

Adding to this sense of alienation from mainstream American culture, the Surgeon General's Report on Mental Health (Satcher, 2001) notes that while Latinos and other members of racial and ethnic minority groups are an increasing part of America's population, many racial and ethnic minority group members find the mental health system to be

> uninformed about cultural context and, thus, unresponsive and/or irrelevant. It is partly for this reason that minority group members overall are less inclined than whites to seek treatment (Sussman et al., 1987; Gallo et al., 1995), and to use outpatient treatment services to a much lesser extent than do non-Hispanic whites. In the interim, culturally competent services—that is, services that incorporate understanding of racial and ethnic groups, their histories, traditions, beliefs, and value systems—are needed to enhance the appropriate use of services and effectiveness of treatments for ethnic and racial minority consumers. (Chapter 8)

A CRITICAL RESPONSE

One of the troubling concepts discussed in this chapter is that of machismo. While the chapter tries to correct the stereotypic view of machismo, more needs to be said on the subject since it is often felt that crises develop in Chicano families because of problems related to the behavior of Chicano men. In correcting the traditional notions of machismo associated with Chicano men, Baca Zinn (2001) writes, "viewing machismo as a compensation for inferiority in effect blames Chicanos for their own subordination" (p. 24). Luzod and Arce (1979) write, "It therefore seems erroneous to focus on maternal influences in Chicano families since Chicano fathers provide important positive influences on the development of their children" (p. 19). Mirande (1979) writes, "There is sufficient evidence to seriously question the traditional male dominant view [in Chicano homes]" (p. 47). In responding to traditional notions of machismo in Chicano men that include dominance and aggressiveness, Chafetz (1974) writes that these characteristics are not only found in Chicano men but, "a strong emphasis on masculine aggressiveness and dominance may be characteristic of most groups in the lower ranges of the socioeconomic ladder" (p. 54).

While many Latino groups have thrived in the United States, Mexican Americans have had a more difficult time. Yzaguirre (1987), for example, notes lower per capita income, low graduation rates, and higher crime rates than among the population as a whole and when compared to other Latino groups in America (p. 494). This suggests that in the transition to American life, Mexican immigrants may require additional supports and services. Cultural biases that influence the provision of services only impede that transition.

This chapter helps the reader understand the cultural issues that may affect Latino clients as they enter a crisis and then utilize the unfamiliar help of professionals. It is important to recognize that just as cultural stereotypes affect many people in the United States, professionals often share those same stereotypes. Notions of machismo and beliefs in the passivity or inferiority of certain populations result in what Delgado (1974) calls labeling for the purpose of social control (p. 6). Riddel (1974) suggests that the machismo myth and similar myths about Latinos are exploited by an oppressive society to keep Latinos in an inferior position, socially and economically. Staples (1978) suggests that minority men often live in the culture of poverty and that their behavior is a consequence of factors associated with racial and social prejudice. These concerns should be part of the professional response to problems encountered by Latino clients as they do what all immigrant groups have done in the United States: Work extremely hard to provide better lives for their families and to co-exist with others in harmony and peace.

SUMMARY

This chapter suggests the need to understand the collective nature of Latino life and to respond to Latino clients in crisis with social and cultural sensitivity. It also suggests that many Latino clients are placed in crisis situations, not so much because of pre-existing pathologies, but because they have difficulty navigating the legal and cultural waters of American life. New immigrants face discrimination from North Americans who value their labor but who often do not value Latinos. This may create situations that increase the possibility of crisis. The chapter notes a number of ideas for culturally relevant treatment and utilizes a strengths agenda in providing treatment interventions for the newly immigrated or culturally traditional Latino client in crisis.

INTEGRATIVE QUESTIONS

1. Although the word *Latino* is used to describe the population helped in this chapter, the material is really mainly about Mexican Americans. Is it fair to use the more encompassing term *Latino* when the material is really mostly about Mexican Americans?

2. Isn't it always problematic to portray people as being similar? One would think that among Latino immigrants in crisis that there is considerable cultural, educational and religious diversity. What do you think?

3. Distrust of state-offered services suggests that Latino clients in crisis may not use public services. What are some of the reasons Latino clients might be reluctant to use public services?

4. The use of *dichos* (wise sayings) seems more spiritual and philosophical than therapeutic. Why do you think *dichos* would or would not be effective with Latino clients?

5. This chapter assumes that Latino clients are less sophisticated in therapy than are other immigrant groups. Doesn't the availability of television offer all immigrants a look at modern therapy through soap operas and popular American programs available to almost anyone with a television set?

REFERENCES

Baca Zinn, M. (1980). Gender and ethnic identity among Chicanos. *Frontiers*, 2, 18–24.

Baca Zinn, M. (2001). Chicano men and masculinity. In M.S. Kimmel and M.A. Messner, *Men's lives* (pp. 24–32). Boston, MA: Allyn & Bacon.

Brooks, M. (July 1994). Individual interview. Cemanahuac Educational Community, Cuernavaca, Morelos, Mexico.

Chafetz, J.S. (1974). *Masculine/feminine or human.* Itasca, IL: Peacock Publishers.

Congress, E. (1990). Crisis intervention with Hispanic clients in an urban mental health clinic. In A. Roberts (Ed.), *Crisis intervention handbook* (pp. 221–236). Belmont, CA: Wadsworth.

Delgado, A. (December 1974). Machismo. *La Luz,* p. 6.

Ewing, C.P. (1978). *Crisis intervention as psychotherapy.* New York: Oxford University Press.

Ewing, C.P. (1990). *Crisis intervention as brief psychotherapy.* In R.A. Wells and V.J. Giannetti (Eds.), *Handbook of brief psychotherapies* (pp. 277–294). New York: Plenum Press.

Gallo, J.J., Marino, S., Ford, D., and Anthony, J.C. (1995). Filters on the pathway to mental health care, II. Sociodemographic factors. *Psychological Medicine,* 25, 1149–1160.

Goff, C. (July 1994). Individual interview. Cemanahuac Educational Community, Cuernavaca, Morelos, Mexico.

Gonzalez, M.J. (October 2000). Provision of mental health services to Hispanic clients. Available online at www.naswnyc.org/d16.html.

Hernandez, R. (September 9, 1990). Please stand up if you are a real Hispanic. *Los Angeles Times,* 5–7.

Latino USA. (May 31, 2002). Julio can't read. Available online at www.latinousa.org/program/lusapgm477.html.

Luzod, J.A., and Arce, C.H. (May 1979). An exploration of the father role in the chicano family. Paper presented at the National Symposium on the Mexican American Child, Santa Barbara, CA.

Mirande, A. (1979). A reinterpretation of male dominance in the chicano family. *Family Coordinator,* 28, 473–497.

Monsivais, C. (August 25, 1996). The immigrant's view of education. *Los Angeles Times,* M2.

Riddel, A.S. (1974). Chicanos and *el moveimiento. Aztlan,* 5, 155–165.

Roger, L., and Malgady, R. (1987). What do culturally sensitive mental services mean? The case of Hispanics. *American Psychologist,* 42, 565–570.

Salgado de Snyder, V.N. (1990). Gender and ethnic differences in psychological stress and generalized distress among Hispanics. *Sex Roles,* 22(7/8).

Satcher, D. (2001). Surgeon General's report on mental health. Available online at http://www.surgeongeneral.gov/library/mentalhealth/chapter8/sec1.html#tailor.

Snyder, R. (July 1994). Individual interview. Cemanahuac Educational Community, Cuernavaca, Morelos, Mexico.

Staples, R. (1978). Masculinity and race: The dual dilemmas of race. *Journal of Social Issues,* 34, 169–183.

Sussman, L.K., Robins, L.N., and Earls, F. (1987). Treatment-seeking for depression by black and white Americans. *Social Science Medicine,* 24, 187–196.

Yzaguirre, R. (November 1987). Public policy, crime, and the Hispanic community. *Annals of the American Academy of Political and Social Science,* 101–104.

Zuniga, M.E. (January 1992). Using metaphors in therapy: *Dichos* and Latino clients. *Social Work,* 55–60.

CHAPTER NINE

THE ETHNICALLY ASIAN CLIENT IN CRISIS AND THE STRENGTHS PERSPECTIVE

A Collectivist Approach[1]

WITH STEVEN M. INO

In this era of acknowledged pluralism, our understanding of Asian clients may be so inaccurate that its relevance for the helping professions may be limited to ethnic stereotypes. Mental health services for Asians based on inaccurate notions of the Asian client may, in reality, result in harm to the client and the client's family. What is clearly needed is an *alternate* conceptual framework from which to interpret and to respond to the Asian life experience. The authors believe that such a model exists and have chosen to call it a "collectivist approach" to intervention. As the reader will note, elements of this approach may also be of value to the worker treating non-Asian clients from what we propose is essentially a strengths approach that demonstrates the significance of culture and ethnicity.

UNDERSTANDING THE ELEMENTS OF COLLECTIVISM

The ethnically Asian client actualizes a fundamental *collective sense* of psychosocial being, which Yu (1989) refers to as a "collective ego identity" in explaining the Asian client's group-oriented achievement motivation. She states, "Thus, the concepts independence and individualism, so strongly emphasized and highly valued in the American culture, are alien to Chinese students socialized in the traditional manner to stress *inter*dependence and affiliation" (p. 184).

[1]Portions of this chapter also appear in Ino and Glicken (2002, 1999).

Hsu (1983) describes the core American national character as "rugged" individualism, which he defines as the intrinsic and unquestionable values of self-containment, autonomy, self-reliance, and self-determinism, which imply that the person takes personal responsibility before taking responsibility for others. The Asian worldview values social collectivism—a social order that is essentially family based and interpersonally or collectively oriented. This worldview is principally explained by versions of Confucianism, Buddhism, and Taoism that have been incorporated into the various Asian cultures.

Confucian philosophy and ethics are concerned with the virtue of the individual as exemplified by his or her participation in appropriate social relationships that lead to social harmony at all levels of society. The Chinese concept of *jen*, or human-heartedness, expressed through social conduct that is strictly prescribed, characterizes the five essential relationships between (1) sovereign and subject (superior and subordinate); (2) parent and child; (3) older and younger brothers; (4) husband and wife; and (5) friends. *Li*, or social propriety, is to be shown in all interpersonal relationships that facilitate and sustain social harmony (Herbert, 1950). Filial piety is central to Confucian thought and practice.

In Asian thought, pragmatism is valued over idealism, and the focus of life activity is in the present time. Furthermore, unlike Western notions of being the master of one's own fate, Asian belief is that one is not in ultimate control. The person is always an integral part of the larger encompassing universe, which has authority over the individual.

Taoism differs from Confucian pragmatism by its concern with the metaphysical and mystical—the cosmic process of *Tao*, or the Way. The person, an integral part of the cosmos, follows the principle of *Wu-Wei*, or nonaction, which means that he or she should always act in accordance with nature, not against it. The notion that "Nature heals, and man (medicine) assists," suggests the belief that nature, not the person, has ultimate authority over the course of one's existence (Chang, 1982). Taoism therefore believes that the person is not in complete control of nature, nor of his or her destiny.

Buddhism concerns itself with the four noble truths: (1) Life is suffering; (2) suffering originates from undue desires; (3) desire originates from ignorance and illusion; and (4) the road to salvation is in enlightenment. Enlightenment is achieved by eight noble paths, including accurate knowledge and correct actions, which lead to the effective or "right" development of the mind. Concentration and meditation are mental processes that help lead to the development of the "right" mind. Buddhism stresses seeking enlightenment through the avoidance of desires of ignorance and teaches the idea of eternal life through rebirth. Proper deportment and social conduct, ancestor worship, emotional restraint, loyalty, and respect for others in the present life have implications for the quality of one's next life (Chang, 1982; Gaw, 1993).

Dynamic social harmony is the major social rule governing all meaningful interpersonal relationships (Ho, 1987). It requires varying degrees of social cooperation, adaptation, accommodation, and collaboration by all individuals in the social hierarchy. In the Asian social hierarchy, social roles are based more on family membership and position, gender, age, social class, and social position than on qualification and ability. However, there is a basic belief that age, training, and life experience are associated with wisdom and competency, although deference and respect from an individual in a subordinate role requires that the person in a superior social position look after that individual.

The formal idea of family in Asian society extends family identity and membership backward in time through all of the ancestors in the male family line, continuing on in the present time, and then on to those future descendants who have yet to appear (Lee, 1996). One's sense of family is not time-bound, nor is it limited only to those important kin who are living. Although the father is the head of the nuclear family household and is responsible for the family's economic and physical well-being, he still shows deference and loyalty to his father and older brothers as well as to his mother and older sisters. Elders in the father's extended family are also respected. The mother becomes included in the extended family of her husband. As a mother, she is the "emotional hub" of her nuclear family of creation, responsible for nurturing her husband and their children. While wielding tremendous emotional power and often acting as the relational and communication link between father and children, she, nevertheless, has little public power and authority and defers to her husband, his mother, and the elders in the husband's extended family.

Self-restraint and stoicism, inhibiting disruptive emotional expression; conscientious work to fulfill one's responsibilities; heightened social sensitivity and other-directedness all contribute to maintaining social harmony. However, a person's breach of social obligation or duty can potentially damage the social harmony of the family, group, or larger community. Significant others will condemn their loss of confidence in that individual's ability to fulfill obligations to the family or group through the mechanism of shaming that person.

From an Asian perspective, the prescribed forms of interpersonal interaction are intended to preserve dynamic social harmony by minimizing direct conflict and social discordance. Communication, as an aspect of social interaction, is highly contextual and tends to flow downward from superior to subordinate, often in the form of directives. Both verbal and written communications are indirect, in the passive tense, and at times may appear convoluted. Furthermore, much of the communication is nonverbal, whereby the conduct of the superior, not the content of the message, is most meaningful. These principles of Asian communication styles serve to maintain vital social harmony in any interpersonal interaction.

The Asian socialization process develops highly differentiated adult individuals with mature levels of deep emotional interdependency and strong feelings of role responsibility and obligation. But within the context of Asian social reality, physical distress may appropriately exemplify psychosocial distress (Root, 1993). For instance, a gastrointestinal disorder can be viewed as a normal expression of psychological stress over an intense interpersonal conflict and is not necessarily seen as a "symptom" or indicator of the client's inability to cope with psychosocial conflict. To alleviate the physical symptom may be an appropriate treatment for a relational conflict over which one has no control.

WHEN ASIAN CLIENTS FAIL TO COPE

Asians, as a group, tend to seek help from mental health professionals only when all other more familiar and usual coping strategies, interpersonal resources, and safer avenues of help have been exhausted. Despite the underutilization of existing services, many Asian mental health professionals believe that there is a significant unmet need for appropriate mental health care (e.g., Sue & Morishima, 1982; Furuto et al., 1992; Gaw, 1993; Uba, 1994). In a study of nonpatient Southeast Asian Americans, Gong-Guy (1987) estimated that 14.4 percent of the sample needed inpatient mental health services and 53.75 percent could benefit from outpatient care, in comparison to corresponding 3 percent and 12 percent rates, respectively, in the general population.

Several reasons help to explain the discrepancy between perceived need and overall service usage: the Asian conception of mental health and mental illness and their management, the strong Asian stigma and shame attached to seeking out-of-the-family assistance for mental illness, the inappropriateness of Euro American mental health care approaches for Asians, shortages of culturally sensitive mental health professionals, and socioeconomic barriers (Sue & Morishima, 1982; Uba, 1994).

Asians seek mental health services only after they are in serious emotional crisis. They will have first exhausted their usual and then their atypical coping strategies and will have sufficiently "overridden" their deeply felt sense of shame and humiliation at breaching family privacy and "loss of face" by seeking help from outside the family. The Asian client who is experiencing the emotional "disequilibrium" of a crisis situation is most responsive to outside assistance (Golan, 1978; Roberts, 1990). However, the same client is also very vulnerable to outside influences, leaving the client concerned about the possibility of worrisome miscommunication and misinterpretation of the need for mental health services by the client's family, friends, and the Asian community.

When an Asian client seeks mental health services, the client is already emotionally disengaged or estranged from family and significant others because the usual collective Asian social support system has failed to remedy the problem or the conflict. Because of strong feelings of shame or a collective need to protect the family and/or significant others, the client may typically be withdrawn and isolated. On the other hand, if the family seeks help for one of its members, then the family has exhausted its own strategies for discreetly helping the family member and must now, regrettably, seek outside assistance and risk considerable shame. The emotional danger for the client is that the family may be prepared to "save face" by disowning or abandoning the client, removing the client's vital "self" support and, thereby, precipitating a second-order crisis.

The high level of stigma associated with intractable emotional problems and mental disturbance has its origin in the strong Asian belief-set that an individual can endure hardship and overcome personal problems through individual perseverance, hard work, stoicism, and the avoidance of morbid and disturbing thoughts and feelings. If the client is unable to benefit from these belief-sets, then he or she is felt to have a weak character, be biologically defective, or is the unfortunate victim of bad luck, a curse, vengeful spirits, or fate.

In discussing the concerns of Southeast Asian refugees, Gong-Guy, Cravens, and Patterson (1991) add that mental illness might also be interpreted as the consequence of past family transgressions. Contributing to its stigma is also a great fear of deportation, loss of government support, and the spread of damaging "gossip" throughout the ethnic Asian community. A family member's serious mental illness can make all eligible family members unmarriageable in the eyes of the community.

The Asian client experiencing unmanageable emotional pain may assume, from a mainstream Euro American cultural viewpoint, a very passive-dependent interpersonal stance as he or she seeks a wise and benevolent worker to act as an authority figure who can advise and assist the client in alleviating the pain. If the client has confidence in the worker's wisdom and respects the worker's authority, timely intervention can provide vital emotional support and guidance, which may lead to more effective and adaptive coping patterns that encourage the client to make corrective life changes.

From the start of treatment, the Asian client should have considerable say in selecting the worker. Maximizing the therapist–client "fit" can strengthen client motivation and facilitate the relationship. However, it is the responsibility of the worker to sensitively inquire about this, because the client may not wish to insult or embarrass anyone by making such a request. There may also be a natural preference for the client to work with an Asian worker who has a similar ethnic and sociocultural life and historical background. Leong (1986) notes the tendency for Asian clients to "describe their therapists as more credible and competent if they are Asian" (p. 198).

Generally, working with an older, professionally trained and credentialed male or female worker can engender an implicit and immediate trust in the clinician. In some cases, however, the client may be very threatened by an Asian therapist sharing a similar background. There is great fear of "gossip," in which the client's family or community finds out about the client's need for treatment. In this case, the client may feel more comfortable with a biculturally aware Asian worker who is "removed" from the client's family and community by virtue of coming from a different ethnic background. On the other hand, both first-generation and highly acculturated Asians may wish to work with mainstream Caucasian workers, believing that they are best-trained and most competent to help. Whatever the background of the workers, they must be prepared to be sociocultural translators or "culture brokers" negotiating between and among multiple social worlds, both in the therapeutic relationship and within the Asian American clients' lives, as the workers help clients understand the nature of their debilitating emotional problems.

A client's feelings about the effectiveness of the initial encounter with a worker will determine the success of that first session and whether there will be further meetings. A substantial amount of material must be covered in the first session as the worker attempts to establish rapport, clarify the problem focus, evaluate the client, and develop a treatment plan. This treatment effort must balance the Asian client's natural reluctance to self-disclose intimate life details to the therapist-as-stranger. Because time and interpersonal activity have a different culturally dictated meaning and pace to the Asian client, the worker must be more flexible in allowing sufficient time—in terms of session length, frequency, and number of sessions—

to accomplish a successful intervention. First and foremost, the worker must be able to ensure that the Asian client feels respected and is able to maintain personal dignity.

If possible, the initial session should last as long as necessary for the client to feel a completion in the disclosure of relevant life issues and the basic establishment of a trusting therapeutic relationship. This may take 30 minutes or three hours. The client may be adamant that this is to be a one-session meeting, which means that the worker must be prepared to provide, in concise form, the entire sequence of interventions in that single session (Ewing, 1990). If it appears that the client is willing to return, it is the worker's responsibility to outline an understandable schedule of further sessions and to articulate clear and reasonable goals to be accomplished, asking, of course, for feedback and clarification from the client to determine whether the proposed plan is acceptable.

A fundamental task for the worker is the need to accurately assess the quality and degree of the client's collective identification. One simple "collective self" assessment question might be, "When you think about yourself, or when you are asked to identify yourself, do you seem to resonate more to your family name or to your first name?" In traditional Asian social situations, personal introductions are made by giving one's family name first and then one's given name. Asian social etiquette implicitly acknowledges and values one's family identity, or collective self, over one's individual identity (Ino, 1985; Ino, 1991).

Workers should not expect Asian clients to be able to readily explain the central problem that brought them into treatment. Fear of losing face, mistrust because of experiences with racism and discrimination, and/or suspiciousness of therapists and mental health services can make clients reluctant to self-disclose personal and family information. When asked, clients may initially focus on physical symptoms or somatic complaints. Consequently, physical complaints must be seen as valid problems to be treated in a competent and respectful way. Explaining the physical symptoms as having an emotional base may initially alienate clients and can create unmanageable conflict.

On the other hand, Asian clients may begin talking so globally about life histories or family situations that it appears only tangential to a clear depiction of the immediate problem. For example, when asked, "What brings you here today?" or "How can I be of help to you?" a client may respond by going into great detail about how he was born in Cambodia, how he and part of his family escaped Cambodia back in 1979, and how they gradually made their way to a refugee camp in Thailand and eventually on to the United States, England, Australia, or Canada. This need to situate the perceived problem in the larger context of the person's entire life history is the client's way of explaining to the worker why he or she has come for help and to provide the relevant information necessary to understand the client's perception of the origins of the problem.

Sometimes, a client may begin by seeking help for a "minor" or less pertinent problem as a way of testing "the therapeutic situation" and the trustworthiness of the worker. If the clinical experience is deemed helpful, the client may then proceed to disclose the true reason for coming.

TREATMENT ISSUES INVOLVING THE COLLECTIVE SELF

Asian American clients often exist in at least two, if not more, interacting, significant social worlds—the collective-based social world of their Asian-identified families, religions, and communities, and the individual-based social order of the larger American society. The American definition of mental health assumes that all mental health treatment approaches have the intent of restoring the vitality, effectiveness, and autonomy of the client's individualistic self. Seldom is culture, family, or tradition considered an important aspect of any treatment plan—nor, for that matter, are the collective attributes that encompass the life experiences of Asian American clients.

To negate the collective part of "self" in treatment may negate the effectiveness of the therapeutic work, for the Asian American self is strongly influenced by the way individual conduct will affect family. And here, family takes on a very broad level of importance, because family in many Asian countries provides the client with a sense of identity that may affect every aspect of life from birth to death. Family is a broad concept that includes an extended nuclear group. What an individual does in Asian societies has broad consequences, for it may affect the way the family may be viewed by the broader community.

Working with the individual self may have little resonance with many Asian American clients. All therapeutic work must therefore consider the impact of change on the extended family. Furthermore, in a family-based society, changes in the client, however small, may have impact on family life and may affect not just the client, but all members of the family in ways that are often unpredictable.

A constraint in therapy with the Asian client is that the client may stay emotionally ill, because to get better may have a negative impact on the family. Or, conversely, the client's improved mental health may positively affect all the family members. Unlike most American therapeutic work, however, the impact of any treatment strategy with the Asian American client must consider how family might be affected and whether the resulting change may adversely affect the client's affiliation with his or her family.

Asian Americans may face up to six common life circumstances that may develop into problems serious enough to warrant intervention: bicultural identity development, significant non-Asian relationships, significant loss, serious loss of face, expulsion from family, and dysfunctional families of origin. In the following sections, several common life circumstances are described, followed by a brief case study to explain the dynamic of the collective self and the way it may affect therapeutic work with the Asian American client.

Bicultural Identity Development

For second- and later-generation Asian Americans, the multicultural socialization process may result in a mix of *self*-identities that are, at times, conflictual and contradictory. For example, an immigrant Asian American may possess a basic sense of collective self and yet practice very acculturated and assimilated attitudes and behaviors and even claim conscious "allegiance" to mainstream American ways of life. At best, bicultural Asian American *self* development can result in resolvable internal psychic confusion and an affective commitment to some form of multicultural *self*. At worst, it may develop into critical intrapsychic disorganization and instability of self. The strength and durability of the client's individual self depends on how psychosocially sound the other significant family members are and on the internal consistency of family interrelationships. An example of a problem with bicultural identity development follows.

JENNIFER: A CASE STUDY

Jennifer is a 26-year-old Korean American, having emigrated with her family from Korea when she was seven years old. She is the oldest of three daughters. Her parents, who were college educated in Korea, run a profitable small retail business. Although Jennifer graduated with a BA in business and has a very successful corporate career, the next youngest daughter is in medical school, and the youngest will enter law school. Her parents had hoped that Jennifer would become a doctor, but she apologetically explained that she did not have the talent for medicine. Her parents also were pressuring her to get married to a successful first-generation Korean American doctor whom Jennifer described as very respectful and generous to her family. Her family had openly voiced their concern that she was getting too old to wait much longer to get married. Jennifer has usually gone along with her parents' wishes, even if she didn't completely agree with them, but she has recently begun to experience very strong resentment and anger and is surprised that she is able to voice these feelings to her parents. Her parents have reacted with greater anger and have accused her of not being a good daughter. Jennifer feels very ashamed.

Jennifer was prompted to come for treatment, after a long delay in which Chinese medicine failed to relieve her symptoms, because of depression and considerable generalized fatigue and anxiety. Despite the focus on her physical problems, Jennifer was able to acknowledge a deeply felt experience of "disconnectedness" from her family and a painful loneliness. Jennifer finds herself uncomfortably rebelling against her parents and has lost her sense of belonging to the family. At 26, she is alarmed to discover that she does not know what she actually wants in life. The troubling tensions in the family interrelationships have strained the dynamic intrapsychic harmony in Jennifer's sense of collective self. This has caused her to further withdraw emotionally from her family in an attempt to help preserve the family's harmony and integrity, but it has also resulted in Jennifer experiencing greater feelings of anomie.

In the course of treatment, Jennifer was able to institute a program of stress management that helped her deal with the effects of family conflict and her shifting self-dynamics. She also developed competence in discussing her goals and aspirations in a way that doesn't alienate or offend her family. Although she has yet to decide about marrying her Korean American suitor, she has begun to develop a new conscious appreciation of the significance of her family to her sense of collective well-being. She also has become more aware of the contradictory expectations her family has placed on her, and has begun to develop the ability to respond to those expectations in ways that promote closer family harmony. Jennifer ended treatment feeling better able to cope with the ongoing family tensions and has begun to use her friends to discuss her feelings about family. As a result, some family harmony has been restored, with a reduction in Jennifer's symptoms.

Although this outcome may be at odds with traditional notions of treatment in which the family would be challenged and even discounted in an attempt to help Jennifer gain autonomy and self-direction, the issue of Jennifer's connection to family and its importance to her in maintaining her sense of identity makes more traditional approaches less likely to help Jennifer mediate between her need for autonomy and her sense of connection to family. The outcome of treatment provides Jennifer with a continued affiliation with her family and the ability to present her goals and desires within a framework that is acceptable to her family.

Significant Euro American–Asian American Relationships

Asian Americans having an essential collective self naturally seek collective as opposed to individualistic relationship involvement with those who become a part of their significant social world. However, individuals may not always be conscious of these needs and may be unaware of who can best fulfill them. Consequently, they may become socially involved with others in an apparently assimilated and acculturated fashion. Serious interpersonal conflicts can arise when a couple having very different *self*-dynamics and accompanying interpersonal needs unwittingly attempt to realize a shared, deep, fulfilling, and intimate bond.

JAMES AND LISA: A CASE STUDY

James is a 41-year-old Sansei (third-generation Japanese American) who has been married for about two years to Lisa, a 35-year-old Euro American. Lisa is very unhappy with the marriage and frustrated that they have not been able to communicate effectively with each other about her unhappiness. Whenever she tries to initiate a conversation about the marriage, James avoids discussing their problems, saying only that their marriage is good and that they just have to work harder at it. He has consistently rejected her earlier requests that they talk to a counselor. James feels very embarrassed about sharing their marital problems with a stranger. Lisa's family is aware of their marital problems and tries to be supportive, but James does not want to disclose their marital problems to his family. As Lisa has become more adamant about separating and as James has become more desperate to save the marriage, he has finally agreed to join Lisa for five treatment sessions.

When they came in for treatment, Lisa was friendly, self-assured, worried, and verbally expressive. James, on the other hand, looked tired, disheveled, tense, constricted, depressed, and on the verge of tears. Separately, both denied any serious physical risk to either James or Lisa, although Lisa continued to worry about James. Both acknowledged that they still cared very deeply for each other, despite the serious marital stress, and that there was more disappointment than animosity in their feelings about the marriage. The short-term goal of the marital counseling, agreed on by the couple, was to help James better deal with the stress of their marital problems and to do some preliminary exploration to help identify the reasons for their conflicts.

In the course of the five sessions, James began to feel more emotionally stable. He was getting considerable support from his older brother and his wife, as well as

(continued)

CONTINUED

from two close friends. Major sociocultural differences were uncovered that neither James nor Lisa thought were present. While James identified himself as "all American" and highly assimilated into mainstream America, his core "self" was collective rather than individualistic in origin. His own Nisei parents, who seemed as "American as apple pie" and only spoke English at home, had nevertheless raised James and his older siblings in a more traditional Japanese way. Even though James had mostly non-Asian friends throughout his life, he developed a "thick" layering of individualistic self that he actualized in his social relationships, but that concealed a core collective self base. As he settled into a secure married life with Lisa, he began to relax his defenses, allowing his collective needs to emerge and seek fulfillment. James had a very traditional view of marriage and was critical of Lisa for not understanding this, even though he had failed to explain the traditions of his culture sufficiently for Lisa to recognize that he expected her to defer to him and place his needs above hers. There were many other unspoken expectations of Lisa that James had not explained but felt she should understand and respect just because she is his wife.

By the end of the five sessions, both Lisa and James realized that they had entered into a much more complex marriage than either had imagined. Both agreed that they needed to talk further with a marriage counselor and accepted a referral to another therapist who was culturally sensitive to both Asian and Euro American ways of being. James left treatment feeling much more in touch with the traditions of his culture and felt ready to enter into a dialogue with Lisa to explain and process those traditions. Lisa left treatment recognizing their cultural differences and agreeing to learn much more about the traditions that had shaped James, but uncertain that she could meet all of James's needs. Both were impressed with the process, which they described as positive. James further noted that the process

> helped me understand not only the problems my cultural heritage created in our marriage, but many of the positives in those traditions which I have a deep appreciation for. It also confirmed my feelings for Lisa and helped me realize the hard work she had done to maintain our marriage. What I thought would be an embarrassing experience turned out to be very touching and I'm grateful to Lisa for not giving up on me.

Significant Loss

For the Asian American who has an important established relationship with someone, the loss of that person, either through death or the dissolution of the relationship, has profound implications for the integrity of individual's collective self. The process of mourning and grieving the loss of that individual and the subsequent emotional reconstitution entails a major psychosocial reconstruction of the collective self. When there is a major loss through death, all Asian cultures have their distinct rituals and practices to help with the healing process of "re"-collective self integration. This reaffirms the collective self integrity of all parties and helps them continue on in life. In the extreme case, a crippling loss may so severely disrupt the person's collective self integrity and desire to live that he or she cannot imagine living without the lost other. Such an individual, who is unable to experience emotional collective self support from others, may be at serious risk of suicide.

■ ■ ■ ■ ■

KEIKO: A CASE STUDY

Keiko is a 32-year-old Japanese permanent resident of the United States. She was brought into the community mental health clinic by two younger Japanese female friends. A Nisei bilingual older female social worker received them. Keiko appeared severely depressed and withdrawn and would only give monosyllabic replies to questions when directly pressed. For the most part, she appeared to allow her friends to speak on her behalf. Her friends told the crisis worker that her 38-year-old Japanese husband Masao, a naturalized American citizen, had just died a week ago in a tragic car accident. The funeral had already taken place. They said that Masao was everything to Keiko and that he was a devoted and caring husband. The two of them appeared to have developed an intense collective involvement that was not moderated by other significant collective involvements.

The friends were very worried about Keiko's lack of social responsiveness or emotion during and after the funeral and by the fact that she often looked vacantly out into space, oblivious to others around her. Neither Keiko nor Masao had any close family in the United States, and Masao had no contact with his family in Japan. Also, Keiko had once mentioned to a friend that she had left Japan for the United States four years ago, against her family's strong wishes, in order to marry and live with Masao. Another friend mentioned a second personal tragedy: a few months prior, Keiko and Masao were expecting their first child, but she had a miscarriage early in her second trimester. They were trying once again to have a baby when Masao died.

The crisis worker spent the session with Keiko and her two friends, whom Keiko indicated she wanted present. Keiko was diagnosed with a major depression, and there was serious concern about suicidal risk. Keiko refused to discuss her actively suicidal thoughts, but she was able to disclose to the therapist that all she felt was a "nothingness," an "empty black hole" inside. The crisis worker arranged for immediate hospitalization, under a suicide watch, and coordinated a daily treatment plan with the hospital psychiatrist. The social worker became Keiko's primary therapist, and she arranged for Keiko's closest Japanese friends to spend as much time as possible with Keiko in the hospital. Her friends were more than willing to be involved in this way. Their actions helped Keiko experience a family-like healing and caring collective involvement.

The crisis counselor also assisted Keiko with immediate financial assistance and initiated contact with her family in Japan. Although there had been only sporadic contact between them, Keiko's family showed great concern for her when informed of her husband's tragic death. Her mother wanted to come immediately to the United States to be with Keiko, but it was decided that a better plan was to have Keiko return to Japan to be cared for by her family and within the entire extended family system. Telephone conversations with her mother and father served to "resurrect" an important collective involvement with her family. Within several weeks, Keiko had regained a sustaining desire to live, and arrangements were made to fly her back to Japan, where she was able to regain a considerable amount of her original functioning under the supportive care of her family.

Although this case demonstrates the importance of family in reintegrating the collective self following a crisis, there is still work to be done with Keiko and her family. The lack of contact over the years has been hurtful to the family, and Keiko's desire to marry her husband and leave Japan against her family's wishes offers a significant set of issues to be resolved. The outcome in this case is satisfactory in the short run, but Keiko has

(continued)

CONTINUED

become Americanized to some degree, and this will be an issue to help the family understand and consider in their "new" relationship with Keiko.

In discussing the case with her American crisis worker, the worker noted,

> Keiko will be cared for by her family in Japan, and she will be able to cope with the loss of her husband. What remains to be seen is whether she and her family can resolve the conflicts that must have existed before and after her marriage. The family may be superb in its helping function as Keiko deals with her grief, but once she is done grieving, many questions remain. Will the family accept the new Keiko? Will Keiko choose to return to America, and will this be acceptable to her family? Once having been helped through a crisis by her family, will Keiko lose the individuality she may have gained in America, and will that cause her unhappiness? I suggested that both Keiko and the family continue the work we did in America with Keiko and contacted a therapist in Japan I know and respect. The family, worried that Keiko will become suicidal again, has agreed to continue her individual therapy and will also enter family therapy. This is a large commitment and one can only hope for a positive result, but the beginnings are certainly very encouraging. I have learned, in my practice, not to give up on families. They can have a powerfully positive impact when approached in a respectful way that encourages their desire to help other family members.

Family Expulsion

In Asian tradition, the son never truly leaves his family of origin. The family he establishes becomes incorporated into the continuous family line as the next generation. Generally speaking, the daughter leaves her family of origin only when she marries, relocates to her husband's family of origin, and establishes a new collective self incorporating his significant family members. Her bond of loyalty and duty to her own father and mother is "transferred" to her husband and his mother. If the son or daughter is "disinherited" or cast out from the family for some perceived travesty by the family before the right developmental time, this can cause a serious emotional collective self fragmentation and a deep sense of *self*-loss.

NGUYEN: A CASE STUDY

Nguyen is an 18-year-old first-generation Vietnamese American, the middle child of five brothers and sisters. She and her family were "boat people"—refugees who fled Vietnam in the late 1970s, interned at a refugee camp in Hong Kong, and then finally relocated to America by church sponsors. She was a very young child when she arrived in the United States. She grew up in a poor, racially mixed urban community in East Los Angeles. Her parents own a small liquor store where all of the brothers and sisters help out. Although her family basically kept to itself and associates only with other Vietnamese, Nguyen's high school friends were Mexican, African, and Southeast Asian

Americans. Nguyen described herself as being "very Vietnamese," close to her family, and not desiring to be more Americanized. She graduated from high school and was working full-time at her parents' store.

Nguyen came into the mental health clinic distraught and crying. She told the worker that her parents had just found out that she had been spending time with an older non-Asian man. Her father was infuriated with her, accusing her of being a "whore." He said that she was no longer his daughter and told her to leave the house. Her father, recalling very negative encounters with U.S. soldiers in Vietnam, feared that his daughter had become like the women kept by some American servicemen. Nguyen told the counselor that she was trying to be a "good daughter" to her parents. She was not sexual with this man and was not planning on "getting serious" with him. He was someone through whom she could confide her most private thoughts and advise her, much like a caring older brother would.

Nguyen had always considered herself to be strong and resourceful, but now she was alarmed at how scared and lost she felt. She acknowledged feeling suicidal but had no clear plan of action. She was too ashamed to ask for help from any of her friends, and came into the clinic because no one knew her there. For Nguyen, the suicidal impulse was mainly due to the deep anguish of loss of her family, a frightening, destabilizing experience in her sense of collective self and an overall feeling of hopelessness and helplessness. She wanted to escape the pain of the loss of her family and the consequent loss of integrity to her *self*.

The crisis worker spent an extended amount of time establishing rapport and trust. Nguyen identified one close non-Asian female friend with whom she could confide. She was able to contact this friend and explain the situation. Subsequently, the friend and her mother came to the clinic to be with Nguyen. The mother offered Nguyen a place to stay overnight, which she gratefully accepted. Nguyen agreed to a nonsuicide contract with the counselor, mother, and friend.

In a meeting with the crisis worker the next day, Nguyen had calmed down somewhat, saying it was comforting to stay with her friend's family because they tried to "include" her in family life. The mother had told Nguyen that she was very welcome to stay as long as needed. The emotional comfort she felt with her friend's family was reminiscent of the collective-based sense of belonging and security she once had but now had lost with her own family.

Fortunately, Nguyen could also identify a favorite uncle—her father's older brother—who would be more reasonable about the situation than would her father. It was decided that she would call the uncle herself, explain the situation, and seek his intervention. The uncle, who was more familiar with American ways, tended to be very understanding and was willing to hear her complete story about her friendship with this other man. He consulted with the crisis worker about Nguyen's emotional condition. The uncle, who commanded respect from her father because of his position of older brother, contacted Nguyen's father on her behalf. He arranged a family meeting between Nguyen and her parents, which he oversaw. The uncle acknowledged his younger brother's outrage and loss of face, but, at the same time, intervened by authoritatively stating that Nguyen had not intended to shame the family. The uncle also introduced the crisis worker into the family, explaining that he was an "expert" on helping Vietnamese families cope with the many difficulties involved in living in America. A series of family therapy sessions facilitated family forgiveness and Nguyen's emotional and physical reentry back into her family.

(continued)

CONTINUED

Nguyen's worker explained the process of working with the family:

Nguyen's father was able to maintain the family through terrible times. Like many survivors of genocide, he believes that complete loyalty to family is the only way to survive the confusing and often disagreeable aspects of American life, aspects that are unfamiliar to him and that seem destined to disrupt old traditions that have helped his family in America experience success and safety. He is worried that Nguyen's relationship with a non-Asian will lead to a disruption in the family and that it will result in family disunity, which may be irreparable. It was important for Nguyen's father to share this with Nguyen and to have her agree completely with his assessment. However, Nguyen was also able to explain that her Americanization was an asset to the family because it would help them in business, and though she had non-Asian friends, she had no desire to enter into serious relationships with those that her family would find unacceptable. She agreed to bring her friend to one of the sessions, and the family could see that the friendship was helpful to Nguyen and had no chance of becoming serious or intimate. At the same time, her Asian friends also attended some of the family sessions and validated Nguyen's deep respect for her father and her commitment to her extended family.

Nguyen comes by the office every so often for chats. After a year, she maintains a very good relationship with her father. She has begun seeing a young man, of whom her family is quite fond. There is a growing feeling of affection between Nguyen and her boyfriend, and Nguyen has accepted traditional courting rituals that please her parents and make her feel safe in the relationship. The Americanization of children in immigrant families is always a stressful experience for families, but when prior genocide is involved, it can be terrifying to parents who believe that the traditions and beliefs that helped them survive will now be lost, and that their survival in America will be at risk.

Dysfunctional Asian American Family

A dysfunctional traditional Asian American family is one in which the significant adult family members are incapable of managing their role responsibilities and obligations and cannot provide a sufficient level of care and appropriate child rearing to promote the development of a healthy collective self. Occasionally, this includes promoting a confusing, contradictory self experience without any inherent coherence and psychosocial integrity, or imposing family roles and responsibilities on its members that are *self*-destructive. When this takes place, a family-level therapeutic intervention is ideally called for.

JANE: A CASE STUDY

Jane is a 23-year-old fourth-generation Chinese American, the youngest of four brothers and sisters. Jane says that she is much more Chinese than American and that most of her social life has been spent within her immediate family. On her own initiative and without any encouragement or financial support from her extended family, Jane enrolled in a local community college. She continued to live at home and took a job to pay for her school costs.

Jane was friendly and motivated, showed an ability to connect with the counselor, but her mind easily wandered off on tangents as she passively talked about her life and related some major concerns. She reported never feeling particularly happy with her life, felt low self-esteem, and has had a continuing pattern of very disappointing romantic relationships. Jane described these involvements with men—both Asian and non-Asian—who were emotionally and, at times, physically abusive.

In time, Jane related to the therapist that her oldest brother had repeatedly sexually abused her. Her father seemed to take delight in humiliating her in front of other family members. At one recent family gathering, she recounted how her father had her stand up in front of everyone so that he could ridicule her for being "overweight and ugly." He had pulled up her sweatshirt to show her "flab," and everyone laughed at her. Jane had become the scapegoat of the extended family and was usually blamed for whatever misfortune affected the family. Nevertheless, Jane had come to accept all of this, saying that she is a part of the family and cannot rebel against them.

When asked if there were any family members who stood up for her and protested her mistreatment, Jane remarked that there were some who objected, but that they could not stand up to her father, who held considerable authority over the extended family. He was the "oldest son of the oldest son" in the family system, and because he was a very successful businessman, he was the primary support for many people in the extended family. Jane also reported that her mother was an "absent mother" who had always been sickly and was usually in the background when it came to family matters. She was ineffectual in protecting Jane from her father and oldest brother. In effect, Jane's *collective self* sacrifice was to relieve other family members of responsibility for misfortune, and to extract and contain any of the family's "badness" onto her *self*.

After determining the severity of this family's dysfunctionality, the crisis worker made the decision that a family intervention would not be practical nor useful, and that Jane must be helped individually. The counselor believed that it was best for Jane, as an adult, to extricate herself from her family. While not concerned about Jane being imminently suicidal, she was very concerned about the ongoing sexual abuse by the brother and the damaging impact her family had on her sense of collective self. Though Jane had enough healthy *self*-survival instincts to be able to want a better life experience, she was collectively committed to her family. It was difficult for her to comprehend disengaging from them. The crisis worker, however, was very concerned about Jane and the other minors in the extended family and filed a child abuse report on both the father and the brother. She carefully prepared Jane for the consequences of an investigation, anticipating that this action could cause the family to strongly reject Jane.

Jane was, in fact, relieved and grateful for the counselor's concern for her and for taking action on her behalf. The counselor, by assuming authority and by attempting to protect Jane, role-modeled a healthy collective self involvement with a parent-figure. This therapeutic action also empowered Jane to seriously consider emotionally disengaging from her family for her own welfare. The crisis worker was careful to support Jane's "selfishness" as necessary for *self*-survival. She was also able to relieve Jane of her role and responsibility in the family as the "bad one," and to help her see how the family, itself, was very unhealthy. The worker managed Jane's collective self dependency needs within reasonable limits, allowing Jane to rely on her during this transition.

(continued)

CONTINUED

In a series of follow-up crisis intervention sessions, the crisis worker and Jane made careful preparations for her to leave her home and to relocate to another state, where she planned to contact some distant and detached relatives who were "healthy" and to continue college. The severing of collective ties to her family was accelerated by the child abuse investigation, which created an intense family crisis. The family's sense of betrayal precipitated their disowning Jane. Jane relocated to an area with a large Cantonese Chinese community, where she continued long-term therapy with a culturally sensitive Chinese American therapist. In her new living environment, she established a family-like set of relationships with a Chinese family and was informally "adopted" by them. In this way, Jane was able to maintain her collective self, but within a healthier family system. Jane kept in regular contact with the counselor, who had become an integral part of her sense of collective self, and maintained, from a distance, an appropriate but vital sense of collective self connectivity with the counselor.

In a letter to her original therapist, Jane wrote,

> I still feel guilty about leaving my family. I have been disowned and, in my family, that means that I will never have contact with them again. I fought the idea of leaving home for a long time and hoped that, magically, someone in the family would make everything right, but that never happened and the abuse and ridicule continued. It's hard for me now to know why I accepted it all those years. I think the importance of family can't be overstated. When I felt part of the family, even though I was being abused, I felt that I had the strength of all of the family members combined. Thinking about leaving the family made me feel very weak. For a long time, I put up with my brother's abuse and my father's ridicule because the option of leaving didn't exist in my mind. You [her worker] helped me see that I was a competent and intelligent woman and that the things that were being done to me at home were mean and troubled and came, not from love or a sense of being a member of the family, but from my family's dislike and rejection of me. It hurt to accept this, and I fought the idea for a while, but in time, I was able to make the break and I'm much better for it. Do I grieve the loss of my family? Every day. Do I feel guilty about what has happened to my brother and father? Yes. They both have been punished by the court and my father's business has suffered. Did I do the right thing? Yes, I think I did. It isn't easy being by myself, but my new family provides a connection I never had in my old family, and I feel loved and valued. It's a new and wonderful feeling.

A CRITICAL RESPONSE

An important premise of this book is the significance of both culture and family in the lives of our clients. A certain familiarity with mainstream America culture is required to function in American society. That familiarity is often attractive to the children of parents from more traditional cultures, but problematic for parents who often see American society as conflicted and believe that maintaining traditional values and beliefs will continue to serve them well in the United States. This chapter shows what happens when traditional values and practices of parents clash with those of children who are trying to navigate the muddy waters of American life and still maintain their allegiance to their families. It is a story that is familiar because it represents the immigrant experience so well. The concept of the collective self offers clinicians a different way of viewing the tensions between the individualism of American society and the collective nature of Asian society. It is a concept that might easily be applied to other traditional cultures and to the immigrant groups who move to America. In a sense, the chapter is also about the confusing nature of assimilation. As Rodriguez(1982) says about the power of assimilation and Americanization.

> Once upon a time, I was a socially disadvantaged child; an enchanted and happy child. Mine was a childhood of intense family closeness and extreme public alienation. Thirty years later, I write this book as a middle class American man. Assimilated. . . . It is education that has altered my life. (preface)

The cases presented in this chapter show the problems and the misunderstandings brought about by cultural conflicts. Further, the chapter shows how sensitive, caring, and understanding work with Asian clients can have a positive impact. Asian clients are an underserved population, and many professionals have only vague ideas about how best to help Asian clients in need. One concern expressed by those who gave feedback on this chapter is the emphasis it places on children making accommodations to parents for the sake of family harmony without similar accomodations made by parents to their children. These cases, however, show very basic movement by parents who are seeking to do the best they can for their children. Both authors of this chapter have immigrant parents and value the experience. We admire the resilience of our parents who endured hardships in America including forced internment during World War II (Stephen Ino), and overt, undeniable, and hurtful anti-Semitism (Morley Glicken). Our parents were traditional but encouraged all that is positive in American life: education, achievement, and service to others. We believe that immigrants come to America and enhance our country. Consequently, concerns about traditional parents asking children to maintain allegiance and loyalty to their families seems a small payment for the heroic efforts made by the immigrant parents who come to America, live through very difficult times, and still manage to raise children who give their energies, commitment, and loyalty to their families, the communities they live in, and to our country. And given the sad state of American family life today, that's saying a lot.

SUMMARY

This chapter discusses crisis work with ethnically Asian-identified Americans. The collective self is presented as an alternate paradigm that more accurately explicates the Asian American life experience. Case examples demonstrate its utility in crisis intervention work. The collective self concept is intended as a legitimate counterpoint to the prevailing Euro American notion of the individualistic self. Its use allows a much more complex therapeutic discourse to take place between the clinician and the Asian American client. It is hoped that further qualitative and quantitative research will be stimulated by its consideration.

INTEGRATIVE QUESTIONS

1. The collective self suggests the unique quality of family life on its members. Do you think the impact of the collective self has a positive or negative impact on children? Explain your answer.

2. In the case of Keiko, whose husband passed away and who became very depressed, do you think returning to Japan was a wise decision? Provide several possible positive and negative scenarios of what might happen when Keiko returns to her family home.

3. America has been described as a melting pot; immigrants come to this country but soon become Americanized. Do you think this impulse to acculturate quickly is good or bad for the immigrants who come here, and for their children?

4. In the case of Jane who was sexually abused by her brother and emotionally abused by her father, does the resolution of this case with Jane moving from home assure us that Jane won't have remaining problems? What might some of those problems be?

5. Family expulsion is a serious act for Asian clients but don't EuroAmerican parents use similar tactics when their children displease them? Can you describe some tactics you've known parents to use when disapproving of their children?

REFERENCES

Chang, S.C. (1982). The self: A nodal issue in culture and psyche: An eastern perspective. *American Journal of Psychotherapy*, 36, 67–81.

Ewing, C.P. (1990). Crisis intervention as brief psychotherapy. In R.A. Wells and V.J. Giannetti (Eds.), *Handbook of brief psychotherapies* (pp. 277–294). New York: Plenum Press.

Furuto, S.M., Biswas, R., Chung, D., Murase, K., and Ross-Sheriff, F. (Eds.). (1992). *Social work practice with Asian Americans*. Newbury Park, CA: Sage.

Gaw, A.C. (1993). Psychiatric care of Chinese Americans. In A. Gaw (Ed.), *Culture, ethnicity, and mental illness* (pp. 245–280). Washington DC: American Psychiatric Press.

Golan, N. (1978). *Treatment in crisis situations*. New York: Free Press.

Gong-Guy, E. (1987). *California Southeast Asian mental health needs assessment*. Oakland, CA: Asian Community Mental Health Association.

Gong-Guy, E., Cravens, R.B., and Patterson, T.E. (1991). Clinical issues in mental health service delivery to refugees. *American Psychologist*, 46, 642–648.

Herbert, E.A. (1950). *A Confucian notebook*. London: Butler & Tanner.

Ho, M.K. (1987). *Family therapy with ethnic minorities*. Newbury Park, CA: Sage.

Hsu, F.L.K. (1983). *Rugged individualism reconsidered: Essays in psychological anthropology*. Knoxville: University of Tennessee Press.

Ino, S. (1985). The concept of an Asian American collective self. Paper presented at the Pacific/Asian American Research Methods Workshop (P/AAMHRC), Ann Arbor, Michigan, August 22, 1985.

Ino, S. (1991). The sense of collective self in Asian American psychology. Paper presented at the American Psychological Association (APA): 99th Annual Convention, San Francisco, August 16–20, 1991.

Ino, S.M., and Glicken, M.D. (June 1999). Treating Asian American clients in crisis: A collectivist approach. *Smith College Studies in Social Work*, 69(3), 525–540.

Ino, S.M., and Glicken, M.D. (2002). Understanding and treating the ethnically Asian client: A collectivist approach. *Journal of Health and Social Policy*, 14(4), 37–48.

Lee, E. (1996). Asian American families: An overview. In M. McGoldrick, J. Giordana, and J. Pearce (Eds.), *Ethnicity and family therapy* (2nd Ed.) New York: Guilford.

Leong, F.T.L. (1986). Counseling and psychotherapy with Asian-Americans: Review of the literature. *Journal of Counseling Psychology, 33*, 196–206.

Roberts, A.R. (1990). *Crisis intervention handbook: Assessment, treatment, and research.* Belmont, CA: Wadsworth.

Rodriguez, R. (1982). *Hunger of memory: The education of Richard Rodriguez.* New York: Bantam

Root, M. (1993). Guidelines for facilitating therapy with Asian American clients. In D. Atkinson, G. Morten, and D.W. Sue (Eds.), *Counseling American minorities: A cross-cultural perspective* (pp. 349–356). Madison, WI: Brown and Benchmark.

Sue, S., and Morishima, J.K. (1982). *The mental health of Asian Americans: Contemporary issues in identifying and treating mental problems.* San Francisco: Jossey-Bass.

Uba, L. (1994). *Asian Americans: Personality patterns, identity, and mental health.* New York: Guilford.

Yu, E. (1989). Chinese collective orientation and need for achievement. *International Journal of Social Psychiatry, 26*, 184–189.

PART IV

THE STRENGTHS PERSPECTIVE WITH SPECIAL POPULATIONS

Chapters 10 through 14 show the application of the strengths perspective to special populations. To demonstrate that the approach can be used with more complex clinical problems, Chapter 10 applies the strengths approach to abusive clients and their victims. This chapter includes such traditionally difficult treatment populations as perpetrators of child abuse, sexual abuse, and family violence, and their victims. Chapter 11 introduces the concept of natural healing with problems of substance abuse. It also shows how the strengths approach might be applied to work with clients who severely abuse alcohol and drugs. Chapter 12 introduces another strengths concept: clients with problems of mental illness helping to manage their own care, as well as the social and emotional difficulties of fellow clients. Chapter 12 also discusses problems of stigma and how incorrect or premature diagnostic labels do harm to clients who often do not suffer the long-term consequences of mental illness but are treated as if they are mentally ill for life. The strengths perspective is applied to clients and their caretakers in this chapter. Chapter 13 applies the strengths perspective to terminal illness, disability, and bereavement. The focus of this chapter is on the existentially meaningful understanding of illness, death, and dying in a death-denying society. Chapter 14 focuses on depression in elderly clients. Elderly clients are often not provided mental health services, and depression is sometimes felt to be a symptom of generalized poor health rather than a mental health issue. The famous Holocaust writer Primo Levi, who committed suicide at age 67, is discussed in this chapter, and questions are asked regarding his depression and whether it was a function of ill health or the consequence of his Holocaust experiences.

The five chapters composing this section of the book include a great deal of data on traditional approaches to treatment. As the reader will note, many of these approaches have limited effectiveness when the research is reviewed. Because this book was written from an evidence-based practice point of view, it's important for the reader to come to his or her own conclusions by independently exploring clinical research effectiveness studies. Many clinicians believe that subjecting therapy to hard analysis is difficult at best, and impossible in many cases. The reader might want to consider the complexity of doing accurate clinical research when these five chapters are read and decide whether the author has given a fair and complete picture.

CHAPTER TEN

THE STRENGTHS PERSPECTIVE WITH ABUSIVE CLIENTS AND THEIR VICTIMS

He'll pinch my pinky until the mouse
starts squeaking.
The floor lamp casts a halo around
his big, stuffed chair.
Be strong Be Tough! *It is my father speaking.*

I'm four or five. Was he already drinking?
With its tip and knuckle between
his thumb and finger,
he'll pinch my pinky until the mouse stops squeaking.

Stop, Daddy, stop (it is more like screeching)
and kneels down before him on the hardwood floor.
Be strong Be tough! *It is my father speaking.*

What happened to him to do such a thing?
It's only a game, he's doing me a favor
to pinch my pinky until the mouse starts squeaking

because the world will run over a weakling
and we must crush the mouse or be crushed later.
Be strong Be tough! *It was my father speaking*

to himself, of course, to the child inside him aching,
not to me. But how can I not go when he calls me over
to pinch my pinky until the mouse starts squeaking
Be strong Be Tough? *It is my father speaking.*

Michael Ryan (1989)

For a long time now, the men and women of America have been engaged in a war that we politely call domestic violence. It is a homogenized term for the punching, the kicking, and the disfigurement of the body and soul of legions of men, women, and children in America. While domestic violence is thought to be violence between two adults, in reality, it is violence to the entire family. Children watch adults in violent interactions, and whether or not the violence affects them physically, it has a predictable psychological impact that is almost as serious as physical violence. The children of America are also the victims of maltreatment, the effects of which may linger on throughout the life cycle. This chapter considers the use of the strengths perspective in the treatment of abusers and their victims, but first, some data on the amount of domestic violence and child maltreatment in America are presented.

FAMILY VIOLENCE: PREVALENCE AND IMPACT OF THE PROBLEM

The data related to the actual amounts of domestic violence are clouded by methodological differences among researchers (Glicken & Sechrest, 2003). As Elena Neuman (1995) notes, many researchers confuse domestic violence (violence between loved ones) with general violence. The result is that the absolute amount of domestic violence has become confused. Neuman (1995) notes that a study by the Surgeon General in 1992 (in Neuman, 1995) estimated that the number of women experiencing physical abuse in a domestic environment ranged between 2 and 4 million a year. However, a 1993 telephone survey of 2,500 women by Louis Harris for the Commonwealth Fund (Neuman, 1995, p. 69) found that 2 percent had been "kicked, bit, or hit with a fist or some other object." According to Harris, this would amount to an overall rate of violence to women of 1.8 million acts of domestic violence per year.

Neuman (1995) also notes that to come up with the larger numbers of 2 to 4 million cases of domestic violence, the survey would have had to add women to the report who experience less violent acts such as pushing, shoving, grabbing, or throwing something at a partner, acts that are aggressive but are often, unfortunately, associated with adult relationships over the normal course of their lives. Using this definition of domestic violence, almost all of us may be guilty of having committed acts defined as domestic violence.

Reporting for the U.S. Department of Justice, Greenfield (1997, 1998) found that, in 1996, female victims of intimate violence experienced an estimated 840,000 rapes, sexual assaults, robberies, aggravated assaults, and simple assaults at the hands of intimates, down from 1.1 million in 1993. Three out of four of the victims of murder by intimates (1998) were women. In the same year, 1996, one in 10 female victims of domestic violence sought medical treatment for injuries sustained at the hands of perpetrators. In 40 percent of the cases of violence among adult intimates, children were residing at home during episodes of violence. The report also noted that in 1996, 150,000 men were victims of intimate violence, a figure that has remained fairly constant today.

THE EFFECTIVENESS OF TRADITIONAL TREATMENTS WITH FAMILY VIOLENCE

Davis, Smith, and Nickles (1998) found no evidence that mandatory prosecution for domestic violence reduced the likelihood of recidivism in domestic violence misdemeanor cases. Furthermore, they found mandatory treatment in diversion projects for men and women who were found guilty of misdemeanor abuse to be unrelated to additional abuse following treatment: "The likelihood of recidivism was indistinguishable for cases resulting in nolles, dismissals, probation with batterer treatment program, and jail sentences" (p. 440). The authors stated that domestic violence cases are "messy" and involve children, property, and emotional bonds that may not be affected by the punishing aspects of the courts. People stay together for reasons that may override the violent aspects of their relationships, and they are often less than truthful with researchers and therapists regarding the discontinuation of violence in the relationship after any treatment input, including incarceration and therapy. Although the justice system may help in protecting people, it does poorly in resolving complex interpersonal relationships among people involved in domestic violence. As Davis et al. (1998) noted, "Habitual behavior that occurs in the privacy of people's homes and out of the public eye is likely to be highly resistant to change in many instances" (p. 441).

Eisikovits and Edelson (1989) report, "It can still be said that the intervention literature [regarding the treatment of domestic violence] is often atheoretical or it has borrowed its theoretical grounding from other areas" (p. 407). In therapy, the ultimate rejection of the process is to stop attending sessions. Attrition for batterers is over 50 percent in most studies conducted in North America (DeMaris, 1989). While some researchers have looked at demographic reasons for attrition (DeMaris, 1989), others have focused on the degree of masculinization of subjects, believing that the more highly internalized the masculine role, the less likely subjects are to stay in treatment. DeMaris (1989) found that demographic issues that correlated with attrition and noncompliance were employment status, use of substances, arrest record, age, income, desire to reduce violent behavior, age of the partner, and the timing or reason for the abuse. DeMaris found, however, that these demographic explanations explained attrition at a level only 12 percent above chance. In other words, it is difficult to find precise reasons for attrition when one looks at the total number of abusers in treatment, but the door is left open to think that treatment might not be working and that attrition is high, suggesting that the abusive behavior may be continuing.

■ ■ ■ ■ ■

JOHN AND LINDA: A CASE STUDY OF DOMESTIC VIOLENCE

John and Linda have been engaged in family violence for the past six of the eight years they have been married. John is usually the perpetrator of the violence, but Linda admits that she can provide the incentive for John to begin his verbal and physical abuse

(continued)

CONTINUED

by making fun of him and reminding him of his many flaws. The couple say they love one another, but the violence is beginning to affect their two sons, ages 6 and 4. Both children are frightened, seem not to be developing emotionally and socially, and are bed wetters. John and Linda use physical and emotional abuse with one another and feel deeply grieved that their relationship has become so violent and abusive. John has many of the classic signs of an abuser. He is jealous, has low self-esteem, is less verbal than Linda, and feels demeaned at home by Linda's constant criticism. Linda also has many classic signs of a victim. She has very low self-esteem and is frightened that John will abandon her, just as her father abandoned his family. Linda watched her mother and father physically abuse one another throughout their marriage. She deplores the violent aspects of her marriage but finds it familiar and, in an odd sort of way, comfortable.

The couple came for marital therapy after John was arrested and charged with misdemeanor domestic violence, punishable by up to a year in jail. He was offered an opportunity to receive treatment in lieu of jail and is in a perpetrator group and marital therapy. The marital worker listened to both sides of the discussion, urging the couple to tell him as much as they felt comfortable sharing. The picture that emerged was of a loving couple with little skill for expressing loving behavior. For both of them, the honeymoon periods of reconciliation that followed the violence were motivators to continue the abusive behavior. Both felt that the fighting was an indication of the deep love they had for one another. The reconciliation period just reinforced that love. As John said, "We wouldn't stay married if we didn't love each other. The fighting just shows how much in love we are." Linda said, "If you fight and make up and don't get divorced, doesn't that show how much you love each other?"

DISCUSSION

The worker engaged the couple in a discussion of their definition of love. It turned out that neither thought violence really suggested love. He asked them to describe loving behaviors. With some difficulty they were able to do this. He then asked them to carefully compare their descriptions and definitions of loving behavior with the reality of their marriage, and to discuss it at home. When they came back the next week, they began a dialogue with the worker about the distance between what they wanted in their marriage and what they had. The dialogue led to a reevaluation of their marriage and pointed out many strengths in the marriage that neither thought existed. Although their sons were having beginning indications of the impact of the fighting, they were loving children who were respectful and had good values. Their home was well furnished and, in many ways, a real improvement over anything John and Linda had ever thought possible in a marriage. They had wonderful friends and had deep religious and spiritual values. There were siblings on both sides of the marriage with whom they had caring relationships. They were doing well in their respective jobs and were both financially responsible. Their intimate moments were physically and emotionally satisfying. They held similar beliefs about many social and political issues, and they found each other attractive.

Focusing on the positives in the relationship led to a discussion of the negatives and how they might be resolved. Both partners were pleased when they were able to develop strategies that seemed to reduce the anger in their relationship, and both were able to understand the "buttons" they each pushed that served as catalysts for their anger. John was learning a great deal about his behavior in the perpetrators group, and Linda, seeing the gains John made, joined a group for abused women. From that group she learned about the connection between the abuse in her family as she was growing up and her own behavior in her marriage. Having no other models of love, she used the one she had learned as a child in an abusive marriage. After six months of marital and group treatment, John and Linda are doing well. The physical abuse has stopped, although there is an occasional argument and emotional violence sometimes occurs. The couple believe they need the support of a self-help group for couples that is offered through their church, and attend weekly meetings. They feel the loving messages they get from the group, and the suggestions and examples of others who have been abusive, but have overcome the abuse, are all positive reinforcers and help them stay on track in their marriage. Both sons are doing well, and the fearful behavior and bed wetting have been resolved.

CHILD MALTREATMENT: PREVALENCE AND IMPACT OF THE PROBLEM

Sedlak (1997) indicates that there were 2.1 million reports of abused and neglected children in a 1986 study. The average abused child was 7.2 years old, ranging from a mean of "5.5 years of age for physical abuse to 9.2 years of age for sexual abuse" (p. 153). Fifty-four percent of the victims were male children who had been physically abused, and male children also accounted for 23 percent of sexual abuse cases (p. 153), suggesting a much higher figure for male victims of sexual abuse than had previously been thought. In the National Family Violence Survey conducted by Straus and Gelles (1986), it was estimated that 110 of every 1,000 children in the general population experienced severe violence by their parents, and that 23 in 1,000 experienced very severe or life-threatening violence. *Severe violence* was defined as kicking, biting, punching, hitting, beating up, threatening with a weapon, or use of a knife or gun (Sedlak, 1997, p. 178). *Very severe violence* resulted in serious bodily damage to a child. Because lower income families are much more likely to have abuse reported by an outside party than are more affluent families, it was estimated by Straus and Gelles (1986) that inclusion of potential abuse by more affluent families could raise the actual amount of abuse by 50 percent.

The U.S. Justice Department (2000) reported that more than 1,000 children died as a result of maltreatment in 1996. Three out of four of these victims were children under the age of 4. Nineteen percent of the victims were age 2 or younger, while 52 percent of the victims were age 7 or younger. About 16 percent of the victims of substantiated abuse or neglect were removed from their homes (U.S. Department of Justice, 1999 National Report Series, May 2000, NCJ-180753).

In 1996, an estimated 3 million children were reported for abuse and/or neglect to public social service/child protective services (CPS) agencies, according to the National Child Abuse and Neglect Data System (NCANDS) project, in its April 1998 report (U.S. Department of Health and Human Services, 1998). The preceding data suggest that abuse and neglect reports were filed on about one child out of every 25 children in the United States. After investigating those reports, over 1 million children were confirmed as victims of actual abuse or neglect situations.

THE EFFECTIVENESS OF TRADITIONAL
TREATMENTS FOR ABUSE AND NEGLECT

In a book review of *Treatment of Child Abuse*, edited by Reece and Ludwig (2001), Lukefahr (2001) wrote,

> Although there is a very strong effort throughout to base findings and recommendations on the available evidence, these chapters highlight the reality that this young, evolving specialty remains largely descriptive. A common theme of several authors is the prominent role of cognitive-behavioral therapy for child abuse victims, but therapists may be disappointed in the lack of specific protocols for implementing CBT. (p. 36)

Kaplan, Pelcovitz, and Labruna (1999) report that the effectiveness of treatment for children who have been physically and sexually abused "has generally not been empirically evaluated. In a review of treatment research for physically abused children, Oates and Bross (1995) cite only 13 empirical studies between 1983 and 1992 meeting even minimal research standards" (p. 1218).

Delson and Kokish (2002) reported the following conclusions about the effectiveness of conventional therapy with abused children:

> Conventional wisdom recommends early treatment for child victims of sexual abuse and professional literature is rich with articles describing treatment methodology and anecdotal case reports. But controlled studies of treatment outcomes are rare. Here's one of the few. Eighty-four sexually abused children ages 5–15 were assessed at intake, along with a group of community controls (Oates & Bross, 1995). When reassessed 18 months later, 65% of the abused children had received therapy—35% had not.
>
> The abused group was more dysfunctional at intake than the control group. As time went by the abused children made greater strides towards normalcy than the controls. At the end of eighteen months, the abused group was still more dysfunctional, but had closed the gap considerably. The greatest improvement was in depression. Self-esteem did not improve and actually deteriorated over time in many of the victims, regardless of treatment. The use of "avoidance" as a coping strategy by mothers correlated positively with deterioration in children's self esteem.
>
> The best predictor of improvement was adequate maternal and family functioning. It may be that supportive social services and counseling for care givers would prove more effective than direct counseling for victims, at least in terms of short-term adjustment. (p. 1)

■ ■ ■ ■ ■ ▬▬▬▬▬▬▬▬▬▬▬▬▬▬▬▬▬▬▬▬▬▬▬▬▬▬▬▬▬▬▬▬

LYNN: A CASE STUDY OF CHILD ABUSE USING THE STRENGTHS
PERSPECTIVE

Lynn is a 9-year-old child who has been physically abused by her mother, Jolene, since Lynn was age 4. Jolene has been diagnosed with schizophrenia and is currently in a state hospital where she is being treated to achieve competence to stand trial for abusing Lynn. The worker sees both Lynn and her mother, though separately. Children have loyalty to parents, even abusing parents, and Lynn hopes that her mother will get well and that they can live together again. The purpose of the treatment Lynn is receiving is to help her understand her mother's behavior, disassociate it from anything Lynn has done, and to help Lynn develop positive feelings about herself.

Lynn believes that she is responsible for her mother's abusive behavior and thinks that there is something evil about her. These are messages given to Lynn by her mother, who believed that Lynn was possessed by the devil. The worker has allowed Lynn to express these feelings, while noting her many positive achievements, even in the midst of abuse, which would be more than most children could endure. The worker brought a note from Lynn's mother saying how much she loves Lynn, how sorry she is for what she did, and that it had nothing to do with Lynn but was something that had to do with her illness. She thinks Lynn is a very special child and prays for her every day and asks God His forgiveness for her bad behavior toward Lynn. Lynn is very moved by her mother's notes and returns from treatment feeling very loved and cherished. "I forgive my mom," she told the worker, "and I pray every night that my mom will get well and we'll be together."

Lynn lives with her grandmother, who is a stable and positive support. Her grandmother is religious, and Lynn has begun to find solace in the religious experiences she shares with her grandmother. The church she attends has been very loving and caring, and many of the children she meets at services have been abused or neglected and are living with relatives or foster parents who attend the church. She has chosen her friends wisely and has developed a small support network of friends who have been abused and neglected and know, without needing to have it explained, that a certain level of sadness never quite leaves an abused child. Some days are difficult for Lynn, but with the kindness of her grandmother and friends, she does well in school and has discovered a gift for music.

In describing her therapy, Lynn said,

> I like seeing Mrs. Redman. She's always nice to me and treats me like an adult. Sometimes when I'm really upset and can't talk much, she's patient and we can sit together and she lets me cry. She makes me feel that I can do anything in life. I like that she's helping my mother and understands that it's her mental illness that makes her act so bad. My mom is a wonderful person when she's not sick, and even Mrs. Redman tells me so. When I see Mrs. Redman, she always tells me about the good things I can do. When I get really sad, she tells me that many children haven't done as well as I have and there must be something pretty special about me. I don't know if that's true because sometimes I feel awful inside, but it sure makes me feel better. The people I have at church and at school help a lot too, and Mrs. Redman always says that nice people are attracted to each other. I hope my mom is OK, and I hope she can see me a lot. She's still my mom and it doesn't matter what she did. You only have one mom in your life and if God meant for her to have this sickness, it must be for a reason. Maybe it helps me care more about other people. I hope so.

DISCUSSION

Like many abused children, Lynn is loyal to her mother. She understands the harm her mother did to her but also recognizes the impact of her mother's mental illness. This understanding attitude is one that will very likely have a positive impact on Lynn as she matures. The treatment she is receiving is supportive, positive, and caring. Lynn feels that her worker is a very sensitive person and that her treatment helps her feel better about herself. She is honest about the feelings of sadness she experiences and has been wise in

(continued)

her choice of friends. Her grandmother and the religious experiences they share together have been strengths that have helped Lynn cope with the abuse and the loss of her mother. Rather than focusing on the harm done to her by her mother, her grandmother and the therapist have focused on Lynn's many positive attributes. By doing this, Lynn is beginning to internalize a positive view of herself that helps offset the many times that she has negative thoughts about herself. Sometimes Lynn feels sad and the worker allows her to feel this way without suggesting that it's a dysfunctional behavior. She sits and allows Lynn to process her feelings, even if it involves long silences. Helping Lynn feel she's in control of her treatment is a way of helping her feel she's in control of her life. In many important ways, the therapist is modeling for Lynn what a kind and supportive mother would be like, and Lynn has begun to understand that being nurtured and loved are important qualities in any relationship. This understanding helps Lynn separate her fantasies about her mother from the realities of coping with a mother who may have a limited capacity to nurture or to love.

SEXUAL ASSAULT: PREVALENCE AND IMPACT OF THE PROBLEM

For the year 1995, the U.S. Census Bureau (1998) estimated that during a woman's lifetime, there is an 18 percent possibility of being raped (a 15 percent completion rate and a 3 percent attempt rate). However, when other aspects of violence including physical assaults were added to the rape data, American women had a startling 55 percent probability of being raped or assaulted sometime during their lifetime. Men have an even greater probability of some form of physical violence. Sixty-seven percent of all men face the probability of being victims of some form of violence during their lives (U.S. Census Bureau, 1998).

In actual terms, the 1995 Census Bureau data indicate that 302,091 women were raped in the United States but when nonreported rapes were added to that figure, the estimate increased to 876,000 rapes and 5.9 million physical assaults (U.S. Census Bureau, 1998). When the data consider only an intimate partner (current and former spouses, opposite-sex cohabiting partners, same sex cohabiting partners, dates and boyfriends/girlfriends), 8 percent of all women will experience rape by an intimate partner and 22 percent will experience some form of physical assault from an intimate partner during their lifetime. In absolute numbers, 1.5 million women were raped and/or physically assaulted by intimates in 1995. To make the physical assault data more vivid, women are 7 to 14 times more likely to have been beaten, choked, threatened with a gun, or actually had a gun used on them by intimates than men. In actual percentages, women experience 3 times the level of physical assault by intimates. Women are stalked 8 times more often than men. Of the 18 percent of women facing a probability of being raped in their lifetime, 54 percent will have been raped before the age of 18. Women raped before the age of 18 are significantly more likely to be raped as adults (U.S. Census Bureau, 1998). Current Justice Department data for the year 2000 (Crime Victimization in the U.S., NCJ 188290, 2002) shows that there were 260,950 rapes, rape attempts and/or sexual assaults in the United States.

Greenfeld (1997) reports that the majority of rape victims (70%) took some form of self-protective action during the crime. While 4 percent of the victims of violence needed medical attention, 6 percent of the known rape victims required medical attention. This does not factor in the number of rape victims who are unknown to us and who seek medical and psychological services after the rape. The estimates are that more rape victims seek medical and psychological service than the population of victims of violent crime, and that these services are used for a much longer period of time. Seven percent of all victims of sexual violence report losing time at work. About 40 percent of the victims of violent sexual abuse suffered injuries with 5 percent suffering major injuries such as fractures, internal injuries, and concussions (Greenfeld, 1997).

THE EFFECTIVENESS OF TRADITIONAL TREATMENTS OF SEXUAL OFFENDERS

Looman, Abracen, and Nicholaichuk (2000) reported that the most common treatment techniques for work with sexual offenders are confrontation, role-plays, supportive psychotherapy, and empathy training, usually provided for about six months. When considering the effectiveness of these techniques, the authors found that the treated group in their study had a sexual recidivism rate of 23.6 percent, while the untreated group had a sexual recidivism rate of 51.7 percent. However, when it came to recidivism for nonsexually related offenses, both groups had high recidivism rates. Treated sexual offenders had rearrest rates of 62 percent, compared with 74 percent of the untreated group, raising questions about the overall treatment effectiveness of the therapeutic techniques used.

Loza and Loza-Fanous (1999a, 1999b) note that, despite the questionable relationship between anger and violent behavior, many correctional facilities require that inmates attend anger management programs. This is particularly true of rapists because of the assumption that anger at women is a primary cause of violent sexual acts. However, when the authors (Loza and Loza-Fanous, 1999b) tested this assumption by reviewing the effectiveness of anger management programs in reducing violent behavior, including the violent behavior of rapists, they found

no differences between violent offenders and nonviolent offenders and between rapists and nonrapists and nonviolent offenders on anger measures. These results supported the previous reports (reported earlier) that disputed the link between anger and violent behavior. The results also indicate that 73% of incarcerated violent offenders and 81% of incarcerated rapists were referred to an anger treatment program (in addition to the sex offender program) and that 74% of the nonviolent offenders and 76% of nonrapists and nonviolent offenders were not referred to anger programs. These results reflect the prevalence of the belief among correctional professionals that there is a link between anger and violence, rape, and recidivism. This situation exists despite the (a) supporting evidence against a link between anger and violent behavior among noncriminal populations and criminal offenders in particular, (b) lack of relationship between anger and criminal recidivism (Loza & Loza-Fanous, 1999), and (c) shortage of researches examining the role of anger in violent behavior and crime (Kroner & Reddon, 1992; Kroner et al., 1992). (Loza and Loza-Fanous, 1999b, p. 497)

■ ■ ■ ■ ■ ▬▬

A SERIAL RAPIST: A CASE STUDY

John is a 36-year-old serial rapist who has raped and physically and emotionally assaulted more than 100 women by his own count. The authorities believe it's more than that because John has been raping and molesting children and women since he was 10. Like many sexual offenders, John began molesting his own sister when she was 5. By any standard, John is a violent, devious, and emotionally labile man who has been in and out of jail for sexual assaults and drug-related crimes. The authorities who supervise John dislike him intensely, not only because of the crimes he's committed, but because he's not a likable person. In a prison full of unlikable people, John stands at the very top of the list.

Because the state in which John lives requires treatment for all felons convicted of sexual assault, John is being seen by a clinical psychologist in individual and group treatment. The prospects for improvement are not very promising, but John dutifully goes for treatment twice a week and attends a sex offender group once a week. The clinician is unlike anyone John has ever worked before, and he has seen many therapists over the years. At first, John thought he was manipulating the therapist because, in addition to being genuinely nice to John, the therapist let John talk. John often lied but the therapist didn't seem to call him on anything. But in time, John got tired of lying and despite his best attempts to never tell the therapist the truth, John found himself telling the therapist everything. At first, he did this to get the therapist's sympathy, which never seemed to happen. Then he began telling the therapist the truth because it felt good to unburden himself. When John was truthful, there was a shift in the therapist so subtle that John missed it at first. But after a time, John could feel the therapist becoming so in tune with him when he was truthful, that it felt to John as if the therapist were reading his mind and that he could feel John's emotional pain.

Truthfully, John is disgusted by his behavior. The fact that he can't control his impulses causes him to be full of self-loathing. To be so universally disliked is often too much for John to contain, and sometimes he breaks down and cries in the therapist's office. It felt terribly feminizing to John to cry and, yet, it felt wonderfully freeing. John began to realize that unlike other therapists he'd seen, this one never focused on his sexual offending. Instead, he seemed to focus on what John did well, on his dreams and aspirations in life, his regrets, and his feelings of disgust and guilt. When John shared these feelings with the therapist, a change began to take place in him that others noticed. He became open in his group treatment and spoke for many of the men in the group when he described the way he felt about himself. He sought men out in prison for advice. He helped a sick prisoner get treatment. As John began to change, so did the reaction to him by the people around him.

When John was released to go to a supervised halfway house after serving seven years for rape, he promised the therapist that in exchange for the help he'd received, that he would never rape or molest anyone again. After eight years, he has kept his word. When asked about the help he received in prison, John said,

No one thinks that people like me have feelings. We do. I began molesting my sister when she was 5. She's a drug addict today. I did that to my own sister, and God only knows the pain I brought to many other women and children. I'm full of regret over what I did. I don't want pity and I don't want anyone to think I didn't enjoy what I did, because I did enjoy it. Rapists have free rein to satisfy their impulsive needs for sex anytime they feel like it. Don't think that's not a powerful feeling, because it is. Any rapist who says they don't get off on it is a liar. At the same time, it's a disgusting feeling to think of what I've been doing to people. I saw one of the women I'd raped in a store six months after I'd raped her, and this beautiful woman of 20 looked like an old haggard witch. I couldn't sleep for days. Gradually, I couldn't get it up when I raped, and then I couldn't rape anymore. People think that once a rapist, always a rapist. It's not true. Like any sick behavior, you start to feel repulsed by it.

Gary, my therapist, seemed to understand what I was feeling right away. He never lectured me or told me how many lives I'd ruined. He knew I already knew that. What he did do was to listen, give me suggestions when I asked for them, tell me good things about myself that no one had ever said before, and he was patient. He didn't fall for my cons and he didn't push. He said we had lots of time and we could go at a pace that was comfortable for me. I had a lot of unburdening to do and I had a lot of sorrow inside. Gary listened, he was supportive, and I think more than anything, he genuinely liked me. Rapists are treated like scum in the "joint," and to have someone like Gary helping me, made me feel loved. I'd never felt that way before unless it was early in my life when I thought of my child molesting as a form of love. Rapists tell themselves lies all the time, and Gary just seemed to expect the truth. Pretty soon, so did I. Have I changed? Yes, I think I have. Will I ever be able to make up for the pain I've caused or help those poor women and children I molested? I'm sure I won't be, but I try every day to do something good. It'll never be enough but, like Gary said, you can only try and you're only human. He said that a lot.

THE STRENGTHS PERSPECTIVE WITH ABUSIVE CLIENTS

Van Wormer (1999) reminds us, "At the heart of the strengths perspective is a belief in the basic goodness of humankind, a faith that individuals, however unfortunate their plight, can discover strengths in themselves that they never knew existed" (p. 51). Van Wormer (pp. 54–56) goes on to suggest the use of the following strengths techniques with clients in correctional settings:

1. Seek the positive in terms of people's coping skills, and you will find it. Look beyond presenting symptoms and setbacks and encourage clients to identify their talents, dreams, insights, and fortitude.
2. Listen to the personal narratives. Through entering the world of the storyteller, the practitioner comes to grasp the client's reality, at the same time attending to signs of initiative, hope, and frustration with past counterproductive behavior that can help lead the client into a healthier outlook on life. The strengths therapist, by means of continual reinforcement of positives, seeks to help the client move away from what van den Bergh (1995, p. xix) calls "paralyzing narratives."
3. In contradistinction to the usual practice in interviewing known liars, con-artists, and thieves, which is to protect yourself from being used or manipulated, this approach would have the practitioner temporarily suspend skepticism or disbelief and enter the client's world as the client presents it. Showing a willing-

ness to listen to the client's own explanations and perceptions ultimately encourages the emergence of the client's truth.
4. Validate the pain where pain exists. Reinforce persistent efforts to alleviate the pain and help people recover from the specific injuries of oppression, neglect, and domination.
5. Don't dictate: collaborate through an agreed upon, mutual discovery of solutions among helpers, families, and support networks. Validation and collaboration are integral steps in a consciousness-raising process that can lead to healing and empowerment (Bricker-Jenkins, 1991).

Moxley and Washington (2001) suggest that the advantage of using the strengths perspective with chemically dependent clients, many of whom are abusive, is that it provides an alternative to labeling, which has dubious validity or value, and that it doesn't blame the client or focus on the client's deficiencies:

> Labeling, diagnosis, and blaming the victim can introduce into the process of treatment and into the treatment relationship itself a cynicism about the potential for change that can contaminate the thinking of both helpers and recipients and, as a consequence, limit their willingness to engage in the transformational process of change the practice of recovery demands. (p. 251)

Haun (1998) suggests a "restorative" approach to working with clients in the criminal justice system. The approach focuses on the positive nature of kindness, mercy coupled with justice, and forgiveness. This, Haun believes, will lead to repairing our fractured communities and reduce the social reasons for abusive behaviors that lead to involvement with the criminal justice system.

Brun and Rapp (2001) report that quantitative studies suggest positive outcomes when strengths-based case management is used with people who have substance-abuse problems. Substance abuse is sometimes associated with physical and sexual abuse, particularly domestic violence. Those outcomes reported by the authors include lessened drug use, retention in treatment programs, and improved functioning at work.

A CRITICAL RESPONSE

It has always been a belief in the helping professions that abuse is harmful to people, particularly children. The essence of this chapter is the implication not only that abuse is harmful, but that treating victims and perpetrators may not be effective using traditional approaches. But what if the assumption regarding the harm done by abuse is false and most people are able to cope with abusive behavior without professional help and without long-lasting harm? Rind and Tromovitch (1997) conducted a meta-analysis of the impact of child sexual abuse on the emotional functioning of adult victims and concluded that the impact was limited. They wrote,

> Our goal in the current study was to examine whether, in the population of persons with a history of CSA [child sexual abuse], this experience causes pervasive, intense

psychological harm for both genders. Most previous literature reviews have favored this viewpoint. However, their conclusions have generally been based on clinical and legal samples, which are not representative of the general population. To address this viewpoint, we examined studies that used national probability samples, because these samples provide the best available estimate of population characteristics. Our review does not support the prevailing viewpoint. The self-reported effects data imply that only a small proportion of persons with CSA experiences are permanently harmed and that a substantially greater proportion of females than males perceive harm from these experiences. Results from psychological adjustment measures imply that, although CSA is related to poorer adjustment in the general population, the magnitude of this relation is small. Further, data on confounding variables imply that this small relation cannot safely be assumed to reflect causal effects of the CSA. (p. 253)

If the authors are correct, and their work has resulted in intense negative feedback from professionals, perhaps the assumption that early life traumas generally cause emotional difficulties is incorrect and the data used in this chapter to show the negative impact of all three forms of abuse are also incorrect. Whether or not that's true, however, the main concern with this chapter is the lack of evidence that the strengths perspective works, either with victims or perpetrators of abuse. Certainly, this is a new approach to helping, but without some empirical evidence of treatment effectiveness, the strengths perspective, compelling as the case studies and the descriptions of treatment approaches make it, is still an untested approach. One would think that the agenda for researchers using this approach would be to do as much solid empirical research as possible. This doesn't seem to be the case, and Brun and Rapp's (2001) contention that the strengths perspective is effective with substance abusers is far less compelling than evidence offered in Chapter 7 on the very positive impact of self-help groups with substance abusers.

A positive aspect of this chapter is Van Wormer's work on the strengths approach with clients in the criminal justice system. Her work shows recognition of how degrading and dehumanizing the correctional system can be and how even abusive and violent people need to be treated with respect and dignity to create an environment that encourages change. In a fascinating article on the meaning of facial movements in determining whether someone is telling the truth, Gladwell (2002) describes an approach used by a police detective that sounds as if it's right out of the work done by Van Wormer:

> Harms gave the impression that he was deeply interested in me. It wasn't empathy. It was a kind of powerful curiosity. "I remember once, when I was working in prison custody, I used to shake prisoners hands," Harms said. "The other deputies thought that I was crazy. But I wanted to see what happened because that's what these men are starving for, some dignity and respect." (p. 48)

In a nutshell, the detective in Gladwell's article described the essence of the strengths perspective—dignity and respect. How few people have either in their lives, and how powerful both would be in creating an environment of change for even the most violent and abusive among us.

SUMMARY

This chapter considers the use of the strengths perspective with victims and perpetrators of abuse. Three types of abuse are discussed: domestic violence, child abuse, and sexual violence. Data regarding the effectiveness of traditional forms of helping are provided, and case studies are included to show the use of the strengths perspective with victims and perpetrators of abuse. The critical response included in this chapter notes the absence of empirical data supporting the effectiveness of the strengths perspective with abusive clients, and raises the issue, through a very controversial article, of the actual damage done by sexual abuse. The data seem quite clear, however, that physical and sexual abuse do great harm to children and adults. In another book written by the author (Glicken, 2004) on violence in very young children, more than 95 percent of the reason for early childhood violence can be tied, through a number of compelling research studies, to early-life physical and sexual abuse and neglect. It seems clear that abusive behavior does damage, and although some people are amazingly resilient, no one who has worked with clients who have been abused or neglected can deny the terrible toll it takes on their lives.

INTEGRATIVE QUESTIONS

1. Do you agree with Rind and Tromovitch (1997) that child sexual abuse results in limited long-term harm to adults abused as children? Perhaps you might find the entire article, noted in the reference section, and critique it.

2. How would you define the behaviors associated with domestic violence? Do you agree that many "normal" relationships include some degree of violence (throwing things, slapping, emotionally hurtful verbal statements, pushing, shoving)?

3. Doesn't it seem naïve to think that being nice to people who do terrible things can result in a change in behavior? Do you believe that what happened in the rape case study is very likely to happen to most rapists in treatment?

4. The lack of research data to prove the effectiveness of the strengths perspective is troubling. The data we do find are not as significant as the data noted in the use of self-help groups run by nonprofessionals. Is it possible that the strengths perspective is more a philosophy of treatment rather than a well-organized and proven theory of treatment?

5. Davis et al. (1998) believe that people in abusive relationships stay together for reasons that transcend the abuse. If this is the case, how can any treatment approach truly help the victims and perpetrators of abuse?

REFERENCES

Bricker-Jenkins, M. (1991). The propositions and assumptions of feminist social work practice. In M. Bricker-Jenkins, N.R. Hooyman, and N. Gottlieb, *Feminist social work practice in clinical settings* (pp. 271–303). Newbury Park, CA: Sage.

Brun, C., and Rapp, R.C. (2001). Strengths-based case management: Individuals' perspectives on strengths and the case manager relationship. *Social Work*, 46(3), 278–288.

Davis, R.C., Smith, B.E., and Nickles, L.B. (July 1998). The deterrent effect of prosecuting domestic violence misdemeanors. *Crime & Delinquency*, 44(3), 434–442.

Delson, N., and Kokish, R. (2002). Treating sexually abused children: Disturbing information about effectiveness. Article found on the Internet, November 25, 2002: http://www.delko.net/CSA%20kid%20treatment.htm.

DeMaris, A. (March 1989). Attrition in batterers counseling: The role of social and demographic factors. *Social Service Review*, 63, 73–94.

Eisikovits, Z.C., and Edelson, J.L. (September 1989). Intervening with men who batter: A critical review of the literature. *Social Service Review*, 63.

Gladwell, M. (August 5, 2002). The naked face. *The New Yorker*, 38–49.

Glicken, M.D., (2004). *Violent young children*. Boston: Allyn & Bacon/Longman.

Glicken, M.D., and Sechrest, D. (2003). *The role of the helping professions in treating the victims and perpetrators of violence*. Boston: Allyn & Bacon.

Greenfeld, L.A. (February 1997). *Sex offenses and offenders: An analysis of rape and sexual assault*. U.S. Department of Justice, Publication NCJ-163392. Washington, DC: U.S. Department of Justice.

Greenfeld, L.A. (March 1998). Violence by intimates: Analysis of data on crimes by current or former spouses, boyfriends, and girlfriends. Washington, DC: U.S. Department of Justice.

Haun, P. (1998). *Emerging criminal justice: Three pillars for a proactive justice system*. Thousand Oaks, CA: Sage.

Kaplan, S.J., Pelcovitz, D., and Labruna, V. (1999). Child and adolescent abuse and neglect research: A review of the past 10 years. Part I: physical and emotional abuse and neglect. *Journal of the American Academy of Child and Adolescent Psychiatry*, 38(10), 1214–1222.

Kroner, D., and Reddon, J.R. (1992). The anger expression scale and state-trait anger scale: Stability, reliability, and factor structure in an inmate sample. *Criminal Justice and Behavior*, 19, 397–408.

Kroner, D., Reddon, J.R., and Serin, R.C. (1992). The multidimensional anger inventory: Reliability and factor structure in an inmate sample. *Educational and Psychological Measurement*, 52, 687–693.

Looman, J., Abracen, J., and Nicholaichuk, T.P. (2000). Recidivism among treated sexual offenders and matched controls: Data from the Regional Treatment Center (Ontario). *Journal of Interpersonal Violence*, 15(3), 279–290.

Loza, W., and Loza-Fanous, A. (1999a). Anger and predicting violent and nonviolent offender's recidivism. *International Journal of Interpersonal Violence*, 14, 1014–1029.

Loza, W., and Loza Fanous, A. (1999b). The fallacy of reducing rape and violent recidivism by treating anger. *International Journal of Offender Therapy and Comparative Criminology*, 43(4), 492–502.

Lukefahr, J.L. (2001). Treatment of child abuse (Book Review). *Journal of the American Academy of Child and Adolescent Psychiatry*, 40(3), 383.

Moxley, D.P., and Washington, O.G.M. (2001). Strengths-based recovery practice in chemical dependency: A transpersonal perspective. *Families in Society*, 82(3), 251–262.

Neuman, E. (1995). Trouble with domestic violence. *Media Critic*, 2(1), 67–73.

Oates, R.K., and Bross, D.C. (1995). What have we learned about treating child physical abuse? A literature review of the last decade. *Journal of Child Abuse & Neglect*, 19, 463–473.

Reece, M., and Ludwig, S. (Eds.) (2001). *Treatment of child abuse*. New York: Lippincott, Williams & Wilkins.

Rind, B., and Tromovitch, P. (1997). A meta-analytic review of findings from national samples on psychological correlates of child sexual abuse. *Journal of Sex Research*, 34(3), 237–255.

Ryan, M. (1989). Milk the mouse. In *God hunger*. New York: Viking.

Sedlak, A. (1997). Risk factors for the occurrence of child abuse and neglect. *Journal of Aggression, Maltreatment and Trauma*, 1(1), 335–354.

Straus, M.A., and Gelles, R.J. (1986). Societal change and change in family violence from 1975 to 1985 as revealed by national surveys. *Journal of Marriage and the Family*, 48, 465–479.

U.S. Census Bureau. (1998). United States Census Department Report. Washington DC: U.S. Census Bureau.

U.S. Department of Health and Human Services, National Center on Child Abuse and Neglect, National Child Abuse and Neglect Data System. (1998). *Child maltreatment 1996: Reports from the states to the National Center on Child Abuse and Neglect.* Washington, DC: U.S. Government Printing Office.

U.S. Department of Justice. (2000). 1999 National report series publication. NCJ-180753. Washington, DC: U.S. Government Printing Office.

U.S. Department of Justice, Bureau of Justice Statistics. (2002). *Criminal victimization in the United States, 2000.* NCJ Report 188290. Retrieved October 13, 2002, from the World Wide Web: http://www.ojp.usdoj.gov/bjs/pub/pdf/cvus00.pdf.

van den Bergh, N. (Ed.). (1995). *Feminist practice in the 21st century.* Washington DC: NASW Press.

Van Wormer, K. (1999). The strengths perspective: A paradigm for correctional counseling. *Federal Probation,* 63(1), 51–58.

CHAPTER ELEVEN

THE STRENGTHS PERSPECTIVE WITH SUBSTANCE ABUSE

THE EXTENT OF THE PROBLEM

Substance abuse is one of the major health and mental health problems in America today. In a survey conducted by SAMSHA, an office of the U.S. Department of Health and Human Services (2000b), in the year 2000, 14.5 million Americans aged 12 or older were classified with dependence on or abuse of either alcohol or illicit drugs, amounting to 6.5 percent of the total population. Of this number, 1.9 million Americans were classified with dependence on or abuse of both alcohol and illicit drugs (0.9 percent of the population). An estimated 2.4 million Americans were dependent on or abused illicit drugs but not alcohol (1.1 percent of the total population), while an estimated 10.2 million Americans were dependent on or abused alcohol but not illicit drugs (4.6 percent of the population). According to *Alcohol Alert*, a publication of the National Institute of Alcohol Abuse and Alcoholism (2000), more than 700,000 Americans receive alcoholism treatment, alone, on any given day. Kann (2001), who used Health and Human Services data, wrote:

> Alcohol and other drug use are among our nation's most pervasive health and social concerns, contributing to leading causes of death such as motor vehicle crashes, other injuries, homicide, suicide, cancer, and HIV infection and AIDS (U.S. Department of Health and Human Services, 2000b). In addition, alcohol and other drug use contributes to social problems such as crime, lost workplace productivity, and lower educational achievement. Alcohol and other drug use among youth is common and contributes to health and social problems during adolescence, and is predictive of substance-related problems in adulthood. Consequently, surveillance of alcohol and other drug use among youth is a critical public health activity. (p. 725)

THE EFFECTIVENESS OF USUAL TREATMENTS
FOR SUBSTANCE ABUSE

Herman (2000) believes that individual psychotherapy can be helpful to substance abusers and suggests five situations in which therapy would be indicated: (1) as an appropriate introduction to treatment; (2) as a way of helping mildly or moderately dependent drug abusers; (3) when there are clear signs of emotional problems, such as severe depression, because these problems will interfere with the substance abuse treatment; (4) when clients progressing in 12-step programs begin to experience emerging feelings of guilt, shame, and grief; and (5) when a client's disturbed interpersonal functioning continues after a long period of sustained abstinence, therapy might help prevent a relapse.

One of the most frequently discussed treatment approaches to addiction in the literature is brief counseling. Miller and Sanchez (1994) identified six characteristics of brief counseling: feedback, responsibility, advice, menu, empathy, and self-efficacy. They suggest that brief interventions are a valuable approach for reducing alcohol addiction. However, Bien, Miller, and Tonigan (1993) reviewed 32 studies of brief interventions with alcohol abusers and found that the average study showed reduced alcohol use of only 30 percent. It isn't clear whether 30 percent of the subjects stopped drinking or whether consumption was reduced by 30 percent, indicating, in the case of alcohol abusers, continued use of alcohol at rates that might still be considered problematic. In a study of brief intervention with alcohol abusers, Chang et al. (1999) found that both the intervention group and the control groups significantly reduced their alcohol use. The difference between the two groups in the reduction of their alcohol abuse was minimal. In a study of 175 Mexican Americans who were abusing alcohol, Burge et al. (1997) noted that treated and untreated groups improved significantly over time, raising questions about the efficacy of treatment versus natural recovery. Seligman (1995), in an evaluation of a larger report by *Consumer Reports* on the effectiveness of psychotherapy, noted, "Alcoholics Anonymous (AA) did especially well, . . . significantly bettering mental health professionals [in the treatment of alcohol and drug-related problems]" (p. 10).

Fleming and Manwell (1998) reported that people with alcohol-related problems often receive counseling from primary care physicians or nursing staff in five or fewer standard office visits. The counseling consists of rational information about the negative impact of alcohol use, as well as practical advice on ways of reducing alcohol dependence and the availability of community resources. Gentilello et al. (1995) reported that 25 to 40 percent of the trauma patients seen in emergency rooms may be alcohol dependent. The authors found that a single motivational interview, at or near the time of discharge, reduced drinking levels and readmission for trauma during six months of follow-up. Monti et al. (1999) conducted a similar study with 18- to 19-year-olds admitted to an emergency room with alcohol-related injuries. After six months, all participants had decreased their alcohol consumption; however, "the group receiving brief intervention had a significantly lower incidence of drinking and driving, traffic violations, alcohol-related injuries, and alcohol-related problems" (p. 3).

Lu and McGuire (2002) studied the effectiveness of outpatient treatment with substance-abusing clients and came to the following conclusions: (1) The more severe the drug-use problem before treatment was initiated, the less likely clients were to discontinue drug use during treatment, when compared with other users; (2) clients reporting no substance abuse three months before admission were more likely to maintain abstinence than were those who reported abstinence only in the past one month; (3) heroin users were very unlikely to sustain abstinence during treatment, while marijuana users were less likely to sustain abstinence during treatment than were alcohol users; (4) clients with "psychiatric problems" were more likely to use drugs during treatment than were clients without psychiatric problems; (5) clients with legal problems related to their substance abuse had reduced chances of improving during the treatment; (6) clients who had multiple prior treatments for substance abuse were less likely to remain abstinent during and after treatment; (7) more educated clients were more likely to sustain abstinence after treatment; and (8) clients treated in urban agencies were less likely to maintain abstinence than were those treated in rural agencies.

■ ■ ■ ■ ■ ▇

JIM, A PERSONAL OBSERVATION ON SUBSTANCE ABUSE TREATMENT: A CASE STUDY

Jim is a 43-year-old alcohol and drug abuser who has had multiple treatments for substance abuse. Jim told the author the following about his experiences in treatment:

> I've been using alcohol since I was 10 and drugs since I was 13. I knew I was addicted the first time I used alcohol. A feeling of invincibility came over me that could only be sustained by using more alcohol and, later, more drugs. I've been pretty successful at work but a lot less successful in my personal life. I'm just ending my third marriage, and I've failed at many relationships, often with other drug and alcohol users. I've been in AA, residential programs, outpatient therapy, day programs, evening lockups, and behavior modification. Nothing seems to work. I can't quit by myself, and when I'm in residential treatment or lockups, I'm always able to get alcohol or drugs. A therapist is currently seeing me, and while I'm doing better than ever emotionally, I still use substances. The therapist I'm seeing is very sympathetic. We seldom talk about my drug use and focus instead on my failed marriages and relationships. He never criticizes me and often suggests ways to figure things out using the skills I have in other areas of my life, like work. This often helps, and I've been able to see that I can do things well in some parts of my life. The way I deal with those parts of my life sometimes helps with problems I have because of my substance abuse. For example, I was able to negotiate a very fair settlement with my current wife in our divorce because I use negotiating a lot at work. I think this will be a very amicable divorce. It feels good to do something right, even if it's ending a relationship I thought would last a long time.
>
> The therapist thinks the drinking and drug use will get better as I feel better about myself, but I don't know. I'm a drunk and a drug abuser. I like the lifestyle. Almost all my friends are drug and alcohol abusers. We support each other in bad times. We're like family in a way. My therapist has encouraged me to go to AA or some other group, but those groups are all so religious and preachy that they make me uncomfortable. I was told about a group made up of professionals like me that wasn't preachy or religious, and it sort of surprised me how comfortable I felt going there. We all still use alcohol and drugs, but it

(continued)

> seems to me I use a lot less these days. The group isn't so concerned with substance abuse and is more concerned that we live happy and productive lives. In that area, I'm not so happy with myself, and the people in the group seem realistic to me. They all have messed their lives up pretty badly and they think of themselves as failures. After about four months of going to the group, something started clicking in me and in the other people. We started to see that we were pretty successful people and just because we drank and used drugs, that didn't make us failures. Maybe that's dishonest, but we all started feeling better and we all found less reason to drink or do drugs. My substance use is way down. I haven't walked away from it completely, and there are days when I use too much, but it feels like I'm gradually getting better. I never thought I could go cold turkey. None of us do, but we're all gradually tapering off. My therapist thinks this is significant, and I just take it one day at a time and keep my fingers crossed.

THE STRENGTHS PERSPECTIVE AND SUBSTANCE ABUSE TREATMENT

Granfield and Cloud (1996) estimate that as many as 90 percent of all problem drinkers never enter treatment and that many suspend problematic use of alcohol without any form of treatment (Hingson et al., 1980; Roizen et al., 1978; Stall & Biernacki, 1989). Sobell et al. (1993) report that 82 percent of the alcoholics they studied who terminated their addiction did so by using natural recovery methods that excluded the use of a professional. In another example of the use of natural recovery techniques, Peele (1989) indicates that most ex-smokers discontinue their tobacco use without treatment, while many addicted substance abusers "mature out" of a variety of addictions, including heavy drinking and narcotics use (Snow, 1973; Winick, 1962). Biernacki (1986) reports that addicts who stop their addictions naturally use a range of strategies that include breaking off relationships with drug users, removing themselves from drug-using environments, building new structures in their lives, and using friends and family to provide support for discontinuing their substance abuse. Trice and Roman (1970) suggest that self-help groups with substance-abusing clients are particularly helpful because they tend to reduce personal responsibility with its related guilt and help build and maintain a support network that assists in continuing the changed behavior.

Granfield and Cloud (1996) studied middle-class alcoholics who had used natural recovery alone without professional help or self-help groups. Many of the participants in their study felt that the "ideological" base of some self-help programs was inconsistent with their own philosophies of life. For example, many felt that some self-help groups for substance abusers were overly religious, while other self-help groups believed in alcoholism as a lifetime struggle because of the disease model held by many self-help groups. The subjects in the study by Granfield and Cloud (1996) also felt that some self-help groups encouraged dependence, and that associating with other alcoholics would probably make recovery more difficult. In summarizing their findings, Granfield and Cloud (1996) reported,

> Many [research subjects] expressed strong opposition to the suggestion that they were powerless over their addictions. Such an ideology, they explained, not only was coun-

terproductive but was also extremely demeaning. These respondents saw themselves as efficacious people who often prided themselves on their past accomplishments. They viewed themselves as being individualists and strong-willed. One respondent, for instance, explained that "such programs encourage powerlessness" and that she would rather "trust her own instincts than the instincts of others." (p. 51)

To further underscore the idea of natural healing, Waldorf, Reinarman, and Murphy (1991) found that many addicted people with supportive elements in their lives (a job, family, and other close emotional supports) were able to "walk away" from the very heavy use of cocaine. The authors suggest that the "social context" of a drug user's life may positively influence the ability to discontinue drug use. Granfield and Cloud (1996) added to the social context notion of recovery by noting that many of the respondents in their sample had a great deal to lose if they continued their substance abuse:

> The respondents in our sample had relatively stable lives: they had jobs, supportive families, high school and college credentials, and other social supports that gave them reasons to alter their drug-taking behavior. Having much to lose gave our respondents incentives to transform their lives. However, when there is little to lose from heavy alcohol or drug use, there may be little to gain by quitting. (p. 55)

Humphreys (1998) studied the effectiveness of self-help groups with substance abusers by comparing two groups—one receiving in-patient care for substance abuse and the other attending self-help groups for substance abuse. At the conclusion of the study, the average participant assigned to a self-help group (AA) had used $8,840 in alcohol-related health care resources, as compared with $10,040 for the inpatient treatment participants. In a follow-up study, Humphreys (1998) compared outpatient services with self-help groups for the treatment of substance abuse. The clients in the self-help group had decreased alcohol consumption by 70 percent over three years and used 45 percent fewer health care services (about $1,800 less per person). Humphreys (1998) argued, "From a cost-conscious point of view, self-help groups should be the first option evaluated when an addicted individual makes initial contact with professional services (e.g., in a primary care appointment or a clinical assessment at a substance abuse agency or employee assistance program)" (p. 16).

Writing about the strengths perspective and the treatment of substance abuse, Moxley and Olivia (2001) note that recovery requires the client and the clinician to focus on the meaning of life and the higher purpose that binds us all together. The use of the strengths perspective to achieve this purpose does not deny the damage done by substance abuse or the pain it causes others. Furthermore, it doesn't deny the social conditions that often lead to substance abuse and the social forces that frequently disempower people who become addicted to substances. To achieve the goal of helping people with substance abuse problems find meaning in their lives, Moxley and Olivia (2001) wrote,

> [N]othing in life effectively helps people to survive even the worst conditions as the knowledge that one's life has meaning. A salient challenge is to ensure that individuals articulate their own perspectives concerning what the transpersonal means to them.

But it is the responsibility of the transpersonal practitioner to offer people in recovery opportunities to awaken. That is, to help individuals coping with recovery not only to make sense of a greater purpose and meaning in life but to do so within the context of their own individuation. (p. 259)

BARBARA: A CASE STUDY

Barbara is a 46-year-old woman who has been severely addicted to alcohol since age 13 and cocaine since age 17. She has had numerous experiences with inpatient and outpatient treatment and is currently a member of AA. Barbara has been unable to stop using drugs or alcohol and feels a despair coming over her. She wants to stop. A new and hopeful love relationship has been developing, and there are opportunities at work that appear very positive. Barbara doesn't think she can successfully handle either the relationship or the work assignments while she continues to abuse substances. Barbara is a solitary drinker and drug user. She is careful never to abuse drugs or alcohol in public and does all of her substance use in the privacy of her home. She is also very careful not to come to work showing signs of her substance abuse and uses her sick days and some of her vacation time to stay home when she has hangovers that would be noticeable to her co-workers, all of whom think that Barbara is quite a special woman and would be very surprised to know of her solitary abuse of alcohol and drugs.

Barbara is being seen in individual treatment using the strengths perspective. She is showing a number of signs of depression and has resisted many of the treatment techniques used by the therapist. Barbara wants the therapist to tell her what a terrible person she is and to focus on what is wrong with her. The therapist has patiently explained that this isn't the approach she uses and has slowly begun to help Barbara move from a negative point of view about herself to a more positive point of view. In one breakthrough session, the therapist and Barbara discussed her inability to stop using drugs and alcohol:

Barbara (B): This is going nowhere. I'm still drinking too much.

Therapist (T): And you're doing better than ever at work and you've begun a wonderful new relationship. I'm thrilled for you that you're doing so well.

B: But what about the drinking?

T: Barbara, I'm convinced that your drinking will modify itself in time. I think right now, you're experiencing the giddy realization that even though you're using substances and you'd like to stop, that you're a wonderfully resilient person and that you're coping well with many aspects of life.

B: But don't you think it would be better if I stopped?

T: I think right now you're making a plan to walk away from substances, and when you're ready, you'll do just that.

B: How can you be so sure?

T: Because you've made very positive changes in your life and reducing your substance use will just be another positive change when the right time comes.

B: You think it'll come?

T: I think it will, but I think you should recognize that it might not come overnight, but that it will happen gradually.

B: Maybe. I don't seem to be using it so much all the time.

T: I think that's a wonderful sign, and you should be proud of what you've accomplished.

B: You know, I am proud. I just thought you were supposed to stop all at once.

T: Some people do, but some people are able to decrease their substance use over time. That's what works best for them.

B: I've stopped using cocaine all together. It's expensive and I'm beginning to dislike the way I feel when I use it.

T: Why that's wonderful, Barbara.

B: But I'm still drinking a lot at home, and I still have mornings when I can't make it to work. I'd like to stop that sort of drinking.

T: It's something that will come in time, Barbara, and many of the same skills you use at work to resolve complicated organizational problems will be helpful to you in reducing or eliminating your alcohol use.

B: Do you honestly think so?

T: Yes, I do.

B: The other therapists I've seen have worked on my not using drugs and alcohol, or trying to show how my early life led to substance abuse. Why aren't you doing that?

T: Because I think people need to feel optimistic and positive about themselves to make positive life changes. I think they need to see the goodness they have inside and their many successes, not the failures in their lives. Just as you've begun to see the many substantially positive things you've accomplished in your life, and it's led to not using cocaine anymore, as we keep working together, your alcohol use may get a lot more manageable.

B: I think so, too. I'm not happy that I can't stop drinking now, but I feel a lot better physically, and you know, I haven't missed as much work as I used to. Johnny, my boyfriend, has been such a help. He's like a cheerleader, and I don't want to let him down. And AA is helping, too. It's inspirational, and I finally have started going to meetings a lot. It's amazing how many successful professional people I see at work. Some of them are like me and they are still drinking, but they're doing a lot better in their lives.

T: I'm very happy for you. It takes a strong person to do the kind of difficult work you've done.

B: I sure don't feel strong when I drink.

T: Perhaps, but you're strong in many other areas of your life.

B: That's true. You know, it really *is* true.

T: I'm glad.

DISCUSSION

The therapist explained her work with Barbara. She responded:

I think it's a mistake to focus on the alcohol and drug abuse. And it's a mistake, in my view, to focus on the pathology that led to Barbara abusing substances. The fact is that this is a

(continued)

CONTINUED

very strong, resilient, and successful woman who has many strengths. That she drinks and uses drugs and is still successful is a wonderful indication of her will to succeed despite great odds. And that other therapies haven't worked for her suggests that using those same approaches won't work in our therapy, either. Barbara discounts her successes and focuses on her negative behaviors. She needs to separate her substance use from her many achievements. When she's ready to stop abusing substances, she'll stop, hopefully, but there are no guarantees and there's no way to prevent her from using substances in the privacy of her home. That's a decision that has to come from her. Focusing on substance use is a "no win" approach, in my view. What does one say when she can't stop? My approach is to focus on her strengths and to improve her support network. Rather than being at home alone at night, she's in a relationship. She attends AA meetings at nights and has begun to develop a support network. Her opportunities to use substances have decreased, and a good deal of contact with new friends has become a substitute. She drinks out of loneliness. One way to decrease her drinking is to improve her social life. Few professionals have given her positive messages about herself. Instead, they define her as an alcoholic. No one stops drinking for long who defines themselves as a drunk. That's how Barbara saw herself before treatment began. She now sees herself as a successful person who drinks too much, and she's motivated, out of a feeling of liking herself, to reduce her alcohol and drug use.

That's the way I think treatment works with substance abusers, and, as you can see with Barbara, it seems to be working for her while many other treatment approaches haven't worked at all. But I want to be realistic. Substance abuse is a difficult problem to resolve. I haven't any magical solutions other than not to give up on people and to help them define themselves in much more positive ways. Will it lead to sobriety and abstinence? I surely hope so, but the decision to walk away from substances is a highly personal one, and I wish Barbara well and I keep my fingers crossed. I'm realistically optimistic. If she isn't able to stop using substances, I won't give up on her or feel that treatment has been a failure. I'll certainly keep helping her with life issues and to live with a problem that's often difficult to cure. I won't deny the possibility of medications to help her and have referred Barbara to a psychiatrist who has used antidepressants effectively with some substance abusers. My job is to remain positive and to refer her to resources that might be of additional help.

A CRITICAL RESPONSE

The idea that people can recover from severe alcoholism and drug dependence through natural recovery approaches is certainly one worth considering, although the majority of alcohol- and drug-dependent people we've spoken to say that it's an unlikely approach for severely alcohol- and drug-dependent people. One person with whom the author spoke managed a bar for seven years and suggested that there was a difference between those who quit their substance abuse spontaneously and those who never quit. She said,

> Real addicts never quit. They may try, but it's not successful. The people who quit are those who aren't really addicted. For sure, they drink or use drugs in excess, but they can walk away from it or go for periods of time without using alcohol or drugs. I think

that describes most substance abusers. The hard cases are the ones who will never quit no matter what, and maybe they're a smaller number of alcohol and drug abusers. If the definition of abuse is the amount and the frequency of alcohol and drug use, we forget that even though people use and abuse substances, they may not be physically dependent. I drank a quart of liquor four days a week on the job, and the other three days a week, I rarely drank at all. I don't think I was dependent, even though I abused alcohol.

Humphreys (1998) says that self-help groups may be more effective than professional help for addictions but doesn't tell us how many people stop attending self-help groups, how many substance abusers never quit using substances, or actual changes in socially responsible behaviors as a result of self-help groups. One hears the term *dry drunk* used to describe substance abusers who no longer abuse substances but still act as if they were. Their social behavior is infantile, they relate badly to spouses and loved ones, they have difficulty maintaining jobs, and they are involved in other addicted behaviors such as gambling or overspending. Humphreys fails to provide compelling evidence that self-help groups improve social behavior. If the only measure of the effectiveness of self-help groups is reduction in the use of substances, that's one thing, but Seligman (1999) and Sandage and Hill (2001) argue that treatment without improvement in social responsibility of clients is not really effective treatment. Reduction in the use of health care, the measure Humphreys uses to show self-help treatment effectiveness, may be a function of many other factors unrelated to treatment effectiveness. As measures of improved social functioning, we wonder about such variables as income levels, DWIs, reports of spousal and child abuse, and job performance, as a few examples. Can Humphreys show consistent improvement in these areas of functioning as a result of self-help groups? We wonder.

Another problem with the treatment of substance abuse is the lack of theoretical information about the most effective ways of helping people. While the research does seem to suggest that professional help is not as effective as we would like it to be, do we want self-help groups to take the place of professional treatment? Shouldn't we be trying desperately to come up with new and better approaches to treatment instead of a growing sense that self-help groups are the only viable alternative? Imagine anyone saying about the medical community what Felix-Ortiz et al. (2000) say about the mental health community and its lack of response to problems of addiction: "The emergence of self-help groups may reflect a societal response to failures within the mental health community. Self-help groups have developed where society has fallen short in meeting the needs of its members" (p. 339).

We also have serious doubts about the research on short-term treatment, including help given in the emergency room, leading to reduced use of alcohol and drugs. We doubt if one (1) educational session on the dangers of drug and alcohol abuse will lead to any substantial change in substance abuse, and we think, as Clifford, Maisto, and Franzke (2000) suggest, that many research studies on the effectiveness of treatment for substance abuse are full of methodological pitfalls. As Clifford and colleagues (2000) indicate,

It is recommended that treatment outcome studies be interpreted cautiously, particularly when the research protocols involved frequent and intensive follow-up interviews conducted across extended periods of time. The interpretation of data from alcohol treatment outcome studies must take into account potential confounding effects of the research assessment protocol. As noted by Clifford et al. (1997), the potential for research protocols to influence clinical outcomes affects not only the individual patient, it affects the field in general. Decision-making regarding patient referrals to the most appropriate treatment, particularly when empirically based, is contingent upon the quality of the available data. (p. 741)

As an example of the type of research errors made in substance abuse research, Ouimette, Finney, and Moos (1997) compared 12-step programs such as AA with cognitive-behavioral programs and programs that combined both approaches. One year after completion of treatment, all three types of programs had similar improvement rates related to alcohol consumption. Participants in 12-step programs had more "sustained abstinence" and better employment rates than participants in the other two programs, but Ouimette and colleagues (1997) caution the reader not to make more of these findings than is warranted because of nonrandom assignment of patients to the different treatment types. Doesn't this fact negate the importance of the finding completely? A careful look at many other substance abuse treatment studies suggests similar methodological concerns in a field in which empirically based studies are essential to good treatment results.

The lack of research on the use of the strengths perspective with substance abusers is, once again, a concern that needs to be resolved in future empirical studies. The case examples seem to imply that therapists can provide supportive treatment and never mention the need for caution when driving or many other potentially dangerous behaviors associated with substance abuse. How can that be acceptable for the professions who have a social mandate to assist clients in achieving socially responsible behavior?

SUMMARY

This chapter on substance abuse notes the high rates of alcohol and drug abuse in America. Research on the effectiveness of treatment is provided, but concerns about methodological issues should make the reader cautious in their acceptance of the studies. Information about the strengths perspective approach is included, with case studies provided that show the way the strengths perspective might be used to help clients abusing substances. Finally, the critical response raises issues with the actual benefits of self-help groups and notes the paucity of research proving that clients in self-help groups progress in their social functioning as a result of treatment. The absence of improvement in social functioning may result in clients who have stopped their substance abuse, certainly an important area of improvement, but who still function poorly in their personal relationships, on the job, and in the social arena where the term *dry drunk* is sometimes used to describe people who stop abusing substances but who still act immaturely.

INTEGRATIVE QUESTIONS

1. Seligman raises the bar on what is expected in treatment by saying that the result should be virtuous and successful clients who live the "good life." Is this a fair expectation for people who may have been severely drug and alcohol dependent for many years and who have difficulty not abusing substances, let alone living the good life?

2. Focusing on strengths in substance abusers often bypasses the dangerous behaviors associated with drug and alcohol abuse, for example, drunk driving, unsafe sexual activity, and dangerous behavior on the job. Is it fair to think that we can work with people and not focus on their negative and "at-risk" behaviors at some point?

3. Natural recovery and professional substance abuse counseling seem to work best for people who are more highly educated and have higher functioning social and work-related behaviors. Why do you think this is the case?

4. The critical responder seemed to call into question the benefits of emergency room counseling for drug- or alcohol-related accidents. Why wouldn't it be reasonable to assume that substance-abusing patients who had just experienced an accident might be highly motivated to change their behavior?

5. One of the examples given in the critical response suggests that some people either don't want to, or are unable to, stop their substance abusing. Do you think this implies that some people will never stop substance abusing and that any treatment is likely to be ineffective?

REFERENCES

Bien, T.J., Miller, W.R., and Tonigan, J.S. (1993). Brief interventions for alcohol problems: A review. *Addictions*, 88(3), 315–335.

Biernacki, P. (1986). *Pathways from heroin addiction: Recover without treatment.* Philadelphia: Temple University Press.

Burge, S.K., Amodei, N., Elkin, B., et al. (1997). An evaluation of two primary care interventions for alcohol abuse among Mexican-American patients. *Addiction*, 92(12), 1705–1716.

Chang, G., Wilkins-Haug, L., Berman, S., and Goetz, M.A. (1999). Brief intervention for alcohol use in pregnancy: A randomized trial. *Addiction*, 94(10), 1499–1508.

Clifford, P.R., Maisto, S.A., Franzke, L.H., Longabaugh, R., and Beattie, M.C. (1997). Alcohol treatment research protocols and treatment outcomes. Paper presented at the annual conference of the Research Society on Alcoholism, San Francisco. (March 15–19, 1997).

Clifford, P.R., Maisto, S.A., and Franzke, L.H. (2000). Alcohol treatment research follow-up and drinking behaviors. *Journal of Studies on Alcohol*, 61(5), 736–743.

Felix-Ortiz, M., Salazar, M.R., Gonzalez, J.R., Sorensen, J. L., and Plock, D. (2000). Addictions services: A qualitative evaluation of an assisted self-help group for drug-addicted clients in a structured outpatient treatment setting. *Community Mental Health Journal*, 36(4), 339–350.

Fleming, M., and Manwell, L.B. (1998). Brief intervention in primary care settings: A primary treatment method for at-risk, problem, and dependent drinkers. *Alcohol Research and Health*, 23(2), 128–137.

Gentilello, L.M., Donovan, D.M., Dunn, C.W., and Rivara, F.P. (1995). Alcohol interventions in trauma centers: Current practice and future directions. *JAMA* 274(13), 1043–1048.

Granfield, R., and Cloud, W. (Winter 1996). The elephant that no one sees: Natural recovery among middle-class addicts. *Journal of Drug Issues*, 26, 45–61.

Herman, M. (2000). Psychotherapy with substance abusers: Integration of psychodynamic and cognitive-behavioral approaches. *American Journal of Psychotherapy*, 54(4), 574–579.

Hingson, R., Scotch, N., Day, N., and Culbert, A. (1980). Recognizing and seeking help for drinking problems. *Journal of Studies on Alcohol*, 41, 1102–1117.

Humphreys, K. (Winter 1998). Can addiction-related self-help/mutual aid groups lower demand for professional substance abuse treatment? *Social Policy*, 29, 13–17.

Kann, L. (2001). Commentary. *Journal of Drug Issues*, 31, 725–727.

Lu, M., and McGuire, T.G. (2002). The productivity of outpatient treatment for substance abuse. *Journal of Human Resources*, 37(2), 309–335.

Miller, W.R., and Sanchez, V.C. (1994). Motivating young adults for treatment and lifestyle change. In G.S. Howard and P.E. Nathan (Eds.), *Alcohol use and misuse by young adults* (pp. 55–81). Notre Dame, IN: University of Notre Dame Press.

Monti, P.M., Colby, S.M., Barnett, N.P., et al. (1999). Brief intervention for harm reduction with alcohol-positive older adolescents in a hospital emergency department. *Journal of Consulting and Clinical Psychology*, 67(6), 989–994.

Moxley, D.P., and Olivia, G. (2001). Strengths-based recovery practice in chemical dependency: A transpersonal perspective. *Families in Society*, 82(3), 251–262.

National Institute of Alcohol Abuse and Alcoholism. (2000). *Alcohol alert*. NIAAA, 49.

Ouimette, P.C., Finney, J.W., and Moos, R.H. (1997). Twelve-step and cognitive-behavioral treatment for substance abuse: A comparison of treatment effectiveness. *Journal of Consulting and Clinical Psychology*, 65(2), 230–240.

Peele, S. (1989). *The diseasing of America: Addiction treatment out of control*. Lexington, MA.: Lexington Books.

Roizen, R., Cahalan, D., Lambert, E., Wiebel, W., and Shanks, P. (1978). Spontaneous remission among untreated problem drinkers. In. D. Kandel (Ed.), *Longitudinal research on drug use*. Washington, DC: Hemisphere Publishing.

Sandage, S.T., and Hill, P.C. (2001). The virtue of positive psychology: The rapprochement and challenge of an affirmative postmodern perspective. *Journal of the Theory of Social Behavior*, 31(3), 241–260.

Seligman, M.E.P. (1995). The effectiveness of psychotherapy: The *Consumer Reports* study. *American Psychologist*, 50(12), 965–974.

Seligman, M.E.P. (1999). The president's address. *American Psychologist*, 54, 559–562.

Snow, M. (1973). Maturing out of narcotic addiction in New York City. *International Journal of the Addictions*, 8(6), 932–938.

Sobell, L., Sobell, M., Toneatto, T., and Leo, G. (1993). What triggers the resolution of alcohol problems without treatment? *Alcoholism: Clinical and Experimental Research*, 17(2), 217–224.

Stall, R., and Biernacki, P. (1989). Spontaneous remission from the problematic use of substances. *International Journal of the Addictions*, 21, 1–23.

Trice, H., and Roman, P. (1970). Delabeling, relabeling, and Alcoholics Anonymous. *Social Problems*, 17, 538–546.

U.S. Department of Health and Human Services. (2000a). *Healthy people 2010*. (2nd Ed.). *With understanding and improving health and objectives for improving health*. 2 vols. Washington, DC: U.S. Government Printing Office.

U.S. Department of Health and Human Services. (2000b). *National household survey on drug abuse*. Retrieved October 13, 2002 from the World Wide Web: www.samhsa.gov/oas/dependence/chapter2.htm.

Waldorf, D., Reinarman, C., and Murphy, S. (1991). *Cocaine changes: The experience of using and quitting*. Philadelphia: Temple University Press.

Winick, C. (1962). Maturing out of narcotic addiction. *Bulletin on Narcotics*, 6, 1.

CHAPTER TWELVE

THE STRENGTHS PERSPECTIVE WITH MENTAL ILLNESS

THE EXTENT AND IMPACT OF MENTAL ILLNESS

Data from the Centers for Disease Control (1991) indicate that suicide, often associated with major depression, is the third leading cause of death among people ages 15 to 24 and the fourth leading cause of death among people ages 10 and 14. The incidence of suicide attempts among older adolescents is estimated at between 7 percent and 9 percent (CDC, 1991). Druss et al. (2000) indicate that about 3 million Americans have an emotional condition that affects their ability to work or to seek educational opportunities. Approximately 1 percent of the population develops schizophrenia during their lifetime and more than 2 million Americans suffer from the illness in a given year. Although schizophrenia affects men and women with equal frequency, the disorder often appears earlier in men than in women, usually in the late teens or early 20s for men and in the 20s to early 30s for women (National Institute of Mental Health, 1999). The National Institute of Mental Health (2001) estimates that over 2 million Americans experience the symptoms of bipolar disorder each year. Those symptoms include distorted views and thoughts, a lack of will to live, labile emotions that often seem out of control, and difficulties with cognition (Jamison, 1995).

Markowitz (1998) reports that people experiencing mental illness are "more likely to be unemployed, have less income, experience a diminished sense of self, and have fewer social supports" (p. 335). Part of the reason for this finding may be a function of the stigma attached to mental illness. Markowitz (1998) goes on to note, "Mentally ill persons may expect and experience rejection in part because they think less of themselves, have limited social opportunities and resources, and because of the severity of their illness" (p. 343). Markowitz also notes that the impact of anticipated rejection of mentally ill people is largely caused by "discriminatory experiences" in which the person observes an employer perceiving potential problems based solely on a diagnostic label and not on the person's actual behavior. This perception of rejection compounds feelings of low self-worth and depression.

In his discussion of an alternative paradigm for treating clients through a positive approach to people, Seligman (2002) notes that while the physical quality of life for Americans has certainly improved, depression rates are 10 times higher and life satisfaction rates are down substantially, suggesting widespread levels of unhappiness, depression, and more serious emotional disorders.

TRADITIONAL TREATMENTS OF MENTAL ILLNESS: A RESEARCH REVIEW

In a study of treatment attrition for mental health–related problems, Edlund et al. (2002) found a drop-out rate of 10 percent by the fifth visit, 18 percent by the tenth visit, and 20 percent by the twenty-fifth visit. Factors influencing attrition include concerns about treatment effectiveness and discomfort with the mental health treatment process. Commenting on these two issues to explain high attrition rates, Edlund et al. (2002) wrote:

> Results of our analyses of patients' attitudes about mental health care should raise at least two concerns. First, a large proportion of respondents believed that mental health treatments are not effective. Patients who held such a belief were significantly more likely to drop out of treatment. These findings suggest that clinicians should spend additional time and effort to educate their patients concerning the effectiveness of mental health treatments. In our recent study of mental health advocacy group members, we observed that receiving such education from providers was critically important in facilitating patients' acceptance of their treatments. Second, respondents who reported feeling uncomfortable in mental health care were substantially more likely to drop out than patients who reported being comfortable. A likely explanation for this finding is that expressing greater discomfort with mental health treatment is a marker of perceived stigma or other psychological barriers. (p. 850)

Manfred-Gilham, Sales, and Koeske (2002) studied social and vocational barriers to participation in treatment for mentally ill patients as one reason for treatment attrition. They concluded that the more realistically workers prepared clients for barriers they might encounter in the community, the more likely clients were to continue on with their treatment regimen. The authors wrote, "We have some evidence from Kazdin et al. (1997) that therapists' perceptions of barriers predicted client treatment continuation more strongly than did the client's own self-report" (p. 220). Manfred-Gilham, Sales, and Koeske (2002) noted that there is a strong link between the strategies used by the worker to prepare clients for barriers in their lives and the clients' ability to resolve those barriers.

Chambless and Ollendick (2001) reported on the attempt to identify psychological interventions that possess empirically based evidence of effectiveness for the treatment of emotional disorders. This attempt to objectify treatment is called "empirically supported treatments," or ESTs. The following is a summary of their research:

1. It is possible for independent raters to agree with one another on whether a treatment is effective.
2. Concerns about effectiveness studies suggest that nonempirically based research may be rejected as unscientific but, "No matter how large or consistent the body of evidence found for identified ESTs, findings will be dismissed as irrelevant by those with fundamentally different views, and such views characterize a number of practitioners and theorists in the psychotherapy area" (Chambless & Ollendick, 2001, p. 699).
3. Presenting evidence-based information about treatment effectiveness can be problematic because it is difficult to design a manual or report that meets the specific needs of all therapists. Therapists also are often unlikely to use such reports or manuals, even when provided.
4. ESTs are effective in clinical settings and with a diverse group of clients; however, the studies found to support evidence-based treatment were high in external validity but low on internal validity. Consequently, while the authors found no compelling evidence why ESTs could not be used in agencies by trained clinicians, more research on their use was suggested. Economic problems facing many social agencies suggest that manuals prescribing treatments for specific social and emotional problems will be more an issue as the economy softens and social and emotional services are curtailed. The authors wrote, "Whatever the reluctance of some to embrace ESTs, we expect that the economic and societal pressures on practitioners for accountability will encourage continued attention to these treatments" (Chambless & Ollendick, 2001, p. 700).

Using a computerized literature search to determine the impact of psychosocial interventions with the mentally ill, Bustillo et al. (2001) found that family therapy and assertive community treatment helped prevent psychotic relapses and rehospitalization. However, the authors reported that these two treatments have no consistent impact on "pervasive" psychotic symptoms, social functioning, or the ability to obtain and sustain employment. Social skills training may lead to improved social skills, but the authors found no evidence that it prevented rehospitalization, relapse into psychotic behavior, worsening of psychopathology, or improved employment status. Employment programs that placed and trained clients appeared to help them obtain competitive employment. Some studies, according to the authors, showed a decrease in delusions and hallucinations as a result of cognitive behavioral therapy. Personal psychotherapy may, according to the authors, also improve social functioning.

O'Connor (2001) has a more negative view of the effectiveness of treatment when applied to severely depressed clients. He says that research verifies that most depressed people receive care that is "superficial, inadequate, and based on false information" (p. 507). He also notes that close examination of most treatments for severe depression turn out to be inadequate (Mueller et al., 1999; Solomon et al., 2000), and he writes,

Many assumptions commonly held in the professional community—that newer anti-depressants are reliably safe and effective, that short-term cognitive and interpersonal psychotherapies help most patients, that many people with depression can be effectively treated in primary care, that most patients can recover from an episode of depression without lasting damage—on close examination, turn out not to be true at all. (p. 507)

LORNA, SPONTANEOUS REMISSION FROM MENTAL ILLNESS: A CASE STUDY

Lorna Andrews is a 37-year-old mother of three who experienced a psychotic episode at age 31 following the birth of her third child. Lorna had been suffering from severe depression for as long as she could remember. The birth of her third child and the postpartum depression she suffered as a result sent her into a deeply withdrawn and uncommunicative emotional state. She was diagnosed with undifferentiated schizophrenia (DSM-IV Code #295.90; American Psychiatric Association, 1994, p. 289), hospitalized, and placed on antipsychotic medication. Lorna's prognosis was poor, and the doctor treating her told Lorna's husband not to expect "miracles," and although the new medications might be helpful and could decrease some of Lorna's psychotic behavior, she was unlikely to be able to live without supervision and continued medication.

Lorna was hospitalized for three months without any change in her behavior. She was withdrawn, aloof, frequently spoke to herself, and experienced auditory and visual hallucinations. Because Lorna's medical benefits were running out, her husband Johnny decided to take Lorna home and asked his retired parents to help out in the house and to watch Lorna while he worked during the day. The children also were briefed on their mother's condition and were prepared for what her 10-year-old daughter called her "weird" behavior.

Within several days of coming home, Lorna began to pitch in and help around the house. She prepared lunches for her children to take to school and was much more communicative than she had been in the hospital. Within two weeks of release from the hospital, her behavior steadily improved, and she enrolled herself in a day program run by a local mental health clinic. In this program, she attended a patient-run recovery group and was asked to be on the patient-managed program board. She had an opportunity at the day program to see professionals, as needed, and felt comfortable in the setting, using it as an adjunct to the supervision of her medication done by her own psychiatrist. Four months after her release from the hospital, Lorna was functioning at a higher level than she had at any time in the previous 10 years of her marriage. Lorna isn't certain why she had a psychotic experience but wonders if it was connected to her postpartum depression. She said that she was perfectly aware of her surroundings during her hospitalization but felt immobilized and incapable of communicating. This feeling changed almost immediately on her return home.

DISCUSSION

Spontaneous remissions from psychoses are not uncommon, but the intriguing part of Lorna's remission is its relationship to her returning home. She was asked about the experience and why she thought her behavior changed so dramatically and so rapidly.

I don't think I was psychotic in the conventional sense. I was very depressed and withdrawn, and perhaps I was having hallucinations, I just can't really remember. But what I think happened was that I was overwhelmed with the responsibilities of caring for three young children. I was depressed before my pregnancy and it became worse during my pregnancy. After my delivery, I could hardly get up in the morning, and I was always tired. We really couldn't afford help around the house, and my folks and Johnny pitched in when they could. As the days went on, I found that I couldn't do many of the things I did before the baby was born, and I could feel myself going into this really deep depression. It was scary and I felt frightened by the changes I was experiencing. Small things frightened me. Noises seemed very loud. The children looked different. I started seeing colors and shapes that I knew were not real. Finally, I just stopped functioning all together. The antipsychotic medication numbed me. I can't imagine it helping a lot, and after a while, I "tongued" it like many of the other patients do and spit it into the toilet without swallowing. I was able to rest a lot and that helped. Many of the other patients were helpful and supportive, as were some of the staff. One orderly was very comforting and brought me passages from the Bible that gave me hope. When Johnny took me home, I suddenly felt ready to resume my life. The baby needed me, and the kids were quiet and considerate, but they looked so sad, it broke my heart. One day, I just started going again and that was sort of that.

The day program at the clinic has been a big help. The patients are wonderful and the professionals give us so much leeway. We feel very responsible for one another. Depression and mental illness are struggles that we take a minute at a time. Since I've been in the day program, my depression has improved a lot. I haven't seen a single person in the day program return to the hospital. When any of us start to decompensate, we all pitch in. We feel personally responsible for everyone in the program. If anyone goes back to the hospital, it feels like we just didn't help enough. I don't think I'm ever going to be really sick again, but I know that I'm depressed more than most people and that I have to stay on top of it. The day program helps me do that, and after having gone through the experience in the hospital, I value my life and my family more than ever. Insanity is frightening, and no one who has been mentally ill wants to be that sick again.

I can't speak for everyone, but hospitals for the mentally ill keep people sick. Had this happened to me, knowing what I know now, I would have had Johnny let me sleep for a week and then I would have entered the day program, where any behavior is seen as unique and acceptable. Hospitals see you as insane and treat you as if you're helpless. Our day program sees each of us as special and we're treated like adults. Being treated as an adult allows you to get back on your feet without being called mentally ill. And you know what? The people in this program are just as troubled as the people in the hospital. They just get on with their lives anyway. Most of them work and have families and function. In the hospital, we watched TV and we acted crazy. That's what was expected of us. Someone called the hospital I was in a "warehouse for crazy people." And you know what? That's exactly what it was.

APPLYING THE STRENGTHS PERSPECTIVE WITH MENTAL ILLNESS

Chronicity Is an Incorrect Notion

Carpenter (2002) suggests that mental health services have been developed in the belief that mental illness is a chronic disease requiring continual care and supervision. She notes that the DSM-IV (APA, 1994) indicates that schizophrenia will result in progressive deterioration and cautions readers that complete remission of symptoms is rare. However, research studies fail to support the concept of long-term chronicity in patients diagnosed with mental illness. Carpenter (2002) reports that most people with a diagnosis of schizophrenia or other serious mental illnesses experience "either complete or significant remission of symptoms, and work, have relationships, and otherwise engage in a challenging and fulfilling life" (89). In a study of over 500 adults diagnosed with schizophrenia, Huber, Gross, and Schuttler (1975) found that over one-fifth of the sample experienced complete remission and over two-fifths experienced significant remission of symptoms. In a 40-year follow-up study, Tsuang, Woolson, and Fleming (1979) found that 46 percent of those diagnosed with schizophrenia had no symptoms or had only nonincapacitating symptoms. The Vermont Longitudinal Study (Harding et al. 1986a, 1986b), a 20- to 25-year follow-up study of former state hospital patients, found that 72 percent of the people diagnosed with schizophrenia had only slight or no psychiatric symptoms. Despite these very optimistic findings, Carpenter (2002) writes,

> [T]he premise of chronicity continues to be widely accepted in the mental health system, and dismal prognoses continue to be communicated to people with psychiatric disabilities (Kruger, 2000). These prognoses leave little room for a sense of hope on the part of those labeled with mental illness and, as such, may become a self-fulfilling prophecy (Jimenez, 1988). The consumer–survivor recovery movement has sought to restore that hope with an innovative perspective on the meaning and course of psychiatric disability (Kruger, 2000). (p. 89)

Consumer–Survivor Recovery Movement

Carpenter (2002) defines the consumer–survivor recovery movement as one that assumes that people with psychiatric disabilities can and will recover. Recovery is defined as a process of achieving self-management through increased responsibility for one's own recovery. This process is aided by a sense of hope provided by a patient's professional, family, and support systems. Carpenter (2002) goes on to say that "the consumer–survivor definition of the experience of psychiatric disability is as much about recovery from the societal reaction to the disability as it is about recovery from the disability itself" (p. 90). Anthony (1993) believes that recovery from mental illness is aided by what he calls "recovery triggers," which include sharing with patients, their families, and the community the research indicating that many people with psychiatric problems do, in fact, recover. Another trigger involves information about the availability of services and treatment options such as self-help groups and alternative treatment approaches. Using a strengths-oriented assessment approach also helps in recovery and is a strong antidote to the medical model that perceives the person as pathological and often ignores significant growth and change. The experience of Nobel Prize–winner John Nash (Nasar, 1998), who had a gradual remission from many years of mental illness, is a reminder that people change, with time, and that remission of symptoms, if not outright cures of mental illness, are often possible.

Chinman et al. (2001) suggest that one way of improving treatment results and decreasing recidivism is through the mutual support of other mentally ill clients. According to the authors, mutual support groups reduce hospitalization rates, the amount of time spent in hospitals, symptoms, and days spent in the hospital. Additionally, they improve the quality of life and self-esteem, and contribute to better community reintegration of clients with severe psychiatric disorders (Davidson et al., 1999; Kyrouz & Humphreys, 1996; Reidy, 1992). Mutual support groups provide acceptance, empathy, a feeling of belonging to a community, necessary information to help with management of social and emotional problems, new ways of coping with problems, and role models who are coping well. Chinman et al. (2001) indicate, "Mutual support also operates through the 'helper-therapy' principle that suggests that by helping one another, participants increase their social status and self-esteem (Riessman, 1965)" (p. 220).

Beyond mutual support groups, Chinman et al. (2001) suggest that there is growing evidence that consumer-run services may prove to be very effective in helping clients with mental illnesses (Davidson et al., 1999). They state,

> Consumer providers are sometimes better able to empathize, to access social services, to appreciate clients' strengths, to be tolerant and flexible, to be patient and persistent, to be aware of and respond to clients' desires, and to be able to create supportive environments which can foster recovery and the restoration of community life (Dixon, Krauss, & Lehman, 1994; Kaufman, 1995). Other studies found that a consumer-run case management service yielded equivalent outcomes to those generated by a conventional case management team (Felton, Stastny, Shern, Blanch, Donahue, Knight, & Brown, 1995; Solomon & Draine, 1995d [1995]). (p. 220)

Writing about the treatment of severe depression, O'Connor (2001) indicates that we often fail to recognize that what keeps people depressed is their own view of their depression as ongoing, untreatable, and hopeless. These cognitive definitions of their depression, in time, become self-definitions that reinforce the depression and keep it from improving. To help his patients cope with their depressions, O'Connor (2001) provides them with "aphorisms" about depression that he believes serve as a way of changing long-held beliefs about their depression and about themselves. While cognitive in nature, the aphorisms O'Connor provides are also strengths based. Several aphorisms that seem particularly relevant to a book on the strengths perspective are "1) If I change what I do, I can change how I feel; 2) Change can come from anywhere; 3) I am more than my depression" (p. 517). These aphorisms are "assertions about the nature of depression and recovery from it, which help patients move toward taking an active role in questioning how the condition affects them" (p. 507). O'Connor goes on to say that "aphorisms [are] statements that perform an action simply by being spoken" (p. 512).

Writing about the use of the strengths perspective with caregivers of the mentally ill, Berg-Weger, Rubio, and Tebb (2001) state that the caregiver's role can be increased by strengthening the caregiver's sense of achievement. Strategies suggested by the authors include the following:

> (1) providing information and an array of coordinated, tangible services; (2) intervening as early as possible in the care giving process; (3) involving caregivers in the intervention planning process; (4) providing training on needed care giving skills, conflict resolution and behavior management for increased sense of mastery; and (5) encouraging flexibility. (p. 268)

Goals for Treatment

Seligman (2002), who wrote about depression as a form of learned helplessness, believes that a greater understanding of how people achieve happiness is needed in the helping professions and argues that we should be shifting psychology's paradigm away from its narrow-minded focus on pathology, victimology, and mental illness toward positive emotions, virtue, strength, and the positive institutions that increase people's levels of happiness. He lists three main approaches people can take in achieving happiness that may provide direction for the treatment of mental illness:

1. *The Good Life:* Some people are low on pleasure, but high on "absorption and immersion," meaning they take great pleasure in the things that they do. He gives as an example people who are so immersed in their work that time ceases to exist.
2. *The Pleasant Life:* This person achieves happiness through laughter and thriving on contentment, pleasure, and hope.
3. *The Meaningful Life:* These people apply their highest strengths and virtues for the greater good through charities, volunteer work, religious involvement, or politics.

Seligman (2002) believes that to achieve happiness, we must first identify into which of the above categories we fall and then ascertain our individual strengths and virtues and apply them in ways that lead to positive emotions. This uniquely strengths oriented approach is called "positive psychology" by Seligman and is a paradigm for applying the strengths perspective in helping situations. It is particularly appropriate for the mentally ill, and rather than offering a model of remission from illness or management of illness, it offers the possibility of a cure. Seligman goes on to note that psychology has ignored the importance of virtue, religion, and philosophy in the lives of people and believes that there are six core virtues that define the healthy person and that provide direction for the mental health worker: (1) wisdom and knowledge, (2) courage, (3) love and humanity, (4) justice, (5) temperance, and (6) spirituality and transcendence.

■ ■ ■ ■ ■

ROBERT, A MENTALLY ILL PATIENT: A CASE STUDY

Robert Byers is a 17-year-old with beginning signs of bipolar disorder. Robert walks around downtown Palm Springs, California, with his face painted like a mime and has several friends he hangs out with who accompany him on his walks. Robert curses a good deal, and many people find his behavior upsetting. The police try to handle Robert gently. Each encounter with the police to modify his behavior brings torrents of abuse and curse words directed at the police and anyone else within hearing distance. Robert often walks through the streets and obsesses about his "hassles" with the police for days.

Robert's parents are affluent enough to allow Robert to live in an apartment in Palm Springs and to see a private therapist and psychiatrist. They briefly had Robert hospitalized, but the experience was so stigmatizing for the family that they prefer the illusion of telling friends that Robert is attending a good private school and is doing well. In fact, Robert is doing badly. He uses illicit drugs, doesn't take his medications, misses his therapy sessions, and is very close to being in legal trouble because of his confrontations with the local police. Robert's parents seldom see him, and even though he is under age, the police have found the parents uncooperative and unwilling to come to Palm Springs to help develop a plan for Robert's care. Instead, his parents refer the police to his therapist.

After a particularly bad encounter with the police, in which Robert assaulted a police officer, he was involuntarily committed to a psychiatric unit of a local general hospital for a mandatory 72-hour observation period. He was diagnosed with *bipolar disorder* with increasing signs of psychosis and was sent, by the court, to a residential facility in Palm Springs with a day program, which he was required to attend or be remanded to court and charged with assault of a police officer, a class A felony in California.

Robert was initially a very hostile and uncooperative patient. Visits with friends were withheld because of fear of drug exchanges. His medication needs were met by giving him shots because it was felt that he wouldn't take his medication orally. Over a two-week period, his behavior began to moderate and he was integrated into the day program while still under close observation in the clinic's locked inpatient unit. Initially uncooperative and belligerent in the day program, within a month Robert began cooperating. His behavior moderated so that the bipolar symptoms were almost unnoticeable. He attended high school in the facility and turned out to be a highly intelligent young man with very strong math and science skills. The patients in the residential facility were accepting and positive, and Robert began feeling that he was part of a family, a unique experience for him. He contacted his parents by phone and, astonished by the change, they began to come for visits. In time, his parents agreed to begin family therapy with Robert and to be part of a parents' group to learn more about the management of bipolar disorder. Robert is very involved in the patient-managed day program and helps determine the program schedule for field trips. He is also on the committee that meets to consider violations of the patient rules of conduct, developed and enforced by the patients. Robert feels that it is a privilege to be in the day program and sees the changes in his life as a direct result of his involvement in the day program.

DISCUSSION
Robert spoke to the author about a year after his initial involuntary hospitalization:

> I don't think I even understood how disturbed I was before I was hospitalized. I was angry and using drugs, and I thought the problem was with other people, not with me. When I was sent to the facility, I was very angry and uncooperative. The medication certainly helped calm me down, but more than that, the people in the program were wonderful. I'd never really felt that I was part of a family before since mine is so dysfunctional. Being in the program at the clinic, I started to feel loved and valued by the other patients and the staff. These were new feelings for me, and I began to respond to other people in the same way. During my drug years, I would have thought that being nice to people would result in a knife in my back, but being nice to others and having them be nice to me was like a great experience. And the people in the clinic program, I mean we were all pretty wacky, but most of us are working or going to school. I thought wacky people sat around and vegetated. Not in this program. In this program you work hard, you go to school, you do your job, and you help others. There are days I feel pretty crazy, but others see it and I feel protected. No one is going to let me fall apart and do the things I did before I came here.

(continued)

CONTINUED

I see my family every weekend and, you know, we're a lot better. I've gone for weekend furloughs, and while we don't always click, we do better than before. It isn't a good place for me to be since it's too close to all the things that got me into trouble, but I love my family and I'm pretty happy that things in that area have improved. I'm doing really well in school and they tell me I have ability in math and science. I'm sort of surprised since I always thought I was pretty stupid. And you don't find any bullshiters here. They're very honest about my medical problems and how I have to stay on top of them. Bipolar disorder is something you have to be intelligent about. When I start feeling hyper or down, I talk to the staff and they make certain I get some changes in my medications. It's not rocket science. It's knowing how your body is operating and making sure you don't let it go bonkers. The big difference is that I used to medicate myself with uppers, and downers, and every drug I could find. The staff knows a lot more about medication, and I know a lot more about my body. We work together and we trust that we'll do the right thing. It's pretty great. When I get ready to leave high school and go to college, I intend to stay with the program and live here in the facility. I know I can't do that forever, but it's home now, and you shouldn't leave home until you're ready. At least, that's what I think.

A CRITICAL RESPONSE

It's certainly true that labels can be stigmatizing. With the mentally ill, they are particularly stigmatizing and conjure up images, in the popular imagination, of behavior that is not only inaccurate, but also pejorative and demeaning. On the other hand, a certain number of mentally ill patients are dangerous to others or actively harass people, as one of the case examples demonstrates. These are not people who should be unsupervised, and management by other patients would probably be unsuccessful and, perhaps, dangerous. Still, studies challenging the idea of chronicity are welcome changes in our outlook on mental illness, and new medications bode well for the treatment of even complex and nonresponsive disorders. Mental hospitals have been stereotyped in films like *The Snake Pit* and *One Flew Over the Cuckoo's Nest*. It's not always the case that these stereotypes are necessarily well deserved. Sometimes they create antagonisms between the patient, the patient's family, and the hospital that makes emergency hospital treatment difficult. Although keeping people out of hospitals for mental disorders is admirable, there are times when it is necessary to hospitalize the mentally ill, particularly in cases in which people are dangerous to themselves or others. The first case study paints a fairly typical and certainly negative picture of mental hospitals that is often reinforced by outpatient programs and by self-help groups. Rather than antagonism, we should have a cooperative relationship with residential facilities. Hospitals are still the front line in the treatment of mental illness.

Finally, on the issue of spontaneous remissions, we need not see this as a magical event. Remission in mental illness is a state similar to that of remission in a variety of other illnesses. Just as we are uncertain of the reasons for the remission in those illnesses, we are also uncertain about the reasons for remission in the mentally ill. One easy answer to spontaneous remissions is the all too common mistake of diagnosing a mental disorder when the symptoms are related to a physical problem that either goes away in time or are treated in conjunction with the mental illness. Another reason is that the diagnosis of mental illness may be in error, or the symptoms of mental illness are transitory. Reactions to medications, cultural and religious issues, physical illness, isolation, weather, and a host of conditions may prompt unusual behavior, but a diagnosable mental illness may not, in reality, exist. Certainly, however, it is not wise to think of mental illness as a chronic state, when, much like many physical conditions, the illness gets better in time and the person returns to normalcy.

SUMMARY

This chapter discusses the prevalence of mental illness in the United States and the often stigmatizing effect the label of mental illness has on patients. This stigma frequently inhibits improvement in the condition and may affect employment opportunities and further social and financial possibilities in a person's life. The strengths perspective approach to mental illness suggests that it should be treated as a condition affecting functioning, but that the client should not be made to think that the condition is permanent or that change isn't possible. Several case studies suggest the way in which mental illness may respond to treatment and the possibility of spontaneous remission of the symptoms. The critical response argues for a better working relationship between hospitals serving the mentally ill and the professionals who run outpatient treatment programs. Concern is also raised that spontaneous remission of mental illness may be a misdiagnosis of the problem or that the symptoms may be caused by physical conditions that are likely to improve with time and treatment.

INTEGRATIVE QUESTIONS

1. This chapter argues that most mentally ill people improve and stay improved over time. Do you think this is because of advances in treatment, spontaneous remission, or natural healing?

2. Hospitals for the mentally ill have been described as places where patients are often ignored and little actual treatment takes place. Do you think that this is true, and do you think the mistreatment of the mentally ill is any worse than the treatment of people who enter hospitals for physical reasons?

3. In this chapter, there was little by way of an explanation of the cause of mental illness. It appears, however, that the cause is usually thought to be biochemical. Can you think of examples of other causes of mental illness?

4. If you live in a large city, you often see people whose behavior appears very much like that of Robert in the case study. Isn't it possible that people who live alternative lifestyles are perfectly sane but that our tolerance of their behavior is low?

5. Lorna, in the first case study, doubts that she was mentally ill but wasn't able to communicate this to her family or to treatment personnel. How might we more accurately gauge the extent of troubled behavior when clients aren't able to verbally share their feelings and perceptions?

REFERENCES

American Psychiatric Association. (1994). *Diagnostic and statistical manual of mental disorders* (4th Ed.). Washington, DC: American Psychiatric Association.

Anthony, W.A. (1993). Recovery from mental illness: The guiding vision of the mental health service system in the 1990's. *Psychosocial Rehabilitation Journal,* 16, 12–23.

Berg-Weger, M., Rubio, D.M., and Tebb, S.S. (2001). Strengths-based practice with family caregivers of the chronically ill: Qualitative insights. *Families in Society,* 82(3), 263–272.

Bustillo, J.R., Lauriello, J.H., Keith, W.P., and Samuel, J. (2001). The psychosocial treatment of schizophrenia: An update. *American Journal of Psychiatry,* 158(2), 163–175.

Carpenter, J. (2002). Mental health recovery paradigm: Implications for social work. *Health & Social Work,* 27(2), 86–94.

Centers for Disease Control. (1991). Attempted suicide among high school students—United States, 1990. *Journal of the American Medical Association,* 266, 1911–1912.

Chambless, D.L., and Ollendick, T.H. (2001). Empirically supported psychological interventions: Controversies and evidence. *Annual Review of Psychology,* 52, 685–716.

Chinman, M.J., Weingarten, R., Stayner, D., and Davidson, L. (2001). Chronicity reconsidered: Improving person–environment fit through a consumer-run service. *Community Mental Health Journal,* 37(3), 215–229.

Davidson, L., Chinman, M., Moos, B., Weingarten, R., Stayner, D.A., and Tebes, J.K. (1999). Peer support among individuals with severe mental illness: A review of the evidence. *Clinical Psychology: Science and Practice,* 6, 165–187.

Dixon, L., Krauss, N., and Lehman, A.L. (1994). Consumers as service providers: The promise and challenge. *Community Mental Health Journal,* 30, 615–625.

Druss, B.G., Marcus, S.C., Rosenheck, R.A., et al. (2000). Understanding disability in mental and general medical conditions. *American Journal of Psychiatry,* 157(9), 1485–1491.

Edlund, M.J., Wang, P.S., Berglund, P.A., et al. (2002). Dropping out of mental health treatment patterns and predictors among epidemiological survey respondents in the United States and Ontario. *American Journal of Psychiatry,* 159(5), 845–851.

Felton, C.J., Stastny, P., Shern, D., Blanch, A., Donahue, S. A., Knight, E., and Brown, C. (1995). Consumers as peer specialists on intensive case management teams: Impact on client outcomes. *Psychiatric Services,* 46, 1037–1044.

Harding, C.M., Brooks, G.W., Ashikaga, T., Strauss, J.S., and Breier, A. (1986a). The Vermont longitudinal study of persons with severe mental illness: I. Methodology, study sample, and overall status 32 years later. *American Journal of Psychiatry,* 144, 718–725.

Harding, C.M., Brooks, G.W., Ashikaga, T., Strauss, J.S., and Breier, A. (1986b). The Vermont longitudinal study of persons with severe mental illness: II. Long-term outcome of subjects who retrospectively met DSM-II criteria for schizophrenia. *American Journal of Psychiatry,* 144, 727–735.

Huber, G., Gross, G., and Schuttler, R. (1975). A long-term follow-up study of schizophrenia: Psychiatric course of illness and prognosis. *Acta Psychiatrica Scandinavica,* 52, 49–57.

Jamison, K.R. (1995). *An unquiet mind.* New York: Alfred A. Knopf.

Jimenez, M.A. (1988). Chronicity in mental disorders: Evolution of a concept. *Social Casework,* 69, 627–633.

Kaufman, C. (1995). The self-help employment center: Some outcomes from the first year. *Psychosocial Rehabilitation Journal,* 18, 145–162.

Kazdin, A.E., Holland, L., Crowley, M., and Breton, S. (1997). Barriers to treatment participation scale: Evaluation and validation in the context of child outpatient treatment. *Journal of Child Psychology and Psychiatry,* 38(8), 1051–1062.

Kruger, A. (2000). Schizophrenia: Recovery and hope. *Psychiatric Rehabilitation Journal,* 24, 29–37.

Kyrouz, E., and Humphreys, K. (1996). Do psychiatrically disabled people benefit from participation in self-help/mutual aid organizations? A research review. *The Community Psychologist,* 29, 21–25.

Manfred-Gilham, J.J., Sales, E., and Koeske, G. (2002). Therapist and case manager perceptions of client barriers to treatment participation and use of engagement strategies. *Community Mental Health Journal*, 38(3), 213–221.

Markowitz, F.E. (1998). The effects of stigma on the psychological well-being and life satisfaction of persons with mental illness. *Journal of Health and Social Behavior*, 39(4), 335–347.

Mueller, T.I., Leon, A.C., Keller, M.B., et al. (1999). Recurrence after recovery from major depressive disorder during 15 years of observational follow-up. *American Journal of Psychiatry*, 156, 1.

Nasar, S. (1998). *A brilliant mind: The life of mathematical genius and Nobel laureate John Nash.* New York: Simon and Schuster

National Institute of Mental Health. (1999). Schizophrenia. Publication 99-3517. Bethesda, MD. Retrieved October 13, 2002, from the World Wide Web: www.nimh.nih.gov/publicat/schizoph.cfm.

National Institute of Mental Health (2001). Bi-polar disorder. Publication 01-3679. Bethesda, MD. Retrieved October 13, 2002 from the World Wide Web: www.nimh.nih.gov/publicat/bipolar.cfm#intro.

O'Connor, R. (2001). Active treatment of depression. *American Journal of Psychotherapy*, 55(4), 507–530.

Reidy, A. (1992). Shattering illusions of difference. *Resources*, 4, 3–6.

Riessman, F. (1965). The helper-therapy principle. *Social Work*, 10, 27–32.

Seligman, M.E.P. (2002). *Authentic happiness: New positive psychology to realize your potential for lasting fulfillment.* New York: Free Press.

Solomon, D.A., Keller, M.B., Leon, A.C., et al. (2000). Multiple recurrences of major depressive disorder. *American Journal of Psychiatry*, 157, 229–233.

Solomon, P., and Draine, J. (1995). The efficacy of a consumer case management team: Two year outcomes of a randomized trail. *Journal of Mental Health Administration*, 22, 135–146.

Tsuang, M.T., Woolson, R.F., and Fleming, M.S. (1979). Long-term outcome of major psychoses. *Archives of General Psychiatry*, 36, 1295–1301.

CHAPTER THIRTEEN

THE STRENGTHS PERSPECTIVE WITH SERIOUS ILLNESS, DISABILITY, TERMINAL ILLNESS, AND BEREAVEMENT

My strength is in my vulnerability
—Psalms

THE SEARCH FOR MEANING

In this chapter, four health-related issues are considered: serious illness, disability, terminal illness, and bereavement. Much of the chapter discusses the importance of life meaning as a way of coping with all four conditions. As the literature so clearly states, significant personal growth often takes place when people deal with illness, disability, and bereavement. Kubler-Ross (1969, 1997) reminds us that coping with the possibility of death and disability often leads to life-changing growth and new and more complex behaviors that focus on the meaning of life. Greenstein and Breitbart (2000) write, "Existentialist thinkers, such as Frankl, view suffering as a potential springboard, both for having a need for meaning and for finding it" (p. 486). Frankl (1978) believed that life meaning could be found in our actions, our values, and, significant to this chapter, our suffering. Commenting on the meaning of suffering, Frankl wrote,

> This is why life never ceases to have and to retain a meaning to the last moment. Even facing an ineluctable fate, e.g., an incurable disease, there is still granted to man a chance to fulfill even the deepest possible meaning. What matters, then, is that the stand he takes in his predicament . . . the attitude we choose in suffering. (p. 24)

One aspect of the search for meaning is the development of spirituality in the midst of trying to understand life-changing or life-ending disabilities or illnesses. Finn (1999) writes that spirituality leads to "an unfolding consciousness about the meaning of human existence. Life crises influence this unfolding by stimulating questions about the meaning of existence" (p. 487). Balk (1999) suggests that three issues must be present for a life crisis to result in spiritual changes: "The situation must create a psychological imbalance or disequilibrium that resists readily being stabilized; there must be time for reflection; and the person's life must forever afterwards be colored by the crisis" (p. 485).

TERMINAL ILLNESS

Hardwig (2000) suggests that people with terminal illnesses often suffer from an inability to find meaning in the last moments of their lives and are unable to deal with significant issues related to family and other loved ones. Often they feel "cast out" because they are no longer healthy or productive and feel that they are a burden to others because they are unable to care for themselves, in even very basic ways. Hardwig notes that people with terminal illnesses often feel isolated and angry about their lives and frequently feel abandoned by friends, family, and by God. Most of all, they feel betrayed by their own bodies and often have no way of dealing with the physical and emotional changes they are experiencing. Hardwig (2000) goes on to say, "Facing death brings to the surface questions about what life is all about. Long-buried assumptions and commitments are revealed. And many find that the beliefs and values they have lived by no longer seem valid or do not sustain them. These are the ingredients of a spiritual crisis, the stuff of spiritual suffering" (p. 29).

Hardwig (2000) indicates that the following problems facing people with terminal illness frequently create difficulty in finding meaning in the last moments of life: (1) The medical care system often takes important treatment decisions out of the hands of terminally ill patients; (2) use of pain-killing drugs leave dying patients unable to think clearly, and distort the days and weeks before death occurs; (3) no one listens to terminally ill patients or helps them resolve unfinished business; (4) in a death-denying society, families may not allow terminally ill patients to discuss issues that often help the terminally ill person find important life messages and also help the family with bereavement; and (5) family members may not want to "let go" of a loved one and may ignore the terminally ill patient's desire to end life naturally without intrusive life supports or treatments.

Caffrey (2000) confirms the role of psychotherapy in work with terminal illness. He believes that "palliative" care alone, the reduction of anxiety and depression related to dying, is shortsighted. In discussing his experiences with a dying Vietnam veteran, Caffrey wrote:

> As illustrated by Bruce's deep, positive transference, voluntary exposure to his trauma, striking life improvements, and personal and social integration, end-of-life psychotherapy can go well beyond conventionally understood palliative care. I hope that Bruce's therapeutic success will inspire therapists working with terminally ill persons

to keep their sights high, feel confident that major growth is possible, and communicate that confidence to their patients. (p. 529)

BEREAVEMENT

Balk (1999) believes that bereavement, the loss of a significant person in one's life, can result in physical and emotional problems, the most significant of which may include

> intense and long-lasting reactions such as fear, anger, and sorrow. Bereavement affects cognitive functioning (e.g., memory distortions, attention deficits, and ongoing vigilance for danger) and behavior (e.g., sleep disturbances, excessive drinking, increased cigarette smoking, and reckless risk taking). It impacts social relationships as outsiders to the grief become noticeably uncomfortable when around the bereaved. And bereavement affects spirituality by challenging the griever's very assumptions about the meaning of human existence. (p. 486)

Balk (1999) suggests that bereavement is a catalyst for spiritual change because it triggers a life-threatening crisis that, in turn, threatens "well-being, challenges established coping repertoire, and over time, produces harmful and/or beneficial outcomes" (p. 486). While agreeing that loss of a loved one creates a life-changing crisis, Stroebe (2001) challenges the "grief work" we usually associate with the treatment of bereavement. She points out a number of problems with grief work. Her first concern is the limited empirical evidence that working through grief is a more effective process than not working it through. A second concern is that grief work notions lack universal application. There are very different ways of working through grief prescribed not only by cultures, but also by religion, by genders, and by socioeconomic groups. She writes, "There is no convincing evidence that other cultural prescriptions are less conducive to adaptation than those of our own" (p. 654). A third concern is that grief work limits itself to dysfunctional adaptations and has symptom removal rather than a broader understanding as its end goal. A final concern is that grief work lacks a precise definition and is poorly operationalized in research studies. This results in Stroebe (2001) asking, "What is being worked through? In what way?" (p. 655).

In answering these questions, Stroebe (2001) identifies the following major issues that might help in our understanding of bereavement: (1) How do people who have suffered the loss of a loved one cope with their loss? (2) How do we differentiate between normal and what Stroebe calls "complicated" or dysfunctional grief? (3) What are the defining causes of traumatic and nontraumatic bereavement? (4) Can people who cope with the death of a loved one do so in ways that are unrelated to meaning-of-life issues and focus primarily on coping with the removal of typical grief-related symptoms (depressions, sleep problems, inability to take over functions formerly performed by a loved one, grief that lasts a very long time, etc.)? (5) Does nontraumatic grief with no underlying symptoms following the loss of a loved one suggest denial or other behaviors that may result in later and, perhaps, more severe grief?

DISABILITIES

Finn (1999) reports that there are as many as 24 million Americans with a severe disabling condition. Nationally, Finn indicates that "there are an estimated 1.7 million people with disabilities who are homebound and an additional 12.5 million who are temporarily homebound. There also are many caretakers of disabled and elderly people who are essentially homebound as a result of their responsibilities at home" (p. 220). Finn (1999, p. 220) goes on to say that a number of social and emotional problems develop from being "alienated" or "socially quarantined" from the larger society, including depression, loneliness, alienation, lack of social interaction, lack of information, and lack of access to employment (Braithwaite, 1996; Coleman, 1997; Shworles, 1983).

In a study of the impact of physical and emotional disabilities, Druss et al. (2000) write,

> Combined mental and general medical disabilities were associated with high levels of difficulty across a variety of functional domains: bed days, perceived stigma, employment status, disability payments, and reported discrimination. . . . Respondents with deficits across multiple domains have few areas of intact function available to make up for their existing deficits. The uniquely high levels of functional impairment associated with combined conditions speak to the potential importance of integrated programs that can simultaneously address an individual's medical and psychiatric needs. (p. 1489)

Finn (1999) studied the content of messages sent by people with disabilities using the Internet as a form of group therapy. He found that most correspondents wanted to talk about their health and about specific issues of treatment and quality of care but that, overall, the correspondents acted as a support group, helping others cope with emotional, medical, and social issues. These issues ranged from "highly technical descriptions of medications, procedures, and equipment to subjective accounts of treatment experiences. There also was considerable discussion of interpersonal relationship issues such as marital relationships, dating, and sexuality" (p. 228). Finn (1999) reminds us that many disabled people are homebound and that the Internet becomes an important part of the communicating they do each day. This is particularly true for homebound people who may also have difficulty speaking or hearing.

COPING WITH SERIOUS ILLNESS: A PERSONAL VIEW

The following discussion of coping with a serious illness was written by the author's daughter (Glicken, 2002, p. A-15) and describes her way of coping with childhood-onset diabetes:

> Two weeks after my tenth birthday, on the joyous occasion of St. Patrick's Day, I was diagnosed with diabetes. Back then, the average life span of those with Type I Diabetes was 27 years. If anyone had informed me at the time that I would only live 17 more

years, things might have turned out differently. But no one told me that. The message from that very first day was this: you are strong, you will handle this, and you will survive. And I have.

The nurses who helped me learn the ropes of diabetes gave me the power to control my own diabetes. They gave me blood sugar diaries, they taught me how to give my own shots, and they showed me how to use a sliding scale for insulin shots. Most of all, they said, "Do not let diabetes define you."

People living with chronic illnesses are reminded every day of their differentness from those who are healthy. They are reminded in small ways: the newspaper headline that touts a new cure, being asked by security to remove your pager (which is actually an insulin pump), a low blood sugar reaction after yoga class. So, we exert our power over the small things. We say, "I have diabetes," rather than, "I am a diabetic," lest we become little more than a label. We say the words out loud when other people won't. We proudly display our medication on our nightstand. We educate the mother who is worried about her child developing diabetes simply because he eats too many carbohydrates. We take pride in knowing our blood sugar count, or our chances of survival when other people walk through the world, ignorant of their mortality.

With new technologies like blood sugar monitors, human insulin, and continuous insulin pumps, having diabetes is no longer a death sentence. Having diabetes is, rather, an impetus to stay healthy. An impetus to not let it beat us. An impetus to make our short time here on Earth meaningful.

After having diabetes for fourteen years, it has become more than a chronic disease for me, more than a steady companion; diabetes is very much a part of who I am. Diabetes is not a burden, nor is it a crutch. It is just a disease that I, and millions of others, live with every moment of every day. When we face the fact of surviving with diabetes, as many have to face the fact of surviving with cancer, or HIV, or heart disease, we find strength in our uniqueness; we find strength in our ability to share our knowledge with others; we find strength in our ability to control our illness rather than letting it control us. I live with diabetes as though it were my troubled child—a lot of work and occasionally painful, but in the end, oddly beautiful and uniquely mine.

COPING WITH POTENTIALLY LIFE THREATENING SURGERY: A PERSONAL OBSERVATION

A colleague wrote the following observation. It describes the way he dealt with a potentially life threatening surgery.

I've been lucky all my life. I've never had anything serious happen to me. I thought I was invincible. One day I was getting out of a hot tub after hiking 10 miles, and I had a pain in my leg so sharp and so intense that I involuntarily began crying. As someone skilled in denial, I sought out a friend for painkillers, took a few, continued to hike, and refused to think that anything was wrong. As the pain continued and worsened, I sought out chiropractors and went for acupuncture. Finally, after the pain became so intense that I could hardly put my clothes on, I saw my doctor and was sent for an

MRI. My doctor, knowing my tendency toward denial, called as I was walking into my office at work. "Well," he said, "you have discs that look like they're cantaloupes and you could certainly lay off the tennis for a while. And, yes, you have a large growth in your spinal cord. The radiologist is concerned it might cause stenosis and block the flow of blood to your lower extremities."

What? I mean I was dumbfounded. I couldn't understand what he was saying. I thanked him, went back to work with a mild sense of foreboding, and then had an all-out panic attack. Was he saying I could become paralyzed? A call back confirmed that yes, that's exactly what he was saying. Was the growth malignant? They weren't sure. Could I die? He didn't want me to get anxious but, yes, it was a serious matter.

I went home and got drunk. At least I tried to. You reach a certain level of pain and nothing affects it. My pain was now so intense that walking to the car in anything faster than a shuffle was impossible. It took 10 agonizing minutes to put on my pants. I couldn't put on socks and went to work without them. Walking to class to teach made me cry from pain. I went to see a neurosurgeon. He found the growth fascinating and showing it on the screen, circled it from many different positions. He wanted to operate the next day. I was in shock and I didn't like him. No way would I have surgery. You have spinal surgery, I told myself, and you're never the same. This was confirmed by several people who'd had similar surgery and several other doctors I saw who told me that I would never be able to ski, or play tennis, or do many of the things I did before the growth occurred. I tried everything I'd done at the start of my spinal problems all over again, including epidurals. It just made the pain worse.

Six months from the onset of my pain, I saw a third neurosurgeon. He asked me what he could tell me that two other people hadn't and I said, "That I'll live." A look came over his face. I don't know but his look was so tender and kind that I think I fell in love with him for that moment. He told me that I needed the surgery badly, that there was a possibility of paralysis if I didn't get it soon, that there was only a small chance that the pain would go away after surgery, but that he'd try his darndest to make it better and that, "Yes, Professor, you'll live." I could have kissed him and I trusted him.

Through these months of pain, I couldn't sleep. I'd lie in bed and at some point in time, I began to have silent discussions with God about my life. I suddenly loved God. I couldn't talk to Him enough. I never negotiated with Him or said that if I got through the surgery I'd change my life, but I did see some things about my life that needed to be changed and vowed that I'd change them however the surgery came out. I told God that being alive with pain beat being paralyzed or being dead, but of course, when you talk to God, you can't con Him and I had to admit that I was an active person and if the pain was severe and limited sports or other activities, that I wasn't sure I could make it. I wondered, in these talks with God, about suicide. I wrote an e-mail to my tennis partner and told him about the growth in my spinal cord, only I wrote the word "Card" instead of Cord. He wrote me back a sarcastic and thoroughly insensitive note. I never played tennis with him again. I began to see that many of the people around me were cold and uncaring, and I sought out new friends. I had little skill at this, but lots of motivation. The woman I was seeing didn't come to my surgery. I ended our relationship. I went to synagogue and tried to enjoy the experience, but didn't. Through this period, I spoke to God about my life and the changes I was making in relationships. I thought of God as a good father who listened patiently and lovingly, and He did. I believe in God. I trust my conversations with Him. I shared my concerns, my sorrows, and my worries with Him, and He listened.

My surgery was a large success. I'm pain free except when I overdo activity. I have a new appreciation of the need for supportive people in my life. I try to act with kindness and love, but when I don't, I try and explain my behavior and apologize. It takes no effort to apologize. I do it often and I mean it when I say I'm sorry. I'm only human and I make mistakes that I regret. I think I have a strong appreciation for the wonders of life and the need not to waste it. When I sense pain in others, I am much kinder than I used to be. A good friend of mine with whom I'd had a disagreement that ended in us not speaking for a year and half, wrote me before the beginning of the Jewish New Year and reminded me that we Jews try and resolve our differences before the beginning of the new year, and that he hoped we could do that. We met, embraced, and spoke to one another for six hours. Letting go of anger and recognizing the negative aspects of vanity have been the strongest lessons I've learned from my surgery. You realize how important life is when you're facing death, and no one who goes through it is ever the same.

THE STRENGTHS PERSPECTIVE

Just as the approaching end of a therapy session often stimulates candor and disclosure in a patient, so the approach of death can focus and stimulate life forces in a dying person. Kubler-Ross (1969, 1997) identified the "unfinished business" that so often keeps dying persons temporarily alive. The unfinished business can be simple or complex, but it usually has deep personal roots. The dying person is concerned with death, of course, but they're also concerned about death as a constraint on life matters that need attending to. A student at Kubler-Ross's Death and Dying Seminar expressed amazement that the dying patients and hospital staff at her seminar "talked so little about death itself." In a summary remark, Kubler-Ross (1969, 1997) said, "We can help them die by trying to help them live" (Caffrey, 2000, p. 519).

Greenstein and Breitbart (2000) write that existentialist thinkers, such as Frankl, see suffering in those who are experiencing life-threatening illness as a catalyst for needing and finding meaning in their experience. Terminal illness offers a patient the opportunity for personal growth in the process of learning to cope with pain and the possibility of death. Fromm, Andrykowski, and Hunt (1993) and Andrykowski, Brady, and Hunt (1993) found positive emotional and social changes, as well as an increased sense of meaning in life, in people diagnosed with malignancies and following bone marrow transplantations. Greenstein and Breitbart (2000) write that "patients report reordering their priorities, spending more time with family, and experiencing personal growth through the very fact of having had to cope with their traumatic loss or illness" (p. 486).

Suffering may lead to empathy and the willingness to reach out to others. Morris Schwartz, the subject of *Tuesdays with Morrie* (Albom, 1997), used his illness to teach his student important lessons about life, and as Greenstein and Breitbart (2000) wrote, "Frankl felt that one of the things that helped him to cope with and ultimately survive his concentration-camp experience was his responsibility to publish the manuscript that was destroyed upon his arrival there, and to lecture at universities about the psychology of the concentration-camp experience" (p. 486).

One of the curative functions of treating clients with serious or terminal illnesses and disabilities in a group context is that the sense of connectedness between people often becomes an overriding positive that helps group members cope with painful and distressing conditions in ways that prolong life and add to its meaning.

In describing the shift clinicians must make in order to use the strengths perspective with clients in crisis, Blundo (2001) believes that we must "de-center" ourselves from old traditions that assume "that 'truth' is discovered only by looking at underlying and often hidden meanings, making causal links in some sequential order leading to the 'cause' of it all" (p. 302). Instead, Blundo believes that we need to engage clients in crisis in a highly collaborative dialogue that may result in surprising outcomes for the client and the worker. He also thinks that a strengths-oriented approach to clients, without preconceived ideas of underlying pathology, will yield the most positive and meaningful results. When applied to the client with serious or terminal illness, this means that the process of a truly client-centered dialogue may achieve startling information that moves the client into new areas of understanding about their situation and its relevance to their lives.

USING THE STRENGTHS PERSPECTIVE IN TREATMENT: AN EXAMPLE

Early in my career as a social worker, and much before I had a usable theoretical framework to help people, I worked for the Sister Kenny Foundation in Minneapolis, a rehabilitation center. Quite without knowing why, I would buy ice cream after work and go from room to room visiting my clients in the evening. Many of my clients had serious disabilities brought on by strokes, illness, or accidents. There was a rawness to these evening visits, and my clients would often despair about their lives as we sat together in their rooms. I was too young to know what a disability was like, physically, but my patients would struggle through their daily regimens of physical therapy and sometimes they would collapse in exhaustion and despair. The physical therapists would coax my clients on. It was tragic, and it was wonderful.

In my evening visits, my clients would tell me about their fears, their sorrows, their deepest anguish. Something in me reached out to them, and we held hands in the night and comforted one another. I was wise enough to listen and to remain silent, for the most part, but the urge to be a cheerleader was very strong and sometimes I would say something so palpably optimistic and positive that my clients would smile, nod their heads, and say, in that way clients have of telling you how off base you've been, "Bravo for trying, but maybe you don't quite know what you're talking about." The impulse to say something positive is strong in most of us, and it may help, but I've come to realize that listening and sitting with a client in the moment can do wonders. These brave people endure such pain that I want to embrace them all and give them little love messages. Wisely, I've learned to listen, to be empathic, and to respond only when I'm invited to. In a sense, this is a very optimistic and positive approach, because no one listens to people in pain, or to the people who are afraid of death, or to the people who will never do the things again that we all take for granted.

The knowledge of what life is like for our disabled and terminally ill patients always touches me deeply. Like most of us, I cannot imagine a life of immobility and pain, or the terminal illness that takes a life before anyone can possibly be ready for death. And like most of us, I don't think I could cope, and it makes me very humble when I work with people who are not only coping well but are, in a real sense, evolving. The process of evolving in the midst of pain, disability, and possible death seems quite beautiful to me and I am in wonder of it.

Clients with whom I have worked ask me my notion of death. I haven't a very firm one, and I can never give them a very good answer. Instead, I wonder about their idea of death. Often, like me, death bewilders them. They haven't thought about it and admit that it's a subject they've always avoided. But often, they want to finish unfinished business with family, some of it very painful and disturbing. Frequently, they want to remember the good moments in their lives and to have someone confirm that they're good people. Often, they want to talk to a religious figure and share their worries about the afterlife. And quite frequently, they are angry. Why shouldn't they be? And I listen to their anger, some of it directed at me because I represent someone healthy when they are not, and I think it's a small price to pay for what they're enduring.

In the end, death isn't clean, or pleasant, or uplifting. It is often filled with pain, and misery, and fear. The one thing you realize when you work with dying patients is that they want to make their time with you meaningful. What they talk about, the empathic way you respond, the gentle listening you do can help them move gracefully from this place to the next. As one of my clients wrote me as he faced the end of a long and painful illness:

> *I will go to the river and I will lie in peace.*
> *And when the sun sets, I will sleep the peaceful sleep*
> *of a child.*
> *And when it is dark and night comes,*
> *I will go from this place to the next.*
> *And I will be with God, and I will know*
> *His tender mercies.*

A CRITICAL RESPONSE

There are a great many beautiful and inspiring thoughts in this chapter, and we should remember the many people who find meaning in life's tragedies. They are certainly the resilient people among us who persevere in moments of great personal challenge and crisis. At the same time, it might be helpful to remember that many people find no meaning in severe pain, debilitating disability, lingering or terminal illness. They believe that the most helpful thing that anyone can do for them is to make their lives pain free and hopeful. For many people, dying is not a meaningful experience. Terminal illness is often diagnosed so late in the illness that patients seldom get past being confused and angry about what is happening to them. Disability may occur in a nanosecond and it may be the result of an accident that is someone else's fault. It's difficult to expect patients to take this philosophically, even happily, in the hope that the event will give them life meaning. Many people, who have long and painful illnesses and disabilities, suffer. Their lives deteriorate and they live out the remaining years in misery. Perhaps what Caffrey (2000) calls "palliative care," the reduction of pain, fear, depression, and anxiety is exactly what might prove most beneficial for many terminally ill and severely disabled clients. One respects Frankl's work, and he is right about finding meaning in life tragedies. It's just that the healthy among us trying to promote life meaning seems a little presumptuous and, at times, not a little insensitive when people among us live in great pain and a sense of hopelessness that sometimes precludes meaning.

SUMMARY

This chapter discusses a strengths approach to serious and terminal illness, disability, and bereavement. Much of the chapter focuses on finding meaning in the crisis of illness and death. The critical response, however, notes an opposing view that, briefly stated, suggests that it is presumptuous of the healthy to assume that something as traumatic and painful as illness and death can be meaningful. Instead, we should put our energies into life-saving technologies that actually offer people hope for long and normal lives. As helpers, the critical response suggests, our role should be to reduce anxiety and depression and to eliminate symptoms associated with illness and disabilities.

INTEGRATIVE QUESTIONS

1. Some people with terminal illness find great strength in finishing unfinished personal business. Can you think of unfinished business that might be important to resolve for anyone with a terminal illness?

2. The critical response argues that we should offer people hope rather than meaning as a way of dealing with terminal illness and disabilities. How do you feel about this distinction in our role as helpers?

3. Coping with the loss of a loved one may never be possible for some people. Can you imagine how the death of a loved one might be terribly difficult to cope with and could have traumatic repercussions?

4. Viktor Frankl survived the Holocaust and wrote about his experiences as a survivor. Do you think people who have survived genocide do so because they find meaning in the experience or because they have a tremendous will to live and do whatever it takes to survive?

5. The critical response argues that disabled people often live lives of quiet desperation. Do you know of disabled people who live fulfilling and successful lives? What is it about them that permits them to cope with a disability when others are unable to?

REFERENCES

Albom, M. (1997). *Tuesdays with Morrie: An old man, a young man, and life's greatest lesson.* New York: Doubleday Press.

American Diabetes Association. (2002). Facts and figures. Retrieved October 13, 2002, from the World Wide Web: www.diabetes.org/main/application/commercewf?origin=*.jsp&event =link(B1).

Andrykowski, M.A., Brady, M.J., and Hunt, J.W. (1993). Positive psychosocial adjustment in potential bone marrow transplant recipients: Cancer as a psychosocial transition. *Psychooncology,* 2, 261–276.

Balk, D.E. (1999). Bereavement and spiritual change. *Death Studies,* 23(6), 485–493.

Blundo, R. (2001). Learning strengths-based practice: Challenging our personal and professional frames. *Families in Society,* 82(3), 296–304.

Braithwaite, D.O. (1996). Exploring different perspectives on the communication of persons with disabilities. In E.B. Ray (Ed.), *Communication and disenfranchisement: Social health issues and implications* (pp. 449–464). Hillsdale, NJ: Lawrence Erlbaum.

Caffrey, T.A. (2000). The whisper of death: Psychotherapy with a dying Vietnam veteran. *American Journal of Psychotherapy,* 54(4), 519–530.

Coleman, L.M. (1997). Stigma: An enigma demystified. In L.J. David (Ed.), *The disability studies reader* (pp. 216–231). New York: Routledge.

Druss, B.G., Marcus, S.C., Rosenheck, R.A., et al. (2000). Understanding disability in mental and general medical conditions. *American Journal of Psychiatry,* 157(9), 1485–1491.

Finn, J. (1999). An exploration of helping processes in an online self-help group focusing on issues of disability. *Health & Social Work,* 24(3), 220–231.

Frankl, V.E. (1978). *Psychotherapy and existentialism: Selected papers on logotherapy.* New York: Touchstone.

Fromm, K., Andrykowski, M.A., and Hunt, J.W. (1993). Positive and negative psychosocial sequelae of bone marrow transplantation: Implications for quality of life assessment. *Journal of Behavioral Medicine,* 19, 221–240.

Glicken, A.J. (2002). Building on our strengths. *Park Record,* 122(59), A–15.

Greenstein, M., and Breitbart, W. (2000). Cancer and the experience of meaning: A group psychotherapy program for people with cancer. *American Journal of Psychotherapy,* 54(4), 486–500.

Hardwig, J. (2000). Spiritual issues at the end of life: A call for discussion. *The Hastings Center Report,* 30(2), 28–30.

Kubler-Ross, E. (1969, 1997). *On death and dying.* New York: Touchstone.

Shworles, T.R. (1983). The person with disability and the benefits of the microcomputer revolution: To have or to have not. *Rehabilitation Literature,* 44(11/12), 322–330.

Stroebe, M.S. (2001). Bereavement research and theory: Retrospective and prospective. *American Behavioral Scientist,* 44(5), 854–865.

CHAPTER FOURTEEN

THE STRENGTHS PERSPECTIVE WITH ISSUES RELATED TO AGING

Do not go gentle into that good night,
Old age should burn and rave at close of day;
Rage, Rage against the dying of the light.

—Dylan Thomas (1943)[1]

AGING AND DEPRESSION

This chapter explores issues that affect people as they age and the application of the strengths perspective. Much of the discussion centers on depression in elderly clients and the cause and treatment of late-onset depression. Two case studies provide added information about the cause and treatment of depression in the elderly.

Mills and Henretta (2001) report that more than 2 million of the 34 million older Americans suffer from some form of depression. Yet, late-life depression, they note, is often undiagnosed or underdiagnosed. When the authors looked at self-reports of health as one variable related to depression, they found significant differences along racial and ethnic lines. More Hispanics and African American elderly from ages 65 and above reported that their health was only fair or poor, as compared with non-Hispanic white elderly. Axelson (1985) reports that Mexican Americans tend to see themselves as "old" much earlier in life than other groups (e.g., at about age 60, as compared with ages 65 for black Americans and 70 for white Americans, respectively). Axelson (1985) believes that these types of attitudes and expectations about aging "may put the Hispanic elderly at increased risk of what has been called psychological death, or a disengagement from active involvement in life" (found in Mills & Henretta, 2001, p. 133).

1. By Dylan Thomas, from THE POEMS OF DYLAN THOMAS, copyright ©1952 by Dylan Thomas. Reprinted by permission of New Directions Publishing Corp.

Robert and Li (2001) note that despite a usual belief in the relationship between socioeconomic status (SES) and health, research actually suggests a limited relationship between the two variables. Instead, there seems to be a relationship between community levels of health and individual health. Lawton (1977) suggests that older adults may experience communities as their primary source of support, recreation, and stimulation, unlike younger adults, who find it easier to move about in search of support and recreation. Lawton and Nahemow (1973) believe that positive community environments are very important to older adults who may have emotional, physical, or cognitive problems. The need for healthy and vital communities is particularly relevant to older adults who have health problems that limit their mobility. A tragic example of the impact of unhealthy communities is the Chicago heat wave of 1995 in which 739 older and less mobile people died. The reason for that large death rate is that many elderly and less mobile people were afraid to leave their homes and be exposed to environments they felt were dangerous and unsafe (Gladwell, 2002). One elderly woman, in explaining why she was afraid to leave her home, even though she was literally dying of heat prostration, said, "Chicago is just a shooting gallery" (Gladwell, 2002, p. 80). Furthermore, Chicago had no emergency system for helping elderly and less mobile people. So many people died during the heat wave that

> callers to 911 were put on hold. . . . The police took bodies to the Cook County Medical Examiner's office, and a line of cruisers stretched outside the building. . . . The morgue ran out of bays in which to put the bodies. The owner of a local meat-packing firm offered the city his refrigerated trucks to help store the bodies. The first set wasn't enough. He sent a second set. It wasn't enough. (Gladwell, 2002, p. 76)

Rather than thinking in terms of a relationship between individual SES and health among an aging population, Robert and Li (2001) suggest three indicators of healthy communities that relate directly to individual health: (1) a positive physical environment that provides an absence of noise, traffic, inadequate lighting, and other features of a community that may lead to functional loss in older adults; (2) a positive social environment that includes an absence of crime, the ability to find safe environments in which to walk, and easy access to shopping; and (3) a rich service environment that includes simple and safe access to rapid and inexpensive transportation, the availability of senior centers, and easy access to meal sites.

Studying the impact of natural disasters on a population of elderly adults demonstrating pre-disaster signs of depression, Tyler and Hoyt (2000) noted that elderly adults reporting high amounts of social support had lower levels of depression before and after a natural disaster. They also reported that "older people with little or no social support, perhaps due to death of a spouse and/or loss of friends, may have a more difficult time dealing with life changes and, as a result, are particularly vulnerable to increases in depression" (p. 155).

In their research on successful aging, Vaillant and Mukamal (2001) believe that predictors of longer and healthier lives can be made before the age of 50 by using the following indicators: parental social class, family cohesion, major depression, ancestral longevity, childhood temperament, and physical health at age 50. Seven variables indicating personal control over physical and emotional health that are also related to longer and healthier lives include alcohol abuse, smoking, marital instability, lack of exercise, excessive body mass index, poor coping mechanisms, and lower education. The authors conclude that people have much greater control over their postretirement health than had been previously recognized in the literature.

For purposes of understanding what is meant by *successful aging*, Vaillant and Mukamal indicate the following:

1. Although elderly people taking three to eight medications a day were seen as chronically ill by their physicians, the cohort deemed to be aging successfully saw themselves as healthier than their peers.
2. Elderly adults who age successfully have the ability to plan ahead and are still intellectually curious and in touch with their creative abilities.
3. Successfully aging elderly adults see life as being meaningful, even very elderly adults above the age of 95 who are able to use humor in their daily lives and to compare themselves positively with those who are more afflicted.
4. Aging successfully includes remaining physically active and continuing activities (walking, for example) that were used at an earlier age to remain healthy.
5. Elderly adults who age successfully are more serene and spiritual in their outlook on life than are those who age less well.
6. Successful aging includes concern for continued friendships, positive interpersonal relationships, satisfaction with spouses, children and family life, and social responsibility in the form of volunteer work and civic involvement.

■ ■ ■ ■ ■ ▬▬▬▬▬▬▬▬▬▬▬▬▬▬▬▬▬▬▬▬▬▬▬▬▬▬▬▬▬▬▬▬▬▬▬▬▬

PRIMO LEVI, ELDERLY DEPRESSION: A CASE STUDY

Primo Levi was the remarkable author of *The Periodic Table* (1995a), *If Not Now, When?* (1995b), and other books about the human spirit and the Holocaust experience. In his youth, he was imprisoned for a year at the notorious Auschwitz concentration camp during World War II, a subject about which he wrote with great humanity and sensitivity. Many think his books about the concentration camp experience are among the best examples of the way people can successfully cope with incredible trauma. Levi was prone to depressions throughout his life, and whether his experience at Auschwitz increased his propensity for depression is difficult to say. Certainly it didn't help. In his mid-60s, at the height of his recognition as a writer, Levi suffered his final depression. He was ill with prostate problems, was finding writing increasingly difficult, and was entering a severe and unrelenting late-onset depression.

The biographer Carole Angier (2002), writing about his depression, said, "The real pit of his depression had begun. It was so bad that he had lost interest in everything and didn't want to see anyone" (p. 706). Elsewhere, she reported a letter written to a friend, in which Levi said, "I am going through the worst time of my life since Auschwitz, maybe the worst time in my life because I am older and less resilient. My wife is exhausted. Forgive me for this outburst" (p. 708). And later, he called his doctor and said, "I can't go on" (p. 731), and moments after talking with his doctor, walked outside his apartment

(continued)

CONTINUED

where he had lived all of his life, stood at the railing of the staircase, perhaps paused for a moment, and then jumped five stories to his death. Conjecturing about his decision to commit suicide, Angier wrote,

> [H]e just needed to get out and really thought he might walk downstairs. He opened the door and found himself outside. It wasn't the light and air he had dreamed of, but it was a deep void. I think he looked for [his wife] to stop him. Then he leaned (over the railing of the staircase) and looked, but she wasn't there; and he let go. (p. 731)

Did Levi commit suicide because of his experiences in Auschwitz? Angier wrote, "Primo Levi held up a light for us. . . . And if he had laid down that light himself [because of his suicide], was he saying that he no longer believed in [the light], that he no longer believed in us?" (p. 726). Or was his suicide the culmination of a writer's inability to write, a serious illness, and an increasing age-related depression that many elderly people experience because they are unable to do many of the things they did so well before? Certainly the traumas of the concentration camps contribute to feelings of depression in many Holocaust survivors. But this experience of a famous author taking his life, someone with many social contacts and a rich personal life, should give us pause when we think about the lives of elderly people who no longer work, have, perhaps, lost a mate and live alone, are beginning to have serious physical problems, and experience a deterioration in their ability to do the very things they did well just a few years earlier. Angier (2002) believes that Levi's decision to commit suicide was a private decision. She wrote, "Auschwitz caused him guilt and shame, and torment about human evil; but he contained these in decades of writing and talking, and with the knowledge that he had done everything he could to right them. What we suffer from most in the end is our own private condition. It was his own private condition that killed Primo Levi" (p. XX). Who can ever know Levi's reason for choosing suicide? But this story of Primo Levi should help us understand the complex nature of aging and the inability many of us have to accept the sometimes rapid deterioration in our physical and emotional functioning that accompanies aging for many of America's elderly.

To further suggest that Levi's suicide may have taken place for reasons unrelated to his experiences at Auschwitz, Waern et al. (2002) report that elderly people commit suicide for reasons having to do with depression, failing health, aloneness, changing cognitive abilities, family deterioration, death of loved ones, and a variety of other complex reasons. However, according to Waern et al. (2002), the primary reason for elder suicide is a severe late-life depression that is unresponsive to treatment. This certainly describes Primo Levi, who, in addition to receiving psychotherapy, was also placed on antidepressive medications.

In studies of Holocaust survivors such as Primo Levi, Baron et al. (1996) suggest that survivors who were aware of their ethnic identities and cultural heritage were less vulnerable to emotional traumas. Newman (1979) suggests that religious beliefs were beneficial to Holocaust survivors and that religious beliefs provided many survivors with feelings of personal control over the experience, which helped give it meaning. Angier (2002) described Primo Levi as a highly assimilated Jew who wrote little about the Jewish experience in the death camps but wrote, more precisely, about the human experience. She noted that he told us very little about himself in his books and was often aloof from people, even people he knew well. She wrote, "He very rarely betrays his feelings, and almost never has negative feelings—this is the first and most important thing everyone notices in his great books about the Shoah [the Holocaust]" (p. xv). Angier went on to say that Levi was a deeply conflicted man and that the "torments" of his experiences with the Holocaust, with which he tried to cope by living a highly rational life (he was also a well-known chemist), began to fail him. As Levi aged, the conflicts he saw in other parts of the world that paralleled his Holocaust experience (Cambodia, for example), "at slowly diminishing intervals rose up and dragged him under" (p. xix).

Does this mean that Levi's suicide is an indication that his lack of strong religious beliefs prevented him from coping with his Holocaust experiences? No. Having worked professionally with Jewish Holocaust survivors, the author has known many survivors who were religious and many who were deeply ambivalent toward religion after their experiences in the death camps. What defines survivors who have complete and successful lives is an inner strength, a strong belief in self, and a resilience of the spirit. Does that resilience sometimes change with age? Of course, but that may be true of many people who age. Baron et al. (1996) note that clinicians were highly pessimistic about the survivors they were seeing after the survivor's release from the death camps. They believed that survivors they saw were severely maladjusted and, as one measure of their maladjustment, that they would make poor parents. The children of survivors, they reasoned, would also show major maladjustments (for example, hypervigilence, the inability to form attachments, irrational fears, depressions). But as Baron et al. (1996) note, "Children of survivors have shown no pattern of maladjustment or psychopathology in most research" (p. 513). Perhaps this demonstrates that resilient people can perform many socially successful functions, such as parenting and working, and still suffer episodes of depression similar to those of Primo Levi.

Survivors of genocide from Europe, Cambodia, Bosnia, Latin America, and elsewhere, with whom many of us have worked, while strong and resilient, also show a core of sadness and pessimism about life. Many experience debilitating depressions, and one is strongly inclined to believe that dehumanizing experiences such as genocide have a terribly negative impact on survivors. If we consider the life experiences of many America elderly who experience failure and loss and regrets in their lives, we also find pessimism, depression, and a loss of hope. Primo Levi, while well known and successful, is a good example of the impact of aging and our very beginning understanding of how to help elderly clients experiencing severe depressions. Clearly, Levi's late-life depression parallels the experience of many elderly people in a society that doesn't know, and perhaps doesn't want to know, how best to help people cope with aging.

A STRENGTHS APPROACH TO WORK WITH ELDERLY CLIENTS

Lenze et al. (2002) studied the effectiveness of interpersonal treatment in conjunction with antidepressive medications with elderly depressed clients. Not surprisingly, given the lack of awareness of late-onset depression in elderly clients, the authors reported, "To our knowledge, this is the first report concerning social functioning in a controlled randomized study of elderly patients receiving maintenance treatment for late-life depression" (p. 467). The researchers found improved social adjustment attributable to combined interpersonal psychotherapy and maintenance medication.

Although improvements in social functioning could not be related directly to the therapy, maintenance of the gains made in social functioning seemed directly related to therapy. The most significant gain reported by the authors were in the areas of interpersonal conflict role transitions and abnormal grief.

Kennedy and Tannenbaum (2000) suggest that there is compelling evidence that older patients experience a variety of emotional problems, including depression, anxiety, caregiver burden, and extended bereavement. The authors believe that many elderly clients can benefit from psychotherapeutic interventions. Kennedy and Tannenbaum suggest that adjustments made for effective clinical practice with elderly clients should include consideration of "sensory and cognitive" problems, the need for closer collaboration with the clients' families and other care providers, and a belief by the clinician, shared with the elderly clients and their families, that treatment will result in improved functioning and symptom reduction to offset stereotypes of the elderly client as being untreatable or unlikely to improve. The authors suggest that work with elderly clients also requires skill with a variety of approaches, including work with couples, families, and groups and that pharmotherapy may produce very positive results with late-onset social and emotional problems experienced by elderly clients.

O'Connor (2001) notes that clients usually get better after their first episode of depression, but that the relapse rate is 50 percent. Clients with three episodes of depression are 90 percent likely to have additional episodes. O'Connor suggests that we need to accept depression as a chronic disease and that therapists must be prepared to "give hope, to reduce shame, to be mentor, coach, cheerleader, idealized object, playmate, and nurturer. In doing so, inevitably, we must challenge many of our assumptions about the use of the self in psychotherapy" (p. 508). O'Connor (2001) goes on to say,

> When patients are trying their best but their environment is not rewarding them, one obvious alternative source of reinforcement that we have near at hand is the therapist him/herself. Most depressed patients acutely desire the therapist's approval, and it is an effective therapist who gives it warmly and genuinely. (p. 522)

Denton, Walsh, and Daniel (2002) suggest that much of the therapy used to treat depression has no empirical base to suggest its effectiveness. Before we select a treatment approach, we should consult empirically validated research studies that indicate the effectiveness of a particular therapeutic approach with a particular individual. The authors describe evidence-based practice as the use of treatments with some evidence of effectiveness. They go on to say that evidence-based practice requires a complete literature search and the use of formal rules of proof in evaluating the relevant literature (Evidence-Based Medicine Working Group, 1992, p. 2420). Finally, they indicate that the selection of a practice approach should be shown to be effective with a particular population (Chambless & Hollon, 1998, p. 7).

Timmermans and Angell (2001) indicate that evidence-based clinical judgment has five important features:

1. It is composed of both research evidence and clinical experience.
2. One must be able to read the literature, be able to synthesize the information, and make judgments about the quality of the evidence.

3. The way in which information is used relates to the level of confidence in the effectiveness of the information gathered.
4. Evidence-based practice includes the ability to test the validity of research evidence in the context of one's own practice.
5. Evidence-based clinical judgments require professional conduct and are guided by a common value system.

Gambrill (1999) believes that use of evidence-based practice can help us "avoid fooling ourselves that we have knowledge when we do not" (p. 342). She indicates that a complete search for effectiveness research will provide the following information relevant for work with all clients, including the elderly (p. 343), first suggested by Enkin et al. (1995):

1. Beneficial forms of care demonstrated by clear evidence from controlled trials.
2. Forms of care likely to be beneficial. (The evidence in favor of these forms of care is not as clear as for those in category one.)
3. Forms of care with a trade-off between beneficial and adverse effects. (Effects must be weighed according to individual circumstances and priorities.)
4. Forms of care of unknown effectiveness. (There are insufficient or inadequate quality data upon which to base a recommendation for practice.)
5. Forms of care unlikely to be beneficial. (The evidence against these forms of care is not as clear as for those in category six.)
6. Forms of care likely to be ineffective or harmful. (Ineffectiveness or harm demonstrated by clear evidence.) (Gambrill, p. 343).

LYDIA, A DEPRESSED ELDERLY CLIENT: A CASE STUDY

Lydia Holmes is a 68-year-old retired executive assistant for a large corporation. Ms. Holmes had a long, successful, and happy career, moving up the ladder in her company to one of its most important and highly paid positions. She retired at age 65 in good health and wanted to travel and spend more time with her grown children and her grandchildren. A year earlier, and still in good health and happy with her decision to travel, Lydia experienced the beginning signs of depression. Alarmed, because she had never before experienced prolonged depression, she saw her gynecologist during her annual physical examination and shared her symptoms with him. He immediately referred her to a psychiatrist, who placed her on an antidepressive medication and urged her to consider therapy. Because Lydia had no idea what was causing the depression and thought that it might be something biochemical related to aging and the discontinuation of hormone therapy for symptoms of menopause, she decided against therapy and stayed with the antidepressant. There was little relief from the medication, and a second visit with the psychiatrist confirmed the need for therapy and a change in medication. The second medication made her fatigued and lethargic. After an additional month of feeling depressed, she saw a licensed clinical social worker recommended by her psychiatrist.
　　Lydia was very pessimistic about therapy. She had known many people in her company who had gone for therapy and who had come back, in her opinion, worse than

(continued)

CONTINUED

before they'd entered treatment. She also thought therapy was for weak people and refused to see herself that way. When she began seeing the therapist, she was very defensive and kept much of the problems she was having to herself. The therapist was kind and warm and didn't seem to mind Lydia's unwillingness to unburden herself by discussing the actual problems she was experiencing. This went on for four sessions. On the fifth session, Lydia broke down and cried, and described the awful feeling of depression and her confusion about why someone who had never before been depressed would experience such feelings. The therapist asked her if she had any ideas about why she was experiencing depression now. She didn't. All she could think that might be relevant was that she had been an active woman all of her life and since her divorce at age 55, she had put all of her energies into her work and her children, but now she felt as if she were of little use to anyone. She was bored and thought it had been a mistake to retire.

The worker thought this was a very good theory and suggested that she might want to explore the possibility of going back to work, perhaps part-time, at first, to see if she liked it. She returned to her old company, worked part-time in a very accepting and loving department in which people were genuinely happy to have her back, and found that, if anything, the depression was increasing. Alarmed, she contacted the therapist and they began the work that ultimately led to an improvement in her depression.

The therapist felt that Lydia had put many of her intimacy needs aside when she was divorced. She had not had a relationship since her divorce and felt bitter and angry at her ex-husband for leaving her for a younger woman. She had no desire to date or to form intimate relationships and said, repeatedly, that her good female friends were all she needed in her life. It turned out, as the therapist helped Lydia explore her past, that Lydia was given large responsibilities to manage her dysfunctional family when she was a child. Never having learned about her own needs, Lydia took care of people and now wondered who would take care of her as she grappled with depression and aging. Her very good friends found it difficult to be around her when she spoke about her depression. Increasingly, she felt alone and unloved. Her children were busy with their own lives, and she didn't feel it was right to ask for their help. The therapist arranged for several family meetings, and her children were, as Lydia predicted, sympathetic but unwilling to help in more than superficial ways. The recognition that her family didn't care about her as fully as she cared about them validated feelings she had not expressed to the therapist: that her family and friends were not the supports she imagined them to be and that, in reality, she was alone in life.

This realization led to a discussion of what Lydia wanted to do in treatment. Improving the depression was foremost in Lydia's mind, but she also wanted to make some changes in her life. She expressed interest in social activities and accepted the therapist's suggestion that she join a self-help group for depressed older people going through an adjustment to retirement. Going to the group made Lydia realize that she was a much more healthy and optimistic person than many of the severely depressed people in the group. She also made several friends, who turned out to be true friends, one of whom was male. The relationship didn't become intimate, but they were able to have companionship, to travel together, and to attend events. Lydia found his company very comforting and supportive. She joined a dance group and, through the group, also made several friends. She began to date and experienced a type of intimacy with the man she was dating that she hadn't known in her marriage. In treatment, she focused on what she wanted in her life and how to use her highly advanced skills to achieve those goals. The depression began to lift as her social and personal lives improved.

There are moments when she is still depressed, and the therapist believes these are more biochemical and situational than serious signs of depression. She continues to work with the psychiatrist on finding a better way to manage her depression biochemically. After six months of trial and error, they found a medication and dosage that works well for her. She continues to work part-time, recognizes the primary reasons for her depression, and continues to work on those reasons with her therapist.

DISCUSSION

Lydia is not unlike many elderly people who find that retirement brings with it the painful realization that they are often alone in life. Depression isn't an unusual result of this realization. Lydia is a highly successful woman with many advanced strengths. The one thing she could not easily do was seek help, a not uncommon condition in people who have cared for others throughout their lives with little thought of being cared for themselves. The therapist stayed with Lydia during her moments of denial and rejection of help and allowed her to go at her own pace. Once Lydia confirmed her painful depression and explained why she thought it was happening, the therapist supported her theory, which led to a helping agenda that Lydia could accept. Like many parents, the recognition that her children were only marginally involved in her life was difficult for Lydia to accept, and felt hurtful to her in the extreme. However, Lydia now recognizes that her children have resented her intrusiveness into their lives since her divorce and that they viewed it as a way of filling her life without their asking for or wanting her involvement. She continues to discuss her children with her therapist, and Lydia and her children grapple with their confused feelings about one another.

Lydia, once again, feels in control of her life and, highly intelligent and insightful woman that she is, sees that rebuilding her life is important at this point in time. She has moved to another self-help group of more highly functioning people and feels a kinship with them. Her relationships with her male friends have blossomed, and she realizes that the anger she had for her husband limited her ability to allow men into her life. The new feeling of comfort with her male friends has made her aware that many men find her interesting and attractive, and she is experiencing the pleasant sense of being in demand as a friend and companion. She values her male friends and sees in them the true friendships she wasn't always able to have before her therapy began.

The author spoke to the client about her experiences in treatment. She told him,

> I think I'd been a bit depressed since my marriage started to fail. To cover it up, I was busy every second of the day. I'd work all day and then go to every play, musical event, and function I could find, usually with friends. My relationships were very superficial, and it came as no real surprise that my friends weren't there for me when I became really depressed. The first thing I realized after retirement was that I had free time that I'd never had before. I filled it with everything I could find, but still, I had time on my hands. At some point, I didn't know what to do with myself. It was clear to me that my kids felt confused about having me around, but I talked myself into thinking they needed me and I didn't pick up the signs of their unhappiness over my frequent calls and visits. When the depression hit, I knew I needed help, but I talked myself into believing it was hormonal. I knew better, of course, but I just didn't want to accept that I was depressed because I was living a depressing life.
>
> My therapist was pretty amazing. She let me babble on and avoid important issues until I finally had nowhere to go with my feelings and just fell apart in her office. She involved me in determining the issues we would work on. She was very supportive and encouraging and always seemed to be able to see things in a positive way. In time, I guess

(continued)

CONTINUED

I began to see things more positively. The groups I went to, run by other depressed people, really made a difference in my life. I've made some very good friends through the people I've met in group. They're not superficial people and they care about me. I've stopped bugging my family, and I don't need to be busy every minute of the day. I have moments when I'm depressed, but it's not like the depression I had when I began therapy. That depression felt like I was falling down a deep hole and I'd never get out. My therapist made me realize that I had lots of skills to manage my depression, and the discussion about my life gave me an opportunity to see that I had never really asked anyone to give back to me, emotionally. I think my husband got tired of my always giving, even when he didn't need anything. He'd ask what he could do for me and I'd never know what to say. I think he started to feel irrelevant. I have a relationship in which we give equally, and while it sometimes feels wrong to even ask, I'm getting a lot better at it. Would I have gotten better without therapy? I doubt it very much. Medication helps a little, but it's no magic cure. Therapy pretty much saved my life.

A CRITICAL RESPONSE

This discussion of problems related to aging certainly shows the terrible irony of working hard all one's life and then facing declining physical and emotional health as the reward for years of hard work. It may have strengthened the chapter to focus on other aspects of aging and on the socioeconomic issues related to differences in the way people age as a result of levels of education and income. It's uncertain that personal wealth is as disassociated from healthy aging as this chapter would have us believe, because it does buy much better health care. However, it seems reasonable that healthy communities provide a safe and personally satisfying environment that may be a positive catalyst for healthy aging. Part of that environment includes social contacts and healthy personal relationships. Many elderly people complain about feeling isolated, and senior centers and other programs that bring the elderly together may not be as effective as we would like them to be. Like all of us, no one wants to admit that they are aging, and perhaps many elderly people avoid senior centers and senior activities because they are either stigmatizing to them or they make them feel old. No doubt we can do much better in terms of activities and roles for elderly clients.

Some universities and corporations have programs that may help in this discussion. The University of Arizona, for example, has a "Senior Academy" in Tucson, a housing development for retired academics with ties to teaching and research activities at the University of Arizona. The Senior Academy permits retired academics to work closely with the University of Arizona on program development, research projects, and scholarly activities. A visit to the Academy, by the author, much as the idea is a good one, suggests that it would apply best to academics with considerable financial resources, because housing costs and association fees are out of the range of many retired academics. Still, the idea is a very good one. Some retirement communities, like Ferrington in Chapel Hill, North Carolina, have rich lecture and activity schedules that would be of interest to many educated retirees. But what is available for the less affluent elderly? There isn't very much, and most of what is available is expensive.

Many people don't care to live in subsidized housing for the elderly, because the mix of people isn't comfortable to them. Leaving communities where one has friends and family for better weather often ends in boredom and feelings of isolation, as does retiring before a plan is developed for maintaining an active life. Lydia's case example graphically illustrates this.

Medical care is expensive for many elderly people, and the cost of health services is increasing rapidly, forcing the elderly to make draconian choices about needed medications and other medical services, because co-payments, deductibles, and maximum benefits force decisions that may have a negative impact on health. And what roles do we give the elderly in American society? None that are very clear.

And, finally, the death of friends and loved ones can create a sense of aloneness that often leads to solitary drinking, depression, and suicide among the elderly. With a rapidly increasing aging population in America, we'd best start getting our house in order when it comes to the role of the elderly in American life and the varied services we need to offer older people to promote healthy aging.

SUMMARY

This chapter discusses issues affecting the elderly and the use of the strengths perspective to provide services when needed. Much of the chapter deals with problems related to the aging process that result in depression. The critical response reminds us that many elderly people face a decreased role in life, problems with medical care, lack of affordable housing, feelings of isolation as friends and mates pass on, and the fact that many older adults don't use current services because they feel uncomfortable with the notion that they are aging.

INTEGRATIVE QUESTIONS

1. What impact will the anticipated increase in the elderly population have on social and medical services in the United States?

2. Is the rate of late-onset depression, discussed in this chapter, more a function of the isolation and lack of a social and economic role for the elderly than a function of the aging process, which includes more health-related problems that may contribute to depression?

3. Do you believe that more services should be developed for the elderly, including low-cost housing, employment, and wellness centers, to maintain good health and decrease feelings of pessimism and social isolation? Will the cost of these services reduce funding needed for other populations in need, including children, the terminally ill, victims of family violence, and so on?

4. Could you see committing yourself to keeping in close contact with less mobile elderly people who live in unsafe areas of the community so that disasters such as the one in Chicago don't happen again? Perhaps you can discuss this in a small group and think about the type of commitment this would require.

5. There is an old belief that the way people live their lives before retirement is the way they will live their lives after retirement, and that life experience and age don't lead to increased wisdom. Do you agree or disagree, and why?

REFERENCES

Angier, C. (2002). *The double bond of Primo Levi*. New York: Farrar.

Axelson, J.A. (1985). *Counseling and development in a multicultural society*. Monterey, CA: Brooks/Cole.

Baron, L., Eisman, H., Scuello, M., Veyzer, A., and Lieberman, M. (1996). Stress resilience, locus of control, and religion in children of Holocaust victims. *Journal of Psychology*, 130(5), 513–525.

Chambless, D.L., and Hollon, S.D. (1998). Defining empirically supported therapies. *Journal of Consulting and Clinical Psychology*, 66, 7–18.

Denton, W.H., Walsh, S.R., and Daniel, S.S. (2002). Evidence-based practice in family therapy: Adolescent depression as an example. *Journal of Marital and Family Therapy*, 28(1), 39–45.

Enkin, M., Keirse, M.J.N., Renfrew, M., and Neilson, J. (1995). *A guide to effective care in pregnancy and childbirth* (2nd Ed.). New York: Oxford University Press.

Evidence-Based Medicine Working Group. (1992). Evidence-based medicine: A new approach to teaching the practice of medicine. *Journal of the American Medical Association*, 268, 2420–2425.

Gambrill, E. (1999). Evidence-based practice: An alternative to authority-based practice. *Journal of Contemporary Human Services*, 80(4), 341–350.

Gladwell, M. (August 12, 2002). Political heat. *The New Yorker*, 76–80.

Kennedy, G.J., and Tannenbaum, S. (2000). Psychotherapy with older adults. *American Journal of Psychotherapy*, 54(3), 386–407.

Lawton, M.P. (1977). The impact of the environment on aging and behavior. In. J.E. Birren and K.W. Schaie (Eds.), *Handbook of the psychology of aging* (pp. 276–301). New York: Van Nostrand Reinhold.

Lawton, M.P., and Nahemow, L. (1973). Ecology and the aging process. In C. Eisdorfer and M.P. Lawton (Eds.), *The psychology of adult development and aging* (pp. 619–674). Washington, DC: American Psychological Association.

Lenze, E.J., Dew, M.A., Mazumdar, S., et al. (2002). Combined pharmacotherapy and psychotherapy as maintenance treatment for late-life depression: Effects on social adjustment. *American Journal of Psychiatry*, 159(3), 466–468.

Levi, P. (1995a). *The periodic table*. Stockholm: Raymond Rosenthal.

Levi, P. (1995b). *If not now, when?* New York: Viking Penguin.

Mills, T.L., and Henretta, J.C. (2001). Racial, ethnic, and sociodemographic differences in the level of psychosocial distress among older americans. *Research on Aging*, 23(2), 131–152.

Newman, L. (1979). Emotional disturbances in children of Holocaust survivors. *Social Casework: The Journal of Contemporary Social Work*, 60(1), 43–50.

O'Connor, R. (2001). Active treatment of depression. *American Journal of Psychotherapy*, 55(4), 507–530.

Robert, S.A., and Li, L.W. (2001). Age variation in the relationship between community socioeconomic status and adult health. *Research on Aging*, 23(2), 233–258.

Thomas, D. (1943). Fern hill. In *The poems of Dylan Thomas*. London: New Directions.

Timmermans, S., and Angell, A. (2001). Evidence-based medicine, clinical uncertainty, and learning to doctor. *Journal of Health and Social Behavior*, 42(4), 342.

Tyler, K.A., and Hoyt, D.R. (2000). The effects of an acute stressor on depressive symptoms among older adults. *Research on Aging*, 22(2), 143–164.

Vaillant, G.E., and Mukamal, K. (2001). Successful aging. *American Journal of Psychiatry*, 158(6), 839–847.

Waern, M., Runeson, B.S., Allebeck, P., et al. (2002). Mental disorder in elderly suicides: A case-control study. *American Journal of Psychiatry*, 159(3), 450–455.

A STRENGTHS PERSPECTIVE APPROACH TO HEALTHY COMMUNITY LIFE

Part V of this book contains the concluding chapter, Chapter 15, which serves a dual function. It summarizes the major points made in the book about the strengths perspective, and it discusses the importance of healthy communities. Robert Putnam's book, *Bowling Alone* (2000), sets the tone in Chapter 15 for a discussion of the impact of isolation and loneliness in America and its effect on community strength. Healthy communities are linked to healthier lives in this chapter. The work of Martin Seligman on learned optimism and authentic happiness and the writing of Dennis Saleebey on the importance of healthy communities are additional aspects of this chapter.

It's appropriate that this book end with a discussion of healthy communities. Americans increasingly live in communities in which they have little contact with their neighbors or extended families. Less affluent Americans often live in areas marked by very high levels of crime and violence. The violence Americans endure creates class distinctions, fear, and isolation which increasingly define growing old in this country. It seems a terrible way to end long years of productive work and family nurturing. One hopes that out of the strengths movement and others like it, that older and less affluent Americans can once again enjoy safe neighborhoods and healthy communities.

····· ▬▬▬▬▬▬▬▬▬▬▬▬▬▬▬▬▬▬▬▬▬▬▬▬

CHAPTER FIFTEEN

THE FUTURE OF THE STRENGTHS PERSPECTIVE: HEALTHY COMMUNITY LIFE

POSITIVE AND CAUTIONARY ARGUMENTS ABOUT THE STRENGTHS PERSPECTIVE

In the previous fourteen chapters, the book has shown how to apply the strengths perspective to a number of practice situations common to the helping professions. As a part of the content of the book, critical responses to the material in each chapter have been provided to aid the reader in processing the arguments made about the strengths perspective. Summarizing the *positive arguments* presented in support of the strengths perspective, the following have been noted:

1. There is more to be gained therapeutically with clients by focusing on what is right about them rather than focusing on their pathology.
2. In most cases, there is more that is positive and functional about people than is negative or dysfunctional.
3. There are helping processes in families, cultures, friends, religious and spiritual beliefs, and communities that can assist people in many positive ways.
4. Many people are amazingly resilient, even when traumatized early in life. Focusing on the fact that they have survived traumas rather than assuming that they will forever be dysfunctional is a positive and appropriate clinical response.
5. Focusing on pathology creates a sense of pessimism in clinicians that is contagious to clients. The pessimism of the worker and the stigma attached to many diagnostic categories have a pervasively negative impact on clients.
6. People have self-healing abilities that often create change without the use of therapy.
7. Self-help groups are powerful and positive supports for many clients. A cooperative relationship should be developed between helping professionals and self-help groups.

8. Removal of symptoms is a limited way of understanding the purpose of therapy. The goal of therapy should be to assist people to become more self-fulfilled, socially responsible, and to lead lives that are meaningful.

At the same time, the book has cautioned the reader to recognize the *compelling arguments* against many of the ideas we have presented. We have done this in keeping with Gambrill's (1999) concern that statements made in the helping profession have few, if any, empirically based supportive arguments. Several of the more compelling cautionary arguments about the strengths perspective are the following:

1. There is very little research available to suggest that the strengths perspective is more effective in practice than other helping approaches.
2. Many of the strengths we have emphasized can also be negatives. It was noted, for example, that some people have been badly hurt by religions that find certain widely accepted behaviors in society, offensive. Some spiritual beliefs may interfere with needed medical help. Self-help groups can be rigid and off-putting to many people in need.
3. Attacking the DSM-IV seems pejorative in the extreme because it is not the DSM-IV but clinicians who abuse diagnostic categories and incorrectly apply and interpret them in ways that stigmatize people.
4. The strengths approach may be far too uncritical of the negative behavior of clients. Therapy should always stress positive values and socially responsible behavior.
5. If traditional therapy is as ineffective as it seems to be, there is something very wrong with the training of professionals and the knowledge base used to guide practice.

Still, the strengths perspective is an approach that can significantly help clients through its focus on optimism and individual and community strengths. The critical and often pessimistic stance taken by professionals about such problems as mental illness and alcoholism are an example of how the helping professions actually disserve people. It is embarrassing to note that self-help groups seem to be more effective in treating alcoholism than are professionals, or that self-management by clients diagnosed with mental illness often results in more positive and lasting change than is often provided by professional help.

Self-help groups, new ideas about resilience, and the emphasis on self-healing are exciting and progressive ideas that bode well for the future of the helping professions. With more empirical research, there will hopefully be new findings that support positive outcomes when the strengths perspective is applied in practice. And hopefully, the strengths perspective and movements like it, with a focus on healthy communities, will be a driving force in the reconstruction of our communities as positive places to live for all Americans, but particularly for Americans with special needs. Healthy communities offer healthy environments, or what Taylor (1993) calls "enabling niches." As our communities become healthier, so will their inhabitants, leaving professionals the task of working with those who have the most critical need. Toward that end, the book finishes with a discussion of healthy community life.

THE SEARCH FOR HEALTHY COMMUNITIES: BOWLING ALONE AND AUTHENTIC HAPPINESS

Robert Putnam (2000), writing about the isolating aspects of American life; Martin Seligman (2002), concerned with a helping process that seems to ignore happiness and optimism; and Dennis Saleebey (1996), writing about the importance of healthy communities, all demonstrate a strengths perspective view of the future. Consider Putnam's sense of American life as noted in an interview with Stossel (2000):

> Americans today have retreated into isolation. So argues the political scientist Robert D. Putnam. . . . Evidence shows, Putnam says, that fewer and fewer contemporary Americans are unionizing, voting, rallying around shared causes, participating in religious services, inviting each other over, or doing much of anything collectively. In fact, when we do occasionally gather—for twelve-step support encounters and the like—it's most often only as an excuse to focus on ourselves in the presence of an audience. Supper eaten with friends or family has given way to supper gobbled in solitude, with only the glow of the television screen for companionship. (p. 1)

In describing the impact of social isolation and the weakening of our bond with one another, Putnam provided a particularly relevant strengths notion about the importance of community in the lives of people when he wrote:

> The most startling fact about social connectedness is how pervasive are its effects. We are not talking here simply about nostalgia for the 1950s. School performance, public health, crime rates, clinical depression, tax compliance, philanthropy, race relations, community development, census returns, teen suicide, economic productivity, campaign finance, even simple human happiness—all are demonstrably affected by how (and whether) we connect with our family and friends and neighbors and co-workers.
>
>   And most Americans instinctively recognize that we need to reconnect with one another. Figuring out how to reconcile the competing obligations of work and family and community is the ultimate "kitchen table" issue. As practical solutions to the problem become clearer, the latent public support for addressing the underlying issue will become an irresistible "market" for ambitious political candidates. (p. 4)

On a similar note, writing about the way Americans have gone about achieving happiness, the isolating impact it has, and the way in which the helping professions have failed to provide a positive approach to the achievement of happiness, Seligman (2002) noted:

> [W]e have invented myriad shortcuts to feeling good; drugs, chocolate, loveless sex, shopping, masturbation, and television are all examples. The belief that we can rely on shortcuts to happiness, joy, rapture, comfort, and ecstasy, rather than be entitled to

these feelings by the exercise of personal strengths and virtues, leads to legions of people who, in the middle of great wealth, are starving spiritually. Positive emotion alienated from the exercise of character leads to emptiness, to inauthenticity, to depression, and, as we age, to the gnawing realization that we are fidgeting until we die. (ABCNews.COM, 2002)

Saleebey (1996), writing about the strengths perspective and the importance of healthy community life, notes,

Membership [in a community] means that people need to be citizens—responsible and valued members in a viable group or community. To be without membership is to be alienated, and to be at risk of marginalization and oppression, the enemies of civic and moral strength (Walzer, 1983). As people begin to realize and use their assets and abilities, collectively and individually, as they begin to discover the pride in having survived and overcome their difficulties, more and more of their capacities come into the work and play of daily life. These build on each other exponentially, reflecting a kind of synergy. The same synergistic phenomenon seems true of communities and groups as well. In both instances, one might suggest that there are no known limits to individual and collective capacities. (p. 297)

Continuing with the notion of healthy community life, Kesler (2000) suggests seven core beliefs that underpin the healthy communities movement:

1. "The healthy community movement involves a sophisticated, integrative, and interconnected vision of flourishing of the individual and the human collective in an environmental setting" (p. 272).
2. The healthy communities movement must involve all sectors of society including the disenfranchised.
3. The healthy communities movement is about people connecting intimately with one another and becoming aware of special issues that need to be addressed sensitively and creatively.
4. Healthy communities require a dialogue among people to help formulate public policy agendas.
5. The healthy communities movement must seek consensus and mutual ground among all community groups and political persuasions.
6. The healthy communities movement must function from a broad level of caring, maturity, and awareness.
7. The healthy communities movement seeks to form alliances with other community-based movements.

Kesler (2000) writes that the ultimate goal of the healthy communities movement is to "encourage all concerned to rise to higher integrative levels of thinking, discourse, research, policies, programs, institutions, and processes, so that they might truly begin to transform their lives, their communities, and the greater society" (p. 271).

THE FUTURE OF THE
STRENGTHS PERSPECTIVE

Considering the literature, broadly speaking, on the strengths perspective, there seems to be a ground swell developing, in terms of both research and opinion, that supports many of the beliefs of the strengths perspective. Research on natural healing, chronicity, self-help groups and the impact of spirituality and religion are impressive new views of the change process. Clearly, we are at the beginning of a revolution in the way we think about the way people function, develop, and make life-altering changes. And while the hard evidence on the effectiveness of the strengths perspective in practice has yet to be shown, a number of promising studies support the underlying philosophy of the strengths perspective. The result is a growing enlightenment in the way many of us think about the change process and our belief in what people, training to work in the helping professions, must know for effective practice. For example, the DSM-IV is not inherently bad, nor should it be discarded, but it does seem clear that many therapists are overly committed to a pessimistic view of people that often affects the meaning of diagnostic categories. Certain diagnostic categories suggest long-term problems without any hope of improvement. This has a stigmatizing impact on people and, judging by the research, is incorrect for many types of diagnoses, including mental illness and addictions.

The pathology model is an easy model to teach and to use. Unfortunately, it doesn't work very well, and too many of the studies provided in this book suggest its real limitations in practice. It is, after all, about the client, and it seems clear that much is to be gained by understanding the natural healing abilities of people that are often in conflict with professional views of change. Rather than facilitating change, the pathology model inhibits change. It does so by focusing on what doesn't work and by reinforcing the client's belief that change may be impossible, when in reality, people constantly change. In their darkest moments, they cope. Their ways of coping seem elegant and heroic. Who are we to judge how people solve the traumas they endure? Almost any solution must be viewed with compassion and understanding. Our task is to help clients know that we're thankful and appreciative that they've done as well as they have. These are the heroes of our society, the people who cope with life's anguish and do the best they can. These heroic people are not the troubled, dysfunctional, stigmatized, villainous people so often described in the literature. They are the role models, the people who pick themselves up when they are down, and get on with life. They are the survivors.

One can't help but agree completely with Saleebey (1996) that we've created a mental health complex, a huge corporate organizational entity dependent on the despair of people, while providing little help and then blaming the client for not improving. It's pleasing to see Seligman joining this movement away from a focus on pathology by discussing optimism and virtue. We live in a society in which optimism is the fuel that guides us, and it's a positive sign that someone of Seligman's stature reminds us about virtue and positive values. How can we exist in healthy communities without a sense of correctness in our behavior toward one another?

We live in communities and, if Putnam is correct, they are unhealthy places filled with lonely and isolated people who, in Seligman's words, are "alienated from the exercise of character [that] leads to emptiness, to inauthenticity, to depression, and, as we age, to the gnawing realization that we are fidgeting until we die" (ABCNews.COM, 2002). One of the cornerstones of the strengths perspective is the belief that healthy people must have healthy communities. When communities are, in Taylor's words, "entrapping" (Taylor, 1993), people become isolated, lonely, and depressed. The lack of healthy communities in America is a large contributor to the unhealthy behavior of many of our citizens. Size is not a factor in the health of a community. It is, instead, the inherent desire to be proud of where we live and to commit ourselves to making a community a safe, healthy, and productive place for all of our citizens. The author grew up in such a place, and although there were problems of race, social class, ethnicity, and gender that embarrass me today, I grew up in a diverse and poor neighborhood in which all of us did well in life. As one family broke down under the pressure of financial stress, alcoholism, or abusive behavior, another family reached out to the family in difficulty and took over the healthy functions of family life. Our poor neighborhood was a place of optimism and civic virtue, and the values of our schools and our places of worship substituted for the sometimes-confused and troubled functioning of our families and parents. We all endured terrible stressors, and yet most of us did very well in our lives.

Like many of my friends, I worked in construction, on the railroad, and in menial jobs in high school and college. Not once did I think I would fail in the future. For that, I have the strong guiding hand of some great teachers to thank. They believed in America, they loved our country, and they gave us a sense of optimism. I don't think you can exist happily in a community or commit yourself to civic virtue without a love of country. The renewal of patriotism in this country as a result of the 9/11 events makes me confident that a love of country will provide a new love of community and a commitment to make our towns and cities healthy and caring places. Unhappily, I agree with Putnam that our communities are depressing and isolating places where all too many people live lives of quiet desperation. Creating walled-in and guarded "safe havens" for the affluent among us is no answer to the despair of life in too many American cities.

Social responsibility should guide our commitment to our fellow citizens. People need the support and encouragement of friends, family, neighbors, and public and private institutions. We've been living very isolating lives in America. It is an unhealthy sign, and it serves to negate the underlying strength of our people. It seems to me that the helping professions have removed themselves from issues of healthy environments. One can only hope that the strengths movement will help people remember that clients who live in communities with long, stressful drives to work; where air is polluted and crime is high; where neighbors fail to know their next door neighbors; where discrimination and bigotry and institutional chaos are permitted are environments that function to make otherwise healthy people, unhealthy. The political arenas, civic involvements, board memberships, and involvement in professional organizations are all ways to facilitate change. Helping professionals should make a moral commitment to be involved in activities that are external to their practices and that might lead to healthier environments for all of our people.

A CRITICAL RESPONSE

The argument with this chapter isn't about healthy communities but more about the lack of political involvement of helping professionals in making certain that all people have safe and healthy environments. The tendency to live in "safe havens," as the author calls them, seems driven by a fundamental class system in America in which people of modest means are forced to live in less expensive and often more dangerous areas of many communities. No one should live in unsafe environments, particularly elderly, less mobile, and more needy people. The helping professions must guide this political agenda because, at this moment in time, income drives safety and more affluent people can afford to live in safer, less polluted, and more desirable surroundings. The idea that socioeconomic status doesn't affect health is nonsense. Affluent people can afford a lifestyle that translates into better health and longer life spans. And while Putnam (2000) writes, "The shooting sprees that affected schools in suburban and rural communities as the twentieth century ended are a reminder that as the breakdown of communities continues in more privileged settings, affluence and education are insufficient to prevent collective tragedy" (p. 318), the reality is that violent crime largely remains the domain of America's inner cities (Eisenhower Commission Report, 2002).

If poorer people are to enjoy the benefits of healthier communities, then surely we must provide a level of safety, security, and opportunity not currently available to less affluent citizens. This shift in the way our communities function should be a primary agenda item for the current times, when violent crime is beginning to increase once again in America. Until all of our people live in safe, healthy, and productive communities, the environments of all too many of our clients will act as inhibitors of good mental health and the gains made in treatment will be diminished.

SUMMARY

This chapter discusses the future of the strengths perspective, with an emphasis on the development of healthy communities. Material from the work of Robert Putnam, Martin Seligman, and Dennis Saleebey is offered as evidence that our communities have a long way to go before they qualify as safe and healthy places for our more needy clients to live. The critical response suggests that helping professionals must increase their level of involvement to make certain that their clients leave treatment with a chance of living in communities and neighborhoods that offer safety and health, and benefit from what Hanifan (1916) refers to as "social capital," or "the good will, fellowship, sympathy, and social intercourse among the individuals and families who make up a social unit" (p. 130). The critical response also points out that individual socioeconomic status permits more affluent people to live in communities with more social capital and that community health is actually a function of one's financial status.

INTEGRATIVE QUESTIONS

1. Putnam and Seligman believe that many Americans live lives of quiet desperation and that the unwillingness to affiliate with community groups has left many Americans living isolated and lonely lives. Do you agree?

2. Doesn't capitalism offer the opportunity of living in healthier communities as a function of hard work and achievement? Would hard work and achievement falter if all people were able to live in desirable communities and neighborhoods?

3. The strengths perspective seems more like a philosophy than a theory of change. Would the theoretical aspects of the approach be strengthened if there were more research, or is all therapy so individualistic that the practitioner, and not the approach, determines treatment effectiveness?

4. Putnam believes that the lack of social connectedness to community organizations (e.g., church, PTA, political parties) results in lonely lives. Could it be that the organizations we once thought important enough to join no longer relate to modern life and that new and more relevant organizations need to take their places before people once again become socially affiliated?

5. Seligman believes that the presence of character and personal virtue lead to a more fulfilling and successful life, but we live in cynical times, in which character and virtue may not lead to social or financial success. How shall we rectify the discrepancy between what Seligman believes is a healthy life and our current view that stresses money, social status, and material possessions as measures of happiness?

REFERENCES

ABCNews.com. (2002). Authentic happiness: Using our strengths to cultivate happiness. Retrieved October 14, 2002, from the World Wide Web: http://abcnews.go.com/sections/GMA/GoodMorningAmerica/GMA020904Happiness_feature.html.

Gambrill, E. (1999). Evidence-based practice: An alternative to authority-based practice. *Families in Society: The Journal of Contemporary Human Services*, 80(4), 341–350.

Hanifan, L.J. (1916). The rural school community center. *Annals of the American Academy of Social Science*, 67, 130–138.

Kesler, J.T. (2000). The healthy communities movement: Seven counterintuitive next steps. *National Civic Review*, 89(3), 271–284.

Milton J. Eisenhower Foundation Commission on Violence Report. (2002). *To establish justice, to insure domestic tranquility: A thirty year update of the national commission on the causes and prevention of violence*. Washington, DC: The Milton S. Eisenhower Foundation. Available online at www.eisenhowerfoundation.org/aboutus/publications/fr_justice.html.

Putnam, R.D. (2000). *Bowling alone*. New York: Touchstone Books.

Saleebey, D. (1996). The strengths perspective in social work practice: Extensions and cautions. *Social Work*, 41(3), 296-305.

Seligman, M.E.P. (2002). *Authentic happiness: New positive psychology to realize your potential for lasting fulfillment*. New York: Free Press.

Stossel, S. (September 21, 2000). Lonely in America: An interview with Robert Putnam. *Atlantic Monthly on Line*. Found online at www://magatopia.com/magazine/001atlantic.html.

Stossel, S. (September. 21, 2000). *Bowling alone*. (Interview with Robert Putnam). Atlantic Unbound.

Taylor, J. (1993). *Poverty and niches: A systems view*. (Unpublished manuscript)

Walzer, M. (1983). *Spheres of justice*. New York: Basic Books.

INDEX